The Lives of
RILEY

The Lives of
RILEY

MARK HEISLER

Macmillan · USA

MACMILLAN
A Prentice Hall Macmillan Company
15 Columbus Circle
New York, NY 10023

Library of Congress Cataloguing-in-Publication Data.

Heisler, Mark.
    The lives of Riley/Mark Heisler.
        p. cm.
    Includes index.
    ISBN 0-02-550662-5
    1. Riley, Pat. 2. Basketball coaches—United States—Biography.
    3. Los Angeles Lakers (Basketball team) I. Title
    GV884. R55H45 1994
    796.323'092—dc20   94-23438   CIP
    [B]

Manufactured in the United States of America
10 9 8 7 6 5 4 3 2 1

To Mom, Dad, Gerry, Loretta,

and Emily

And to Pat Riley, who lived this agony and ecstasy

Acknowledgments

Pat and Chris Riley declined to be interviewed so I was obliged to use second-hand sources for their quotes.

I am indebted to Scott Ostler and Steve Springer whose book, *Winnin' Times*, is the definitive work on the Laker rise in the '80s. Also to Riley's *Show Time* and Magic Johnson's *My Life*; to Diane Shah for her 1989 piece on Riley in *Gentlemen's Quarterly*; to Ken Auletta for his in *Vanity Fair* in 1992; to Bruce Newman for his profile on Chick Hearn in *Sports Illustrated*; to Curry Kirkpatrick for his story on the Kentucky–Texas Western game in *Sports Illustrated*; to *People* magazine for its 1987 story on Pat and Chris; to Chris Smith for his 1993 story on the Knicks in *New York Magazine*, and to PBS's Charlie Rose for his hour-long interview with Riley.

I'm indebted to the newsmen who have covered Riley, principally Randy Harvey, Tommy Bonk, Gordon Edes, and Sam McManis of the *Los Angeles Times*; Mitch Chortkoff of the *Santa Monica Outlook*; Rich Levin, Doug Krikorian, and Frank Brady of the *Los Angeles Herald Examiner*; Doug Cress, Jesse Barkin, and Gordon Monson of the *Los Angeles Daily News*; Don Greenberg of the *Orange County Register*; Joe McDonnell of KMPC radio; Curtis Bunn, Peter Finney, Gary Binford, Mark Kriegel, and Bob Raissman of the New York *Daily News*; Dave Anderson, George Vescey, Ira Berkow, Harvey Araton, and Cliff Brown of the *New York Times*; Pete Vecsey, Fred Kerber, and Phil Mushnick of the *New York Post*; Mike Lupica of *Newsday*; Dave D'Allesandro of the *Bergen Record*; Tony Kornheiser of the *Washington Post*; Bob Ryan and Leslie Visser of the *Boston Globe*; Jack McCallum and Billy Reed of *Sports Illustrated*.

I want to thank the people who were kind enough to talk to me or Mike Littwin who researched the Schenectady chapter. In alphabetical order, they were: Dennis Awtrey, Jim Barnett, Bill

Bertka, John and Margie Block, Jerry Buss, Tony Campbell, Altie and Idell Cohen, Jerry Colangelo, Larry Conley, Michael Cooper, Louie Dampier, Warren DeSantis, James Donaldson, Keith Erickson, Mike Francesa, Walt Frazier, Mike Fratello, Teddy Grossman, Bob Gutkowski, Chick Hearn, Mark Jackson, Phil Jackson, Magic Johnson, Jim Kaufman, Lanie and Barry Kramer, Mike Meola, Stu Lantz, Tom Lasorda, Xavier McDaniel, Jon McGlocklin, Pete Newell, Norm Nixon, Mike Ornstein, Randy Pfund, Julie Przybylo, Kurt Rambis, Dennis Riley, Doc Rivers, Darrell Ruocco, Byron and Anita Scott, Lynn Shackelford, Bill Sharman, Mychal Thompson, Gary Vitti, Jerry West, Paul Westhead, Gerald Wilkins, and Dave Wohl.

Thanks to Steve Delsohn for thinking this up; to my editors Rick Wolff, Natalie Chapman, and Jeanine Bucek; to my friend, Rich Hoffer for reading the manuscript; and to my mentor, Littwin, for troubleshooting the project.

And most of all, to my wife, Loretta, for troubleshooting me.

CONTENTS

"...I hunted down, killed and ate a small gazelle. I was utterly primal. I consisted of nothing more than the will to survive, to live through the night, to eat, to sleep. It was the most supremely satisfying time of my life."

—EDDIE JESSUP IN PADDY CHAYEFSKY'S ALTERED STATES

CHAPTER ONE

Riles Doesn't Live Here Anymore

He was 31 when his life ended.

He was alive; it was over. He walked and talked but he didn't know to what end. He had nowhere to go and none of the guys really wanted to see him. Of all the cuts, this hurt most; one moment you're brothers, the next acquaintances.

Everyone was nice but it was different. They were still in The Life. They worried about winning streaks and losing streaks and slumps, griped about the coach, packed for the next trip, or unpacked from the last one. They didn't have time to think of him and if they had, they'd have just murmured, "What a shame." What had he done wrong? He got cut. It was going to happen to all of them, too, and they didn't like thinking about it. He thought of them all the time.

That was the year he started doing his own book.

Day after day he drove down to State Beach in Santa Monica with a yellow legal pad, propped himself up against the back wall next to the parking lot and wrote. Page after page, about the mercenaries and the bullshit loyalty and the short memories. He filled pad after pad. There wasn't enough paper to describe the indignity of it all.

All his life he'd thought he was headed somewhere special but this was where it turned out to be, as if shot from a bow at birth cross-continent to burrow headfirst into the sand. Up against the wall on State Beach.

To the north, the coast curved around to join the Santa Monica Mountains at Malibu; to the south rose the bluffs of Palos Verdes; 26 miles across the sea was Catalina, visible on these clear mornings. Before him were the volleyball courts where the best beach players in the world gathered. Everywhere were the California girls, the whole California deal, and he couldn't share in any of it.

He was young and robust. He had good friends, the beach gang he'd been hanging out with for years. He had a beautiful wife who'd set up a counseling practice, giving them a handy second income. Not that they were hurting financially; he'd gotten good investment advice in his playing days and followed it. They were well set up, with a nice home in Brentwood.

It undoubtedly would have felt good if he could have felt anything.

It was as if he'd made some horrendous mistake, but he didn't know what it was. He'd been raised always to put it all on the line and he had.

Make a stand, his father always told him.

Make a stand? His whole life had been a stand. He never backed down and he still wound up nowhere, just like his father whose baseball career tapped out in the minor leagues. Maybe that was how life was. You dream, you wake up, you live the rest of your life the best way you can.

The son played basketball desperately, as if he was afraid it could be taken away from him, and in the end, it was. He didn't know who he was without it, or worse, he did know. He was no one.

He couldn't imagine what came next.

A friend had offered him a job in a Beverly Hills clothing store. He was going to take it, too, until *that* fell through. It was just the way things were going.

He dreamed of getting back into the game somehow.

Maybe coaching. He'd never thought much about it before; his temperament was too hot, but maybe he could be different. He had no experience so he'd have to start down the line. Like way down the line. Like, past where the line ended and you had to get out and walk. The money wouldn't be much, but he'd be working with kids and it would still be basketball.

He thought maybe somewhere like Oxnard Junior College.

Somebody Up There must have laughed when He heard that one.

▌

Pat Riley prowls the sideline at Madison Square Garden, shining jewel of the Manhattan night, done over in the hot-hot-hot Laker style with cheerleaders named the New York City Dancers and celebrities vying for courtside seats.

This is Pat Riley's own little fiefdom now. The beach is a world away, a memory so faint even his oldest friends aren't sure they remember it.

He's been an NBA coach for 12 seasons without ever once finishing in second place. He's written two best-selling books. Big-time CEOs pay him $40,000 to speak to their employees and get their picture taken with him. *New York Magazine* sends the Pulitzer prize winner David Halberstam to profile him. Tom Brokaw interviews him for NBC. He does Jay Leno's show, plays one-on-one with Mario Cuomo.

How does he do it?

Like, how come the other coaches are contorting their bodies to make shots go in or stay out, and Riley is always so heartbreakingly casual, like a model on the runway? Did someone teach him to cross his arms and get up on that right toe just so? How is it he's rocking and rolling inside and nothing shows on the outside except the inch of cuff at his sleeve and the perfect drape of his jacket?

He always had a lot of style, whichever role he was in—James Dean in *Rebel Without a Cause* as a kid; Mr. Ivy League as a Kentucky All-American; John Lennon's Walrus with long hair and droopy mustache as an NBA journeyman—but he's slipped into this sleek elegance as if waking to a reality that was always there.

When he coached the Lakers, they used to joke he had his young assistant, Randy Pfund, age for him. Indeed, Riley stayed up nights, worked harder than anyone, and always looked great while Pfund had bags under his eyes like a raccoon.

Given the Laker coaching job in a series of freak accidents that suggested only that the gods were getting impatient with the pace of his narrative, Riley became the symbol of Showtime. The unassuming guy who'd been Jerry West's caddy, Chick Hearn's straight man doubling as traveling secretary—here's your boarding pass Kareem, here's yours Jamaal—became the man to finally tame the restless players.

Did they like his program?

"*Loved* it," says Magic Johnson.

"Because one thing he promised when he took over, 'I'll never bad-mouth you in the press. If I'm going to do it, it's going to be in the locker room.'

"And players respect that. They liked him for that. What he made you do, you would go through a wall for him."

The Lakers were living a dream in those days. They weren't just a team but fam-i-ly with Riles as the daddy, intent on giving them the best of everything. Three Lakers at the All-Star game? We can't have our guys riding in NBA shuttle buses like threadbare Celtics or poor-relative Knicks. Rent a limo, send the bill to Jerry West. What to give one's assistant coaches and staff for Christmas? The perfect touch, $1,000 Tag Heuer watches.

Hollywood rolled over and offered its belly. Director Robert Towne asked Riley to star opposite Michelle Pfeiffer in his movie, *Tequila Sunrise*. When Riley decided it wouldn't look right, Towne made do with Kurt Russell whom he instructed to comb his hair back, à la Riles. Oliver Stone had Michael Douglas comb his hair that way as Gordon Gekko in *Wall Street*.

When Douglas won the Academy Award, he sent Riley a telegram that said, "I have to believe it was all in the hair."

4

If Riley ever cared about that stuff, he's so far past it he can't remember it.

All that stuff they write about, the mousse, the Giorgio Armani wardrobe, the dashing figure, it could be someone else. They could be writing about the man in the moon. He doesn't care about that, either. It's all just words.

It's all beside the point. Riles doesn't live there anymore.

Appearances notwithstanding, he moved on years ago, forsaking his old persona, the beach, inner peace, all those California things he was supposed to be *about*, for something rarer.

He was going up his own path, and it was only wide enough for one. He had become someone else, leaner, harder, less frivolous. Fewer people knew him up close and personal as Riles; more admired him coolly through a TV lens as Coach Pat Riley. It wasn't that he was short with old friends or acted as if he thought he was better than they were. He just wasn't there any more.

"When he became so compulsive, there was no time for... *stuff*," says Keith Erickson, a long-time teammate and Riley's successor as Laker broadcaster.

"Old friendships, that wasn't what he was concerned with. He was only concerned with the team, his responsibilities.

"You know, when you're players, it's fun, it's loose, all the crazy stuff you talk about when you're just hanging out.

"There was no more of that. None. It was all business."

Riley had a list of "peripheral enemies" that kept growing. He wandered Forum hallways with his thousand-yard stare, walking past Laker employees without so much as a nod. Mornings after losses, he was fearsome to behold, gaunt, unshaven, so miserable his players complained he wouldn't even look at them.

In the end, they couldn't keep up with him. They kept getting older; he kept getting hungrier. When he leaped nimbly into retirement after an upset loss to the Suns in the '90 playoffs, he had, irony of ironies, his first Coach of the Year award, a $2 million severance package from Laker owner Jerry Buss, and a team near mutiny.

∎

He never thinks about it.

Everything they did together, all those years of yearning and sweating and brotherhood and failing and looking inside themselves to rise above failure—to have that ruined by backbiting and recrimi-nations? It's too painful to think about.

He's the prince of another city although he knows what that's worth. This stuff, they give it to you and then they take it away.

He has something more tangible: summoning that old fear that comes in the night, the test, the moment, the thrill!

His peers betray their torment, wincing, grimacing, politick-ing, intriguing, job-hopping, balding, graying, gaining weight until they flop into the off-season like beached whales.

Somehow, Riley always looks regal. It's a lie, and his genius in a nutshell.

"I never understood where they got this thing that Pat was a cool, calm, collected guy," says Gary Vitti, his Laker trainer.

"To me, he was wound up like a guitar string all the time. All the time. When you finally caught up with him in the off-season or out of this setting, he was a great, great guy to be around....

"You know what? I talked to him about this several times. I was really nervous for Pat. I was really nervous for Pat in the sense of a coronary. His father died of heart disease at a very young age. Pat used to eat a greasy hamburger with french fries by the pool every day.

"The guy looks great, O.K.? He had high cholesterol and didn't exercise. It's all natural. He just looked great—and had a stress level off the map. Now if those aren't primary and secondary characteristics of heart disease, you tell me. I thought any minute in a game, he was just going to come unglued."

He never comes unglued.

No one else can demand as much, dare to aim as high, risk so much disappointment. He likes it, even if one season when the Knicks asked what song he'd like played as he walked on to the Garden floor, he chose "This Old Heart of Mine" with its refrain "Been broke a thousand times."

He lives for those defining moments when his players turn to him because they've got nowhere else to go, and he can make them look inside themselves and he can look inside himself and they can see what they've got.

"The best state you can have," he once said of a Knicks wipeout at Houston, "...miserable, angry, embarrassed, humiliated, fear-ful...."

It's his own life story happening over and over. He knows all about that state, he grew up in it. Hello misery, anger, embarrass-ment, humiliation, and fear, his old friends.

CHAPTER TWO

American Gothic: Lee and Pat

All of us want to have a resolution of that father-son thing. Pat never had a chance to say hello or good-bye.

—KNICKS PRESIDENT DAVE CHECKETTS
TO *VANITY FAIR'S* KEN AULETTA

∎

He's Irish and he keeps it all in.

—CHRIS RILEY
ON HER HUSBAND

One hundred fifty miles up the New York State Thruway from Riley's city that never sleeps sits Schenectady, the sleepy city of his youth.

Schenectady still looks like a Hollywood set for Your Town, U.S.A. There are no tall buildings. A lawyer's shingle hangs from a door. There's a museum of the town's history and a historic district where the old homes have been renovated.

It was a nice place to raise a family but for Lee Riley, father of six and career minor leaguer, finally manager of the local Phillies' farm team, the Blue Jays, Schenectady was where the trail ran cold. He hadn't come to settle down but to work his way up the ladder of the Phillies' minor league system. When he was released, it was as if he'd been shipwrecked there.

Lee's life after baseball was a disappointment his kids could feel in their bones. There was a silence in their home, and Pat, the youngest of the six, would spend the rest of his life trying to shatter it, to fill that house with warmth after the fact.

Pat would travel far, struggle valiantly, and become famous beyond his dreams. He'd tell his story over and over—about his hardscrabble youth, his swerve from juvenile delinquency into basketball, his tough but supportive father—but he'd leave the gritty stuff out. The real story was too painful; talking about it would be outright betrayal.

The grownup Pat would become relentless. He never rested. There was always something more he needed to win, an itch he couldn't ever seem to scratch.

It went back to Schenectady, the town he thought he'd left behind.

∎

In later years, when the Knicks would be at pains to smooth Riley's transition from West Coast icon, they'd note he grew up in Schenectady and was a New Yorker.

Actually, Schenectady could as easily have been in Ohio. It was an upstate General Electric company town of about 150,000, low-slung and spread out like a midwestern city, largely composed of working-class European ethnics. As late as the 1980 census, Schenectady County was 96 percent white.

As in the New Yorker cartoon, Middle America can be said to stretch from the Hudson River to the California state line and it was

Middle America, not anyone's Big Apple, that was Pat Riley's cultural birthplace.

Schenectady was a two-and-a-half-hour drive from the Great White Way. Local people did not trot down to New York after work to catch a Broadway show, and only the people with money went down weekends.

That left out the Rileys.

Lee loved baseball but the game didn't love him back. His glory days consisted of four major league games with the Phillies in the war year of 1944; he batted 12 times, had one hit (a double), and retired with a career average of .083.

He had a mission, getting back to the big leagues as a manager. It was shared by his family who followed along with him in its service.

The life was exciting, Dad's ballpark a toddler's magic kingdom. But the money was bad and the life transient, a summer here, a summer there. The Rileys moved across the land, through the tank towns of the Philadelphia Phillies' farm system, like the family of a carny barker.

Pat was born March 20, 1945, and grew up on two-lane blacktops, riding in the back of the family's Studebaker station wagon with his three brothers and two sisters.

When they reached Lee's new post, he'd rent an apartment for the family. Then he'd disappear into the baseball season.

"He'd come home and then he'd shape us up before he went on the road again," says Pat's older brother, Dennis, who works for GE and lives in Schenectady.

"He could be tough, yeah. He had to be tough. Back in those days, you didn't coddle kids, I guess, like you do today.... He was the all-time disciplinarian. He might give you a pop if you got out of line."

Lee was a no-nonsense man, 6–1 and 180 pounds as a player, a sharp dresser with a thick mane of hair that he slicked back. Iron-willed and competitive, he was considered gentlemanly in the age of baseball managers who came in varying shades of tyranny. These were the '40s, long before "relating to players" or players' unions. The skipper whispered, the player jumped. There were thousands of minor league players and only 400 major league jobs.

"I tell you," says Tom Lasorda, the Dodger manager who played for Lee at Schenectady in 1948, "when I look at Pat, it scares me. He looks exactly like his father. Exactly like his father.

"His father was an outstanding guy to play for, just a tremendous guy. He was a very serious type fella, very disciplined and very strict type of a manager.

"Course, Pat in those days, I guess he was about three years old, him and his brothers used to come around all the time.

"I was telling Pat, one of the funniest things that ever happened between his father and I, we were playing Gloversville. I was pitching for Schenectady and I had 'em beat 2–1, going into the top of the ninth inning. So I came out to pitch the top of the ninth and he came across and handed me the ball and said to me, 'Well, you got three left-handed hitters coming up so you've got no problems.'

"First left-handed hitter hit a double. Second left-handed hitter hit the top of the center field fence for a triple, tied the game. Next left-handed hitter got a base hit to go ahead, 3–2.

"And he comes out to take me out and he looks at me and says, 'Do you know why I couldn't hit in the major leagues?'

"I said, 'I don't know, Skip.'

"He said, 'Because I couldn't hit a left-hander. But if you'd been there, I'd have been a star.'"

Lee had missed being a star but he thought he had a promise to come to the big team. Instead he was released in 1952. In disgust, he threw out every uniform, baseball, trophy, and photo he had and went looking for work after a lifetime that had trained him only to play a game.

"He wasn't thrilled about it," Dennis says. "Things don't always work out for people—not like they do for Pat. We had some hard times. When business was good, we did good. When it wasn't, we didn't."

Said Pat years later to PBS's Charlie Rose: "I could sense his disappointment for years after that...not being able to fulfill maybe his lifelong dream which was to manage a major league team. I never had a chance to sit down with him and talk about it. He never said, Hey this is what they did to me or this is what happened. I mean, even Mother rarely even talked about it. But it ended very bitterly and he carried that with him for a long time."

Lee ran a small restaurant-bar for GE, then opened a little convenience store called Riley's Variety, which didn't last.

The Rileys had few creature comforts. The kids were taught self-reliance. Lee was big on appearance and style; Pat learned to wash, iron, and even tailor his own clothes.

If Lee had his problems, he kept them inside. His youngest son would always remember his father's stern self-control.

Actually Lee was doing all he could do to keep it together. With his vocational problems came a personal one: He was an alcoholic.

Dennis says he was aware of his father's drinking and that Lee overcame it, but theirs was a stoic household where everybody sucked it up and went about his own business.

In later years, when Pat would become a prep All-American, Lee only occasionally went to see him play. Pat's mother, Mary, rarely went. Pat never once brought Lanie Kramer, his high school girlfriend, home to meet his family.

■

Puberty dawned on a defiant Pat, classically dressed for the period, the jeans, the T-shirt, the ducktail. If Lee might give you a pop if you got out of line, his youngest son must have gotten popped because he was dabbling in vandalism, petty theft, and staying out nights.

"Pat was always in trouble," says Mike Meola, a high school friend and teammate in basketball and football. "He was the kind of kid who hung out on the corner.

"You know what I mean, pack of cigarettes rolled up in his T-shirt, a kind of look to him. He was tough. People had to watch what they said to him. He had an attitude. There was always this giant chip on his shoulder."

"I was a product at that time of my environment," Riley said later. "We're in the late '50s. It was about the Del Vikings and it was about *The Wild One* and Marlon Brando and *Rebel Without a Cause*. It was about that time. I wasn't a *bad*, bad kid, you know. The myth grows."

Cinematic fashion notwithstanding, Pat had his own real teenage blues. However, he wasn't cut out for a life of crime. He was too easy to catch.

He took his first and last bust for joining friends in breaking windows at the local public school, breaking into the cafeteria, eating all the ice cream, then, on their way out, breaking the windows they'd missed.

They thought they'd pulled the perfect crime but someone blabbed.

"One day Lieutenant Dominelli and Vincent Monago, the two cops in Schenectady every kid knew, came and picked me up at St. Joseph's Academy, the Catholic school I went to, and called my father," Riley said later.

"They took me to the Mother Superior's office and boy, Mother Superior, she put the fear of Hell in me more than my father.

"Then my dad came down. That was it for me. I had to change my ways.

"This coincided with a basketball game I played. I was in the sixth grade and for some reason we had to play the ninth graders. I don't know how, but we beat them. I scored like 19 points. People were staring at me from the stands wondering, 'Who is this kid?'

"I walked into class the next day and it was the first time I ever got any recognition. The teacher talked about me and I could see the kids looking at me with a little different look in their eyes.

"And I said to myself: 'That's all I gotta do.' So it changed. My life changed. I could feel it."

Lee's sons had inherited his athleticism. The oldest, Lee Jr., would go on to play professional football for the Philadelphia Eagles and New York Giants. Lenny played college basketball.

Lee Sr.'s chief contribution was toughening them up. When Pat started playing basketball, Lee told the older brothers to take him across town to Lincoln Heights to go against the tough kids.

Pat says he was chased home one day by a boy with a butcher knife and roughed up the other days.

"I would get beat up, knocked around," Pat said. "I would run home crying. I would hide in the garage for three or four hours and not come out 'til dinner. One night I did not show up at the dinner table. I was still in the garage.

"My dad asked my brothers, 'Where is he?'

"And finally Lee [Jr.] stood up and asked, 'Why do you make us take Pat down there?'

"My father came out, grabbed me, brought me back to the table. And he said, 'I want you to teach him not to be afraid.'"

█▌

Even in grade school, ladies love outlaws.

Lanie Kramer, the younger sister of Barry, the NYU All-American-to-be, met Pat in the seventh grade and thought he was "cute…adorable. He was a lot of fun. All the girls were wild for him."

Pat was the best basketball player at Central Junior High, but even though he'd given up vandalism, he hadn't foresaken the punk movement entirely. He had an attitude right up until the moment he bumped, almost literally, into the man who'd turn him around. His name was Walt Przybylo and he was the basketball coach at Linton High School.

Years later, back in Schenectady to receive the key to the city and be made an honorary Patroon, Riley told an audience of kids about that day.

"I was a lot like you," he said. "I wasn't sure where I was going. I hadn't gotten to Linton yet but I knew who Walt Przybylo was and he knew me.

"One day at Central Park I walked over to Przybylo to say hello. I had a pack of cigarettes rolled up in my T-shirt sleeve. Anyway, I said, 'Hello, Walt.' Now I can't repeat to you what he said to me, but it got me thinking I hadn't made a great impression."

Przybylo wasn't a big man—"He looked like Wallace Beery, if you remember him," says Barry Kramer who had graduated from Linton a few years before—but he was a disciplinarian who could go off with the best of them. Riley once said of Przybylo, "He'd make Bobby Knight look like a lamb."

At the same time, Przybylo was a fatherly man who took his role as a teacher seriously.

Riley and his teammates would go to practice each day at 3:15 but they'd never pick up a basketball. They'd put their backs to the bleachers and listen as Przybylo talked about some lesson in life. Many years later, Riley would begin his own practices with a talk that he'd prepared diligently.

After school, the Przybylo home was the unofficial team hangout.

"We all lived at the guy's house," says Barry Kramer. "I came back to play at that gym every day when I was in town. Pat did the same thing. He loved his boys. I remember in my senior year when we were taking the SATs and a lot of the guys were nervous. He was like a cheering section. 'You can do it, you're the best.' "

Between Przybylo and Riley, however, there was a stronger bond. In the Przybylo house, a few blocks away from Riley's, Pat found the warmth that was missing at home.

Przybylo died at age 49 but his widow, Julie, remembers, "Walt had a special place in his heart for Pat. I think it was because he knew what it was like to struggle when you're a kid, to not have very much. And also because Pat cared about basketball so much."

"Walt really took Pat under his wing," says Mike Meola. "He cared about all his players, but you could tell how he felt about Pat and it was mutual. Pat was looking for someone like him.

"Pat was skeptical, even as a kid, but he bought into Coach Przybylo's program and it completely changed his life."

"Pat is Walt Przybylo today," says Lanie Kramer. "He took everything this man was and incorporated it into his life. Walt Przybylo was a tremendous figure in Pat's life. His home was Pat's home away from home. It was really his first home.

"The Przybylos were just a real down-to-earth family. I used to baby-sit for them. It was a nice, warm family life. It was mostly a Polish neighborhood. People looked out for one another.

"Walt was probably the most important person in Pat's life."

Pat cut his DA, got a flattop, and unloaded the chip off his shoulder. He became the basketball star at Linton, which made him one of the most famous people in town.

Schenectady loved its prep basketball. The kids played outdoors through the fierce upstate winters, shoveling the snow off the courts first. When Barry Kramer was a high school senior, Howard Cosell came up from New York to interview him.

"High school basketball was really a big deal at the time," says Meola, the Linton point guard. "It was the kind of thing that people, grownups, would talk about. It was that kind of town. And Pat was the star. Everybody knew who Pat Riley was."

"It's hard to stay in contact with reality," says Barry Kramer. "You're 17 years old and a celebrity, a real live celebrity. People recognize you on the street. They come up to you and say hi. You're a star."

In Pat's junior year, Linton played Power Memorial in the Schenectady Holiday Festival. Power brought its star, Lew Alcindor, identified in the Schenectady *Gazette* as a "6–10 frosh phenom."

Riley outscored Alcindor, 19–8, and Linton won, 74–68. The upstate boys got a thrill—"People in New York City were talking about little Linton," says Meola—and Riley had something he could kid Alcindor (who would become Kareem Abdul-Jabbar) about for the rest of his life.

∎

In later years, Lee became a janitor at Bishop Gibbons High School, right across the street from McNeary Stadium where he had managed the Blue Jays.

He also coached the baseball team and, when Pat was in junior high, moved the family into a wood-frame three-story house at 58

Spruce Street, done in the faux Queen Anne style with a porch and bay windows on the top floor.

"That was the first normal house we had," Dennis says, "the first place we lived in that wasn't an apartment. I remember, it was the first place I had my own room."

Pat's friends say he didn't talk about his father. It wouldn't be until the '80s that his yearning for Lee, who had died in 1970, surfaced.

In Pat's 1987 book, *Show Time,* he said of Lee: "He played and coached some pro baseball and scuffled to keep his ambitions alive. He wasn't always an open and talkative guy but he always seemed to be there when it counted."

However, Lee's struggles continued for as long as Pat lived at home.

During a basketball game in Pat's senior year at Linton, Lee became unruly and was ejected from the gym.

"Like all kids from dysfunctional families, there are lots of secrets," says Lanie Kramer. "It's like there's a rhinoceros in the living room that nobody talks about. You stay real busy so you don't have to face the reality. That's very normal and that's what Pat did. Sports are what kept him sane. That's what kept him healthy.

"I had the impression it might have been a pretty violent household. I don't think Pat had any stability in his house. I know he just never wanted to be there."

"I know Pat didn't have an easy childhood," says Barry Kramer, now head of a Schenectady law firm.

"He's a star in town and his dad is a custodian who ran out on the floor one night and had to be removed. Of course, it had an impact on him."

Riley excelled at any sport he tried, including ice skating, but he was still no student and anything but the polished figure he would become. He was low-key and he wasn't outgoing. In the team picture in the 1962 Linton yearbook, he looks dazed, a tall, broad-shouldered young man with a blank look.

"He didn't speak well and he didn't read much at all except maybe the sports pages," says Lanie Kramer. "Now you look at him and he's so poised, so much in control. He doesn't look anything like the guy I used to know."

As a senior, Pat went out for football and became the starting quarterback. He threw himself into that, too and excelled at it, taking the Linton Blue Devils undefeated into their game against their archrivals, the Mt. Pleasant Red Raiders.

"Talk about pageantry," Riley said 30 years later, still into it. "Election Day, the fans, red and blue everywhere. And with 13 seconds left, we were ahead, 13–7. Frank Pigeon was their quarterback. He fades back. They run this little crossing pattern. I was the deep back and I got picked. Joe Massaroni catches the ball with two seconds to go and Frank Pigeon kicks the extra point.

"I can recall every play. Frank Pigeon wore these goggles, like Coke bottles. He was blind."

Riley still calls it one of the two worst losses of his life.

In basketball, he averaged 28 points as a senior and colleges came after him. Recruiting was mostly regional then so most of the interest was from eastern schools, but Kentucky's Adolph Rupp joined the chase.

College football powers were interested, too. Riley took trips to Penn State to meet Joe Paterno and Alabama to see Bear Bryant. Later he would wonder if he shouldn't have chosen football, where he had full-fledged pro size.

"It was almost like my future was predetermined," he said. "I was just going to play basketball. When Adolph flew in, that sealed it."

Now the former dead-end kid was officially going somewhere.

▌

In Lexington, where upstate "Noo Yawk" was akin to Paris, where any Wildcat player was a celebrity and an actual star was a statewide idol, Riley flowered.

He became dashing, a great dancer and, the word soon spread around campus, he was a ladykiller, the guy who walked up to Miss Ohio, a UK coed, and asked her out.

She said yes, of course.

"He was different," says Larry Conley, a basketball teammate a year ahead in school. "He was the only guy I've ever known who ironed his blue jeans.

"That's a true story. I remember walking into his room—we'd go out on dates—and he'd be in there pressing his jeans. And I thought, this man is destined to be one of the great dressers of all time.

"He came in with a cocksure arrogance about him. With some people that can throw you off, particularly when it's in college. But the one thing he could do, whatever he said, he backed it up. I mean, he had the ability to go out there and do it...."

"He can be somewhat of a distant individual. I'm not saying that in an uncomplimentary way. There was a distance Pat had to have. He liked his space. And I think that carried over to today. He wasn't genuinely one of the guys that wanted to go out and do things. We all wanted to pile in somebody's car and go out. Pat was very much of an individual when it came to that. He liked his privacy. And we all honored that. Once in a while he'd jump in and say 'Let's go do this' and we'd all go do it."

The coaches, who decided these things, roomed Riley with another incoming hotshot, Louie Dampier, one of those little Indiana automatons who could shoot for half an hour without hitting the rim.

Dampier never forgot his first vision of Riley in sunglasses, turtleneck sweater, pleated blazer, tight powder-blue slacks, and pointy-toed loafers.

Dampier remembered muttering under his breath: "Look what is here."

Nor was Riley impressed.

"He had one of those little burr haircuts," said Riley. "You know, just like a little kid."

Dampier suspected the coaches paired them off in the hope he'd be a soothing influence on Mr. Boulevard. "He had a wild side that I didn't have," Louie said. Dampier didn't want the job. He was the guy who'd have been in bed for four hours when Riley would come in from a party at 2 A.M.

Dampier asked for a new roommate, as did Riley.

The coaches said no.

"At first I thought Pat was a bit of a cold person," Dampier says. "The day the ice melted was the day President Kennedy was shot. That was the first time I ever saw any emotion out of Pat. It was the first time, to tell you the truth, I realized he had any feelings.

"I think he actually cried a little bit, which surprised me. He was real emotional, real upset....

"We got to be pretty good friends. By our junior year, we started doing a lot of things together. That's when I found out he could hustle pool—and that I could get hurt being there. He was a real hustler in the true sense. We'd go to a pool hall next to the campus and he'd ask some guy if he wanted to play. He'd lose a few games and then when the bets got high, he'd start running the table in nine ball. His game got a lot better when the stakes got higher. I don't know if he ever got in real trouble, but I was there when some guys were pretty unhappy."

17

Pat didn't just hustle pool. In summers he and Mike Meola would go up to Lake George and play basketball for money. In a good day, they could pick up $50.

The money came in handy. The family had nothing extra to send him off with. When he came home for his first Christmas break, he almost stayed.

"We didn't have any money," he said. "There were five other kids. Not one time did my family come down to UK and see me play. We couldn't afford it. I considered coming home and going to Syracuse. That would have made it a lot easier."

He stuck it out because he wanted to play for Rupp.

■|

Be careful what you wish for.

Adolph Rupp was a mixed blessing at best, the last of the great autocrats. His players got the mushroom treatment, kept in the dark with manure thrown over them.

"It wasn't like it is today," Dampier says. "There wasn't the widespread coverage like there is now. The coaches pretty much kept the press away from us. Part of it was Rupp's ego and part of it was to protect us. Rupp liked to get the headlines for himself.

"There were unwritten rules but you learned them pretty fast. We weren't allowed to talk in practice. We weren't even supposed to laugh when Coach Rupp said something funny. He was a dictator.

"They'd run you off. You remember Wayne Chapman, Rex Chapman's dad? He was a heck of a player. He was a free spirit. He enjoyed having a good time and he didn't always go by the rules in practice. They were just unmercifully rough on him. They didn't say, 'You've got to go,' but they made it real uncomfortable for him until he finally decided to leave."

But that wasn't Riley, who held Rupp in awe.

The imperial Baron was no second father as Walt Przybylo had been, and Riley bitched about him as much as anyone else. But he could handle anything Rupp could dish out and thrived in his program.

In later years, Riley would always speak warmly of Rupp.

"He was Schwartzkopf," Riley said. "He was a great, great presence. I take basically a lot of my philosophy from his coaching. I had four years of a drill-type mentality. The players were disciplined enough to where they didn't really despise him but they respected him."

If the players didn't really despise Rupp, they came close.

"I'm not sure Pat would have said that while he was there," teammate Conley says. "We're all in our forties now, heading toward our fifties, and we all look back now and can understand exactly what he was doing to us. But you didn't have the ability to see the larger picture back then. All you know is you've been out there 2½ hours and that son of a bitch has been yelling at you the last 2½ hours and that's all you can think of.

"We were in a situation where we had to perform. We knew who the man in charge was. He let us know that's the way it was. It was a situation where, if you didn't perform, get out of the way and let somebody else take your place. It was strictly adversarial.

"He challenged you every day. He challenged you on everything you did. And you just felt like 'Goddamn it, I'll show you.' "

From the moment Riley showed up, however, he was a star. Freshmen weren't eligible then but everyone at UK knew.

"I watched the guy grow from his freshman year," Conley says. "When he came in, he had all the physical attributes you'd want in a player. I mean, you could see that. Players know it faster than anybody, more so even than the coaches. He had the natural ability but he also worked hard. I mean he *really* worked hard. He was very driven.

"I don't know anybody I ever played with I thought was a better athlete. I mean, he could run, he could jump. He was very, very quick....

"It really amazed me, I gotta tell you, when he got out of basketball that he got into coaching. I really didn't think he was ever cut out to be a coach. He was very impatient. He had a temper. Not in such a manner you'd feel intimidated. He held it inside him. You knew when he got mad. He just had a tremendous drive like that. Sometimes when you've got a player like that, he can pick up and carry a lot of other players. Very hard-nosed. He'd go to war with you in a minute. With everybody."

Riley's development extended beyond the game. The coaches leaned on the players to make grades. Teammates thought Riley only did enough to get by, but his high school girlfriend Lanie Kramer could see a different Pat from Linton.

"He got into communications and he found something he could really sink his teeth into," she says. "He started to grow as a person.

And along the way, I think, he found out that he was really a bright human being."

■

Of course, UK wasn't what it had been.

With Riley and Dampier joining the varsity in 1964, the Wildcats went 15–10, Rupp's worst record to that point.

Little was expected of the '65 squad that had no starter over 6 foot 5. Rupp had Riley jump center; against opponents who came in two sizes, bigger and much bigger, Pat won 46 of 58. He got off his feet quickly and he had a trick; he'd hook his arm over the other player's elbow so his opponent was actually lifting him.

"He was a very strong, physical player in college," Conley says. "You gotta remember, he was trying to make up for some size. We were the same size, we were both approximately 6–3 and we were playing the forward position.

"He had a great body. He weighed about 205, 210 and he really moved people around. Great upper-body strength. And I think it surprised those guys who were 6–6, 6–7, 6–8 who may have weighed more that they just didn't have the ability to move as quick as he did."

The Wildcats, soon to be rechristened Rupp's Runts, embarked on a storybook season. Riley who'd averaged 15 points as a soph, jumped it up to a team-high 22 as a junior and shot 52 percent.

The Runts shot to No. 1 in the country, made the cover of *Sports Illustrated*, and were written up in *Time*. Riley called it "the most exciting time of my life."

They went unbeaten and rolled into the finals of the NCAA tournament against a small school named Texas Western.

Not that anyone expected much of a game or paid much attention to the matchup but Texas Western was all black, a collection of transplanted city kids with colorful names like David (Big Daddy D) Lattin, Neville (the Shadow) Shedd, and Wee Willie Worsely.

The Wildcats were all white, Rupp being a staunch defender of the color barrier. In his book, *Adolph Rupp As I Knew Him*, Rupp's top assistant, Harry Lancaster, said the UK president pressured Rupp to integrate and Rupp confided: "Harry, that son of a bitch is ordering me to get some niggers in here. What am I going to do?"

In a stunning upset that became a landmark, Texas Western won, 72–65.

It wasn't that close. Riley did his little quick-jumping trick and won the center jump but the referees caught him, did it over, and Texas Western got it.

Early in the game, Big Daddy D, a burly forward, got the ball inside UK's 1–3–1 zone trap and dunked horrifically over Riley. Texas Western point guard Bobby Joe Hill took the ball off Dampier and went in for a layup, then stole the ball again on the next possession for another layup.

Riley called it the worst loss of his life, bumping the defeat at the hands of Frank Pigeon's Mt. Pleasant Red Raiders down to No. 2.

"There was an unspoken feeling this was a significant game, even though it wasn't chronicled," he said years later. "It wasn't written about like it would be today.

"First of all, Adolph never let us read newspapers so I wasn't aware of what was being written. And people were more respectful of that kind of commentary, instead of blatantly saying 'five Southern whites against five New York blacks.'

"But you could feel it on the court. Trash talking started there.... I was on the baseline and they kicked the ball to David Lattin on the blocks. There wasn't much dunking then but he dunked over me, ripped the net down, and he said something that let me know he was serious about this game. I won't tell you what he said but you could feel that coming from him. They were committed. Very talented and committed.

"That game opened the door for a lot of ACC and SEC schools. Bob McAdoo, when he came to play for the Lakers, told me, 'I knew from the day Texas Western beat Kentucky, it was O.K. for a Southern black to go to a Southern school.'

"It really did open the door. There wasn't any more of this bullshit going on."

So it was worth it in a way?

"No," Riley said, still carrying his torch. "I've never been that kind of crusader. I believe in equal rights but only when we win."

Rupp never got over it, either.

Nine years later, he told the Louisville *Courier-Journal* his "all-time favorite team" had lost to "a bunch of crooks."

"The last time I saw Adolph Rupp that night," Riley said, "he was walking down the hall toward his hotel room, carrying a brown paper sack by the neck."

∎

That was as good as it got at UK.

The Wildcats were the pre-season No. 1 pick in 1966 but Riley had a bad back, having strained it in a water-skiing accident. He was in constant pain. Doctors put him into traction overnight.

Rupp decided he had to have him in any condition.

"We probably should have held him over," wrote Lancaster. "...It was one of the great mistakes Adolph and I made that year. Pat was just not the same ballplayer his senior year. But we were almost desperate for him. We were bringing in one of our best groups of freshmen and we needed Riley badly that year."

Riley's average fell from 22 to 17, his shooting percentage from 52 percent to 44 percent.

"As soon as Pat warmed up," Rupp said, "he would come over to the bench. He would say, 'Coach, I haven't got it tonight,' or 'I'm going to be all right.' "

One way or another, Riley played them all. UK went 13–13, winning its last game, against Alabama, to keep Rupp from his first losing season. Only then did Riley undergo back surgery for two slipped discs.

In the modern NBA where prospects are measured, weighed, personality-tested, and sometimes investigated by private detectives, his operation would have scared clubs, but this was a simpler time, not far removed from the days when teams drafted players using Street & Smith's *Yearbook*. Riley was a star and the San Diego Rockets, a new expansion team, made him their first No. 1 pick with the seventh choice in the draft.

In 1991, UK brought the Runts back to commemorate the 25th anniversary of their season. Riley, by then more famous as Laker coach, got a rock-star welcome and the biggest ovation.

"Him being the Hollywood type doesn't surprise me at all," Dampier says. "He always had a flair for that. He did like to be in the spotlight. He liked to wear the proper attire.

"But I'm really surprised that he's a coach. He didn't seem to have the personality to coach. I'm really surprised by how hard he works at it. I've heard and read how he really studies the tape and puts himself into it so much.

"That wasn't Pat."

Not yet, anyway.

CHAPTER THREE

Corvette Summer

People always thought of me as a backup for somebody else.... I know people used to see me and say 'Hi Pat' and think nothing further about me.

—PAT RILEY

Young Pat Riley drives west toward the setting sun in a yellow Corvette convertible, top down, radio tuned to old rock 'n' roll, the road stretching out before him like he was George Maharis or Martin Milner, bound for adventure on Route 66.

Imagine Riley's excitement.

For the first time he had money in his pockets and there was more where that came from. He was the San Diego Rockets' first No. 1 pick. Other guys had to go to Detroit or Cincinnati or Baltimore, but he had an expansion team in southern California, which meant he'd play right away, not to mention the tanning possibilities. Crank up the Beach Boys, don't let the music stop.

When he drove up, his new teammates' eyes bugged out. Twenty-five years later, they all remember The Car.

"He drove out in a yellow '67 Corvette, top down across the Southwest," says Jim Barnett, a Rocket teammate. "With a former high school classmate of mine who would go topless across the southwest desert. Truck drivers loved it."

"I think I was driving a Pontiac," says Jon McGlocklin, laughing. "Probably used. And he comes in in that.

"I think he had a four-year contract for 25 grand a year," Barnett says. "I was making, like 14. He had a lot of clothes. I remember him taking me to his apartment, showing me his suits and sport coats. I had, like two, three. He had, like, 15."

Everything about Riley screamed Big Timer. He had that glow. Opportunities leapfrogged over each other looking for him. He'd been drafted not only by the NBA but the NFL, too, though he hadn't played football since Linton. The Cowboys took him on the eleventh round, flew him to Dallas, and treated him like royalty.

"I went down there, met with Tom Landry, Tex Schramm, and Gil Brandt," Riley said later. "They offered me a guaranteed deal with a bonus. There was one problem. I wanted to play quarterback. I was going to be the next Don Meredith. But they wanted me to be a Cornell Green [another basketball player the Cowboys turned into a cornerback].

"I said 'Cornerback? Wait a minute.'

"I remember Tom Landry telling me, 'Well, Pat, we've got Don Meredith, we've got Craig Morton and we have a boy named Roger Staubach coming in this year.' "

Not that Riley really cared. He got a free trip to Dallas out of it. He got to hobnob with the Cowboy biggies. But he was a basketball player, that was how he was going to make it. He'd been a star at Linton, he'd stepped up to the next level and wowed them all over at

University of Kentucky. He'd been everybody's All-American. He'd been on magazine covers.

He drove through the desert in his flashy car toward the setting sun and the start of his life in a world that was all shiny and new.

■

It isn't hard to pinpoint where it went wrong. First day of training camp. First practice.

Jack McMahon, the Rockets' general manager and coach, sent him out to play guard. Riley had been a forward at Kentucky but at an overlisted 6 foot 4, he was small for the NBA. He was sure he could handle the switch but it wasn't going the way he'd hoped.

It wasn't going at all.

"I'll never forget my first day in training camp," Riley said. "After about five minutes, Jack McMahon pulled me over to the sideline and said, 'I drafted you and my job is depending on you and that is the *worst* five minutes of basketball I've ever seen.'

"I said, 'Jack, I've never played guard before.'

"He said, 'You'd better learn.' "

He spent nine years trying.

If it had been in him, he'd have torn it out of himself but it wasn't. At this exalted stage—professional basketball then comprised twelve teams and 144 players—he was simply betwixt and between, too small for forward, too slow for guard, a classic " 'tweener."

Whether it was his size or his surgically repaired back, he was overmatched. His old quickness advantage against bigger opponents was gone. He could barely keep the darting pro guards from taking the ball every time he dribbled it. If he dared to go inside, he ran into monsters like Baltimore's fearsome Gus Johnson, who was two inches taller, 25 pounds heavier, and treated rookies like Riley as hors d'oeuvres.

"He was a different type player than I expected," McGlocklin says. "In college, he was this white leaper. He could get up in the air and play this vertical game. In the NBA, that wasn't the strength of his game at all."

"He didn't have the quickness to guard people," Barnett says. "He was a 'tweener."

If talent had been everything, Riley would have washed out as soon as it was contractually feasible but he was no man to be run off.

He was a fighter with a deep-seated determination, not the surface kind of so many rookies who showed up talking a mile a minute and bowed out the same way, trailing excuses.

The veterans respected that. From the first day, he was someone to be taken seriously.

"Very confident," Barnett says. "Always confident in his basketball abilities. He thought he should be playing. He was better than any guy ahead of him."

"I'll tell you a story," McGlocklin says. "A lot of squirrelly things happened with the Rockets that year. Some guy wrote 'em a letter from Florida or somewhere and told them how good he was and that he wanted a tryout.

"Well, they brought him in and let him try out. The media got hold of it and made it a big thing. And he was a guard!

"And you know, we were all pretty upset about it. This was all outside the system and you didn't do it this way. So we went to the University of San Diego and we had, I think, Riley, Barnett, me, a number of guards. And we played two-on-two or three-on-three. And we were all going to make sure this guy didn't stay around for more than a day.

"We put Riley on him. He killed him. He literally beat him to a pulp. We knew that if we put Riley on him, the rest of us wouldn't have to worry. And it was true. The guy was gone the next day."

The veterans called Riley "Hillbilly" although he was no more Kentucky redneck than New York sophisticate. They put him through the usual rookie routine, sing this, fetch that, but he didn't mind.

"It's not like anyone resented him," McGlocklin says. "Then, rookies were still treated a little like rookies. It's not like today, you come in and you make a few million right off and you don't have to do some of the subservient things. Then you still got a little bit of the treatment. Riles fit in right off.

"It seems to me he handled his first season very well. He got some minutes. You know, the league hadn't expanded much. That was just the second expansion. Chicago was the first one and then San Diego and Seattle. There were still only twelve teams in the NBA. A lot of rookies didn't make it.

"It was a different league back then. There wasn't the exposure. It didn't have the hype it does today. Your adjustment time was a little bit better. You didn't have as much coming at you. You weren't wealthy. Some of us came to the NBA and came down from the college level in the way you were treated and the programs you were in. I'm sure, from Kentucky, he faced that. I certainly did from Indiana. I don't mean in terms of dollars. We didn't get paid at Indiana. [Laughing] They might have at Kentucky."

"He was very likable," his teammate Barnett says. "I liked him a lot. At first, it was difficult for me. You know, we didn't have guaranteed contracts in those days —I never did. It was difficult for me at first to strike up a friendship because he was my rival. I was a little aloof at first. He was a nice guy. He was still ... in control. I mean, he wanted to be in control of your relationship. I just think he always went to his own drum. I think he thought he always had the best way to go, whether you're going to go to this place or that place, what you should do in a ball game, in this situation."

It was a wild first year. The Rockets went 15–67 and lost 31 of their last 32 games but they had the time of their lives.

They still tell the stories: Barnett, also known as Crazy Horse, climbing into the arena rafters to meditate; forward John Q. Trapp feuding with Coach McMahon, showing up 30 minutes before tipoff with his warmups on under his trenchcoat; McMahon surprising Trapp by putting him in a game, whereupon Trapp pulled off his sweatpants and discovered he'd forgotten to put his trunks on.

"That was the happiest team I've ever been on," Riley said later. "We knew our limitations, we sort of understood but we played hard. We were all in it together. There were no guaranteed contracts, none of that stuff. As the season got worse and the team got even worse, we became even tighter."

Riley played all over. McMahon tried him at small forward, even power forward, his old college position, but this wasn't college.

"I remember Pat when he was playing in San Diego," says Keith Erickson, then a Laker. "They would play him at power forward at 6–4. I remember seeing him going against Gus Johnson, which was a mismatch. It was kind of fun to watch that. I liked his fire."

Early in Riley's second season, he injured a knee, went out for a month, and fell down the depth chart again.

He came back for his third season, ready to prove himself but was hurt once more.

"His third year there, he got off in camp, he was really playing good," says Pete Newell, who'd taken over as Rocket GM. "He was shooting better than he'd ever shot and he always understood the game. He adjusted to the two-guard spot.

"And I can see it in my mind right now. I was sitting down at courtside. He went up for a rebound and came down on the ankle or foot of somebody. Honest to God, he had an ankle that looked like it was going to be quadruplets, it was so big.

"And that ankle took forever to mend. And he was really playing well until then. I remember Jack was really enthused about how he'd made the step up and his confidence level had gone real high, too. I don't believe he got back until January or February, that's how severe the injury was. And of course, Alex Hannum was coaching then and the team was pretty well set when he did get back in. And then he was kind of fighting for minutes."

▌

Riley's glow was gone.

Another expansion was coming and the Rockets left him off their protected list. A couple of weeks before he was to marry Chris Rodstrom, a San Diego State coed, Riley was picked by the Portland Trail Blazers. He was about to become a husband and a journeyman.

"We were really upset," Newell says. "Hell, we lost three guys. The only team in the NBA that lost three guys and hell, we were just an expansion team ourselves two years before.

"We lost two and we figured we were safe and I'll be damned if the last pick in the whole thing, Portland picked him."

Riley's parents came out from Schenectady for the wedding, held in a chapel overlooking the Pacific. It was a storybook affair. The bride was beautiful. The groom was handsome, if, for the first time, anxious.

"It was one of those great marriages," Riley told PBS's Charlie Rose. "I was $5,000 in debt. I had a '67 Corvette, pipes on the side. I had four Four Tops records plus three Temptations records, a king-sized bed, a plastic plant, and we were getting married.

"My father came out and we spent a good time talking about it. It was one of the very, very few times that we really had the chance to sit down and for him to really sit across the table and give me some advice about my career.

"He told me not to do what he did, not to leave. I was very bitter about the San Diego Rockets putting me on the expansion draft. I had to leave San Diego. It was my first experience being traded or cut. I was very upset with that.

"The last time I saw him was after the wedding reception. He and mother, we took him downstairs and put him in Chris's parents' old 1965 Chevrolet Caprice, primer on the sides. We put them in the back seat of the car and one of Chris's brothers was riding them back to the house....

"As he was moving away, I can remember him sort of sticking his head out, you know, he was like waving to me and he, at the same time was yelling something. I was sort of chasing after the car.

"We never had a chance to sit down, you know, and really say the things to each other that we wanted to say. I was too embarrassed as a young man to say them and obviously he was probably too much of a dad to want to say them. But I do know that if I was in my 30s, I would have the conversation like in a minute with him. And even if he didn't want it, I would have grabbed him by the lapels and sat him down.

"I say that all the time to players that I talk to about their fathers and any player or person I meet that has a problem with his dad or mom.

"He says, 'They won't listen to me, I don't pay any attention to 'em.'

"I say, 'Hey, do it!'

"You will regret it one day. And I think it's our responsibility to do that as children as we grow. You got to come to peace with it because if you don't, it's gonna be torture, I think, for you later on in life. Especially if you get that telephone call, the one in the middle of the night."

What Lee Riley yelled from the car to his youngest child on his wedding day was nothing new.

Lee had been saying the same thing since Pat was 12, but it was their last moment together. Years later, Pat would summon the echo over and over again when he was afraid and didn't want to be alone. He'd repeat Lee's words to his players and write them in *Show Time*:

"Just remember what I always taught you. Somewhere, someplace, sometime, you're going to have to plant your feet, make a stand and kick some ass. And when that time comes, you do it."

A few months later, Pat got that telephone call in the middle of the night. Lee had died suddenly of a heart attack.

▮

Portland didn't turn out to be the place Pat would plant his feet.

He barely set them down. He was in and out of town in three weeks.

He was a face in the crowd, last pick in the expansion draft. There was a new No. 1 choice, Geoff Petrie of Princeton. There were more guards than the Trail Blazers knew what to do with: Petrie; Barnett and Rick Adelman who'd both been ahead of Riley in San Diego; Stan McKenzie, Shaler Halimon, Claude English. Portland coach Rolland Todd didn't lavish much time or attention on Riley. It wasn't hard to guess what was coming next.

But the Lakers arrived first.

Two weeks before the start of the season, they flew to Portland for an exhibition. Afterward, Riley approached Chick Hearn, the Laker play-by-play announcer, and asked if Hearn could get him to L.A.

Riley's request was completely out of the blue—"I knew him," Hearn says, "like I knew all the guys around the league, you know"— but it wasn't as far-fetched as it would be today.

Hearn was more than a broadcaster. He'd been the team's assistant general manager and he still had clout.

"I came out of the building that night," Hearn says. "You know the players' entrance back there, to get on the team bus. It was pouring rain and there was Pat and his wife, huddled under an umbrella, waiting at the bus.

"He said, 'Mr. Hearn, I was thinking the Lakers might need an extra guard. If there's anything you could do for me, I would really appreciate it.'

"Jeez, my eyes and ears lit up because I'd always liked his play so much and I knew that Fred Schaus (Laker general manager) did, too. I came back the next day and suggested it to management and it was very shortly thereafter they signed him."

The Lakers purchased Riley's contract—for $1,000—nine days before the start of the season.

If Hearn was all alight, it wasn't because he thought he was recommending the next Jerry West, just a nice young guy for the end of the bench.

The Lakers were a collection of legends: West, Wilt Chamberlain, Elgin Baylor. Ahead of Riley at guard were West, Gail Goodrich, Keith Erickson, and Willie McCarter. Of the players who were there all season, Riley would play the fewest minutes.

On the plus side, he'd work his tail off, he'd stay ready, and he'd never complain (where anyone could hear, anyway).

Also, he was white, still a consideration in the '70s.

If Riley never asked for any favors, it was still undeniable that a black player with his limitations would have had trouble lasting nine years. The NBA may have been the best integrated of the sports leagues but it was anything but color blind, loath to try to sell too many black players to predominantly white ticket buyers.

They were not far removed from the days of that old joke about black quotas: "Three at home, four on the road, five if you're behind." It was not uncommon to save the last spot on the bench for a white player.

Riley knew it, too. He said as much to friends.

He would have painted polka dots on himself to stay in the league. Told by his second organization he wasn't good enough, he held on to his good opinion of himself but he needed someone else to believe in him, too.

"He was always a classy guy," Barnett says. "He never lacked for confidence.

"I remember, I talked to him the day Portland let him go. I distinctly remember that day. He thought they were fools. He said, 'They'll live to regret this.' That's verbatim.

"Like me, I would have been a little scared—gosh, no one wants me, that kind of thing. Didn't enter his brain at all. He was confident of his abilities. He was bitter at the Blazer organization, I know that: Stu Inman, who was the director of player personnel; Rolland Todd, who was the rookie coach.

"He never revealed [fear]. I think at times he played scared in games. I know he lost confidence in games. He would never admit that but I could see it."

■I

Riley returned to southern California, but not in the style of his rookie entrance three years before.

"He was very grateful," Erickson says. "I remember that. I remember he and Chris at the time. They were so excited about being in L.A., with this opportunity, being on this franchise with such great players."

Now to see about staying there.

"When I finally realized that I couldn't be a front-line player— and I came to that decision early in my career because I could see the differences in talent—I also came to the conclusion that I wanted a career in the game," Riley said. "I wanted to stay in the NBA.

"Somewhere along the line, a player should realize where he stands in that melting pot of players, then work from that strength.

Of course, I would have liked to be a superstar and all that stuff. You know, not everybody can ride the white horse like Magic or Kareem or Norman [Nixon] or Silk [Jamaal Wilkes]."

Riley introduced a kamikaze spirit to Laker practices. It wasn't just other scrubs he went after on the court but West, himself, the Hall of Famer in waiting, as admired and respected a player as there ever was in the league.

Riley looked at this demigod and saw a human bull's-eye.

"I'll tell you what, he was like a bucking bronc in practice," West says, laughing. "It got to the point where late in my career, when it had started going down the other side of the mountain, I used to tell him all the time, I said, 'Pat, you got to beat the hell out of Gail Goodrich today. I'm tired and I'm sore.'

"He was an unbelievably hard worker. He made our practices. You need people like that to make your practices. You respect people like that."

West and Riley became buddies, hanging out together on the road. West had a financial adviser whose minimum requirement for a bankroll was far above Riley's means but West got him to take Riley, anyway. Riley heeded the adviser's counsel and prospered. When West divorced his first wife after his playing career ended, he moved first into the guest cottage behind Riley's Brentwood home.

Riley averaged only nine minutes a game his first Laker season but things picked up in his second.

Bill Sharman came over from the American Basketball Association to succeed Joe Mullaney as Laker coach. Sharman was an old-school obsessive who raised pre-game preparation to a new level, introducing the notion of the "shootaround."

Players had previously been free to sleep until 5 P.M. the day of games, which came in handy since they'd often played the night before and been awakened to fly to the next city at 6 A.M. the next morning, not to mention the toll taken by recreational activities.

Now Sharman wanted them to go to the arena in the morning for a light workout, get used to the baskets and the lighting.

Not everyone embraced the innovation. Chamberlain, an insomniac who slept late, sent word he was only coming to the arena once. Sharman could take his choice of morning or evening.

It was fine for Riley, who couldn't ever practice long enough, hard enough, or often enough.

Riley looked at Sharman and saw an unbroken line, through Rupp and Przybylo back to his father.

Sharman took a look at Riley and saw something, too.

"I thought Pat Riley, as a player, was definitely what we call an overachiever," says Sharman, now a Laker consultant.

"He didn't necessarily have as much ability as some of the players I had on that team and when I first started the season, I had Gail Goodrich and Jerry West at guards. We had Flynn Robinson who was one of the better shooters in the league at that time. We had Keith Erickson, another guard, but he was kind of hurt. So Pat, when I started out, was down the line. He was the fourth or fifth guard in my rotation.

"I found out that Pat was a tough, physical player, intelligent player. He was not necessarily a good ball handler, good passer, good dribbler, good outside shooter but he played tough, played tough defense. Every night he was going to give you 100 percent. So as the season progressed, I kept moving him up, moving him up and I guess about halfway through the season, he was my No. 1 sub."

Teammates called Riley "Tunnel Vision" for his lack of peripheral vision. Riley gave as well as he got, delighted to be a part of things at last, if one of the last parts. On a bus in Oakland, he confided to a sportswriter he was the lowest paid Laker, joking his salary wouldn't pay Wilt's grocery bill.

It was just great to be there. This was California in the early '70s. Riley's Ivy League haircut crept down his neck and enveloped his ears. He grew a droopy mustache. By the end of his career, he looked like he played in Sgt. Pepper's Lonely Hearts Club Band.

"His Sonny Bono period," said Paul Westphal, then a Phoenix Suns guard.

The Lakers went undefeated from November 5, 1971 to January 9, 1972, winning a record 33 games in a row. They finished with 69, another record, rolled through the playoffs, and won their first title in Los Angeles.

West and Riley ran off the Forum court after the clinching victory over the Knicks, arm in arm.

■❙

So much for the good times.

Erickson returned the next season and Sharman, no sentimentalist, put him back in the No. 3 guard spot.

In 1973, the Lakers got back to the NBA finals but this time without the chemistry. Amid the backbiting and resentment, the Knicks gunned them out in five games.

The next season Chamberlain retired; the season after that, West.

"We had played together for five years," Riley wrote in *Show Time*. "I always used to say I played on parasitic value. I knew how to support and complement the play of the best guard in the NBA.

"We had just gotten beat by the Milwaukee Bucks, eliminated in the first round of playoff competition on April 7, 1974.... Jerry had a muscle tear that would never get better.... Jerry was soaping up in the shower when he turned to me and said, 'This is my last game.'...

"He was the greatest guard the game had known, a complex personality and a loyal friend. When we won the championship, he came into the locker room, had a sip of champagne, shook a few hands and left. I've never been around anyone who wanted to win more than him."

Riley lasted one more season, in which the Lakers went 30–52 and didn't get near the playoffs. That spring, he underwent knee surgery, which is routine these days, but was career threatening then.

The next fall, he fought Laker owner Jack Kent Cooke for a new contract, even holding out a day.

Not that Riley had a lot of leverage, or any. The Lakers made no move to accommodate him. Riley was obliged to return without a contract.

Nor did the Lakers forgive his effrontery. Three games into the season, they traded him to Phoenix for two No. 2 draft picks.

"I know this is a business," Riley said later. "I found out when I was traded that sometimes loyalty doesn't give you any guarantees."

The Suns offered him a 25 percent raise but he turned it down, saying he wasn't going to report. The Suns, in no mood to fool around with a fringe player, immediately suspended him without pay.

"I believe strongly Riley can make a contribution to this team," said Suns president Jerry Colangelo, "but we can do without him easier than he can do without us. We're not going to let the inmates start running the asylum."

It's a tough life out on the margins. Recognizing the truth of what Colangelo was saying, Riley loaded his heavy heart onto an airplane bound for Phoenix.

"He wasn't happy to leave L.A.," says Erickson, who'd preceded him to Phoenix. "He wasn't crazy about coming over to Phoenix. He was still happy to be playing.

"We had some conversations about how much longer we were going to go, wondering what we were going to do."

Riley thought he had time to find out but his future was coming up fast.

He played that one season in Phoenix as No. 4 guard behind Dick Van Arsdale, Paul Westphal, and Ricky Sobers. The Suns, 19–27 at the end of January, went on a 23–14 run and made the playoffs. Then they shocked everyone by advancing to the finals, taking the Celtics to six games before falling.

Riley helped, too.

"We were going to L.A. and we hadn't won there in three years," says Dennis Awtrey, a Suns teammate. "We'd had five games at home and we'd won 'em all but now we had to play in L.A., New York, and Boston.

"We went over to L.A. and it was nip and tuck. And I can remember, Pat got substituted in near the end of the game and he made a running left-handed hook across the middle. I mean, it was about a 10- or 12-footer. And I'd never seen him shoot one, even in practice. He didn't have a hook, left or right.

"I thought it crushed them. So now we've won six in a row. We went up to New York and won so it was seven in a row. I think that propelled us into the playoffs. If I had to pick one spot in the whole year, one play, that stands out."

The next fall, the Suns' doctors refused to give the O.K. to Riley's knee. Faced with being waived, he retired.

His career ended with barely a ripple. The story got five paragraphs in the Arizona *Republic*, on the second page of the sports section, under a diagram of a Billy Casper golf tip ("Toes Out for Full Turn").

"I have done a lot of thinking about it," Riley was quoted in the story. "My knee has been examined by three doctors and it is their thinking that I should retire from pro ball."

Actually, he hadn't been thinking about retiring at all. He went back home to Brentwood and sat by the telephone, hoping for another team to call. No one did.

He'd made his last stand as an NBA player and hadn't even known it. Another Riley's dream had run out.

Another Riley awoke to face a new, harsh dawn.

CHAPTER FOUR

Santa Monica Chainsaw Massacre

Being 31, I thought I could play five more years and when an athlete doesn't—or can't—envision the end, it comes as a shock....

It was a forced retirement. I really wasn't ready to quit. People were afraid of me because of my knee....

After I didn't get any offers from anybody, I just decided to walk away from it. So it was ended. The switch was turned off immediately and I wasn't ready for it emotionally. The last 15 years of my life had been heavy-duty competition in a game I really loved.

I was hurt.

—PAT RILEY

Now for the rest of his life.

After all those years where his movements were planned for him, practice at 10, plane leaves at 4, shootaround tomorrow at noon, bus leaves for the game at 5:15, suddenly there was.... Nothing.

He had suffered his share of indignities, demotions, trades, waivers, the ten thousand snubs a journeyman endures but it was as nothing to him. He loved the life, the excitement, the camaraderie, the sense of mission.

Pat Riley, civilian, didn't have to be anywhere or do anything: practice, stay in shape, think about tonight's opponent. He awoke in the morning with no itinerary, job, or life.

It was as if he was playing the lead in a movie of his father's life. Pat after basketball was Lee after baseball. He had his father's confusion about what to do next. Like Lee, he had been trained only to play a game.

Most days Pat went to State Beach. The Rileys lived in Brentwood, just south of Sunset Boulevard, ten minutes from the water. Just drive over and park, no hassle on weekdays with everyone at work.

It was a beautiful beach, at the mouth of Santa Monica's Rustic Canyon, on the other side of Pacific Coast Highway. The hot volleyball players came from all over southern California to play at State Beach. Famous people hung out there, or people who looked like they were, or people who would be: George Hamilton, Tom Selleck, Sam Elliott.

Riley had been coming around for years with a bunch of Lakers: Keith Erickson, a homeboy who'd been a volleyball All-American at UCLA; Wilt who thought he was as good at the beach game as he was at basketball, *amour*, and everything else; West, whom the other Lakers deferred to; Gail Goodrich, the pouty one. The State Beach regulars thought of Riley as the nice, unassuming one.

∎

The regulars were an eclectic group, bound together by devotion to a lifestyle. Riley's friends included Altie Cohen, a schoolteacher from nearby Pacific Palisades in his forties; Teddy Grossman, a stunt coordinator in the movies or, as they said in L.A., "the industry"; Darrell Ruocco, who sold cars; Bill Gregory, a stockbroker; Jim Kaufman, a dentist, who was married to Barrie Chase, Fred Astaire's dance partner.

Riley fell right in with them.

"He was insecure, not a star," says Altie Cohen. "Never acted like a star. I don't think anybody ever considered him a star.

"He was never anything but a thoroughly nice person. And there was no way in the *world* you could have predicted what was going to happen in his life or any small percentage of it. He never said a hell of a lot. He was not a take-charge guy.

"And [when he was] with the Lakers, he would talk about it a lot. He would say, 'I'm hanging on every day. I'm playing with anger, the anger that I might get cut tomorrow.'

"And he talked a lot about, 'I'm not so sure I'd even be on this team if I weren't white.' "

Nor did anyone think he looked like a star. Altie Cohen's wife, Idell, thought he was a good-looking guy but nothing remarkable. The Cohens' niece, Margery Schwartz, then a teenager hanging around the beach, said the same thing.

Idell thought the long-legged Chris was the looker in the family. Years later, when Riley got famous, Idell's friends would say they were so thrilled she knew Pat Riley, he was so hot, etc. Idell would wonder what she'd missed.

Now it was a morose Riles who haunted the beach. The regulars grew used to seeing him, sitting with his back propped up against the wall of the parking lot, writing furiously.

"I was depressed," Riley said. "I went to the beach every day and wrote. I wrote about ten, fifteen, twenty legal pads.

"I had thoughts about the game. Back then, the money factor was a big deal. I felt that teams were trying to buy loyalty with big contracts. I was bitter about how my career ended. It was typical stuff that would come out of somebody that maybe is mourning the loss of something they really loved...."

Something was going to have to take the game's place but he didn't know what it was. He'd always been a hard worker but now there was nothing to work at.

He discovered the limitless possibilities of home improvements and began working on his house, or working it over.

"What clearly happened to Pat was that he had this body ready to go and no place to go with it," Chris said later. "He dove into home projects in such an obsessive way that it literally drove me out of the house."

She was never sure what she'd find when she got home, either. Finishing up work on her master's at Cal State Northridge, she drove off to school one morning while Pat was starting to take the ivy off the roof of the guest cottage next to the swimming pool.

"The more ivy I took off," Riley said, "the more roof I took off. It was engulfed with ivy.

"So I just said, 'The hell with it,' and started hitting it with a large sledgehammer. By the end of the day the guest house was leveled."

He pruned his trees, too, with a chainsaw.

"He was sawing branches," Altie Cohen says, "and he put the saw into his leg. Terrible gash."

No one let it go as an accident. This was West L.A., as psychiatrically saturated as Freud's Vienna. Riley's buddies leaped to a common interpretation, almost in unison.

"Teddy Grossman called it the chainsaw massacre," Cohen says, laughing. "Part of Riley's self-imposed rehabilitation or whatever he was doing to erase the pain of not playing basketball anymore, and not knowing what's coming.

"We all thought that was Freudian and we kidded Riley a lot."

■I

The game haunted him like an old love.

Heartbreak is the way of sport where all marriages are of convenience and divorces as final as they are sudden. But everyone has to learn the hard way.

At first, he thought he could still come around.

He went to a Laker game, intending to visit the press lounge, the late-night headquarters for Laker officials, broadcasters, writers, friends of the owner, and hangers-on of all shapes and sizes.

The security guard at the door stopped Riley in his tracks.

"I was refused entry," he said. "I played five years with the team, won a championship and now I'm on the outside. You don't think I wrote a lot about that?

"That guy wouldn't let me in. I said, 'What do you mean I can't get in? I want to see Chick. I want to see my old buddies.'

"He said, 'No ex-players.'

"I definitely walked out of there a little crushed."

When he did get in the door, it went no better.

"He went back to the Forum for a practice," Altie Cohen says, "and he told me about it. He said it was the most disillusioning experience.

"He said, 'I was embarrassed to be there. The players were embarrassed to have me there.' He said, 'I'll never go again.' He wasn't wanted.

"Kareem Abdul-Jabbar (who'd just been acquired by the Lakers) sort of half-ass said, 'Hey Riles, c'mon up some time, let's have some this or that!'

"And he went up to visit Kareem one time. Kareem was still playing and Riley was an ex-player.

"Kareem goes 'Riley! I'm on the phone, long distance, I'll be right there!'

"And he came down and talked one minute and got back on the phone. And Riley finally left. He felt so put down, so unwanted."

■|

The hell with them.

Like his father who'd thrown out all his trophies and uniforms, Riley set about casting off his old life, even his clothes.

Once he asked Ruocco if he wanted any of his old shirts. Riley threw open a closet that Ruocco estimated held 250 of them.

"Let me quote Pat Riley at that stage of his life," says Altie Cohen. "I was at the house and I was kidding him about his wardrobe.

"He said, 'That's just leftover stuff. I don't give a shit about clothes. If it's cold, I want to be warm and if it's warm, I want to be cool. I'm most happy if I'm not even aware of what I'm wearing. You didn't know me during my years when I had to get all my suits made. What a thrill, what a weight off my back that I don't have to live like that anymore.' "

Devastated that his basketball friendships hadn't transcended the game, Riley brooded and turned meditative. He grew a beachcomber's shaggy beard.

"One New Year's Eve, we ate dinner at Dante's on Wilshire," said Cohen. "It was Riley and Chris, Bill Gregory and Elizabeth. Teddy Grossman brought Bobby Beathard (then Miami Dolphin personnel director and an old State Beach guy) 'cause he was in town.

"And we went out to Riley's house afterward. Course, people had been drinking.

"And after midnight, Riley said, 'I have something to say.' He clinked a glass or something and he gave this impassioned speech.

"He said, 'We're heading into a New Year and I have some ideas for the New Year and I hope you'll all take them seriously. All of us here together, let's pledge to really be friends in the New Year, to really get to know each other, to care about each other. I don't think we know each other. Let's care about each others' problems, let's share each others' joys.'

"He was pleading. And he went on and on like that. He said, 'That's my New Year's speech.'

"Teddy and Gregory couldn't believe what they were hearing. I thought it was a little inappropriate in that the crowd didn't want to hear that sort of thing but he didn't say anything that wasn't caring. It was quite a thing. That was as intense as I've ever seen him."

The beach guys were a fun-loving group, more used to needling than nurturing each other. Luckily, Pat had Chris, his own live-in therapist, who compared what he was going through to the mourning period after a death. They had had their problems over the years but now he needed her and she stood by her man.

"She used to meet me in the afternoons," Riley said, "and we would make a practice of being on the beach to watch the sun set. After a while, I got the idea that it would be fun to sit on the beach and watch the sun rise.

"We went down there three straight mornings it was fogged in. We sat there, wrapped tightly in our blankets, hugging each other and waiting for the sun to rise. We never saw a thing."

He cast about, looking for something to do.

A guy he knew, Marty Rudnick, who owned a clothing store on Canon Drive in Beverly Hills where Riley had often shopped, offered him a position as store manager.

"Now, why did they want him?" says Altie Cohen. "He had no experience as a retailer. 'Cause he was a Laker.

"But this Rudnick thing fell through, then he was really down. He said, 'I'd be thrilled to get a job coaching at a high school or a junior college. Something like Oxnard or Ventura. I could be happy with that the rest of my life.' "

Idell knew someone at Ventura. She said she'd try to hook Pat up.

■|

Instead fate, or Chick Hearn, lent a hand again.

Hearn's partner, Lynn Shackelford, was leaving to take a job as sports anchor for one of the local TV stations.

Hearn thought of Riley.

Riley, who'd already learned of the job from Shackelford, was salivating at the possibility.

"Shack had a chance to do the nightly news on Channel 9," Hearn says. "He thought he'd gone as far as he could in the booth in seven years. He was a marvelous announcer, all of them have been, and it left us without a color man.

"I don't know why I thought of Pat because he didn't approach me. I approached him and asked if he wanted to make a couple tapes, present them to [then-Laker owner] Jack Kent Cooke.

"He was pretty nasal at that time. I thought, 'Oh, Jesus,' to myself, 'Cooke will never accept this guy.'

"Anyway, we would sit and watch games with the sound turned off. I would do my thing and he would do his as color.

"After we did it many, many times—Cooke didn't even know I was interviewing him—I said, 'Here's a tape I think we can take in to Cooke.'

"So I took it in. I thought we'd get thrown out of his office. And Cooke says, 'My Gawd, Chick! This boy is wonderful! Just what we need!'

"So we hired him."

It was as if the basketball gods had lowered a rope. Riley was back in the life, on the planes, in the hotels, courtside at games. Once again, he could get past the usher at the door of the Forum press lounge.

"This game is in my blood," he said a few weeks into his new gig. "It has been for twenty years. Out of the NBA, I felt terribly awkward, like an outsider. Players would say, 'What are you doing? What are you planning? Do you miss the game?'

"I was too embarrassed to say, 'I'm not doing a thing and I miss it very much.'

"Money wasn't a factor. We invested well. We have no financial problems at all. Had the Lakers said, 'You'll work for free,' I would have jumped."

Of course, it wasn't like being a player.

He was a radio guy doubling as traveling secretary. He didn't just ride the planes and stay in the hotels, he made the reservations, booked the buses and practice gyms and everything else the job entailed.

"I actually had to hand out boarding passes to the players," Riley said. "Players used to throw them back at me—'I don't want 1A, I want 1D. I don't want to sit next to that guy.'"

Then there was his partnership with Chick.

Hearn was a star in his own right, third only to West and Elgin Baylor in the Laker trinity, a towering, hyperkinetic presence on the dial from his Forum perch, "high above the western sideline."

In the media-conditioned Los Angeles market with teams that were recent arrivals, stylists like Hearn and the Dodgers' Vin Scully were giants. The first Dodger employee to earn $1 million a year was not Sandy Koufax, Don Drysdale, or Fernando Valenzuela but Scully. Fans in Dodger Stadium and the L.A. Sports Arena, the Lakers' home before Cooke built his Fabulous Forum, became famous (and were ridiculed elsewhere) for taking portable radios to hear Scully and Hearn describe the games they were there watching.

Chick enjoyed the compliment. Before every Forum game, the p.a. announcer still asks fans with radios to keep them low so the feedback doesn't go out over the air.

Baseball required no selling to Los Angeles, the city all but donating a chunk of downtown real estate for a ballpark. Until Dodger Stadium was built, the Dodgers shattered attendance records in the Coliseum, an awkwardly retrofitted football stadium.

Pro basketball, in comparison, was small potatoes. Los Angeles barely acknowledged the Lakers' arrival from Minneapolis in 1960, making Hearn's magnetism all the more important.

Chick was hired by then-Laker owner Bob Short during the first post-season and flew to St. Louis for Game 5 of the Western finals. The Lakers won, the game was exciting, and so was Hearn. The team that claimed to have averaged 5,045 fans was welcomed home by more than 15,000 in the Sports Arena.

Hearn was a rapid-fire, nonstop talker. In a business where preparation was strictly optional—Tom Brookshier, then one of CBS's top football announcers, bragged that he didn't do any—Hearn did hours of homework, even calling imaginary action to warm up.

When Riley joined up, Hearn was working on a streak of consecutive games that would grow to 2,692 by the end of the 1993–94 season. Not content with just that, Hearn took all the outside work he could get. He acted in movies. He hosted "Bowling for Dollars." He did college football for ABC; his Laker streak would have been longer if bad weather hadn't canceled his flight out of Arkansas in 1965.

He did UNLV basketball on top of his Laker schedule in the 1980s when he was in his sixties, although no one knew for sure what his real age was.

Hearn's demands of a color man were minimal. He was the last NBA announcer to work alone, accepting a second man in the booth only under orders from Cooke in 1967.

Hearn didn't let his first color man, Al Michaels, do anything but read statistics when time was out. Michaels (who went on to become ABC's top announcer) lasted six games with Hearn.

Keith Erickson, who would succeed Riley, seemed to go whole seasons without saying anything but "That's right, Chick." Erickson accepted the role with wry detachment. Asked to speak at a birthday party once, he walked to the microphone and said, "That's right, Chick."

"You can say 'That's all right, Chick,' as many times as you want," said Hot Rod Hundley, Hearn's second color man. "But if you say, 'That's wrong Chick,' you're gone."

Even an old Chickie favorite like Riley knew what the deal was.

"Chick was the kind of guy who would never give his color men a whole lot of rope," Riley said later. "Usually just enough to hang themselves.

"If you're sitting besides him, you'd better be ready because Chick tests you on the air."

Riley had to wait for openings in Hearn's machine-gun delivery, agree intelligently, and get out in a hurry. There was no training program. The time-honored method of grooming a new announcer was to throw him out there and see how he did.

Teamed with a broadcasting giant, fearful of being written off as a jock out of water, a humble Riley begged friends and colleagues for advice.

Joe McDonnell, a young radio reporter, used to see Riley in the press lounge. Riley would ask him if he'd watched the previous night's telecast, and did he have any suggestions?

"He was terribly insecure about that job," says Altie Cohen. "He used to ask me, 'How was I? I know I make mistakes. Would you correct me if I make mistakes?'"

Actually, Riley was doing fine.

Visibly nervous at first, he settled in quickly. His role began expanding. Intrigued by the production end, he started doing mini-features on Laker players, taking a camera crew to their homes on off-days, setting game action to music. He took a production course at USC and even acting lessons. He was grateful to play his second fiddle but he also wondered where it might lead.

∎

Meanwhile, the Lakers faded.

Baylor, Wilt, and West were gone. Cooke had pulled off one of his mega-deals, getting Abdul-Jabbar from the Bucks, who were forced to acquiesce to their dour center's insistence on leaving Milwaukee. But the Lakers had to give up almost an entire team—David Meyers, Brian Winters, Junior Bridgman, Elmore Smith—leaving them with little but Kareem.

Abdul-Jabbar, grateful to be liberated from the Bucks, won the MVP in his first Laker season but even that wasn't enough. The Lakers went 40–42 and Coach Sharman was replaced.

West, restless in retirement, did what he'd said he'd never do and became a coach. He did well in the role, compiling the league's best record, 53–29, in his first season as Abdul-Jabbar won another MVP.

But the furies that drove West as a player consumed him as a coach. As team spokesman, he found things that he thought were off-the-record in the papers. He was quoted as calling Abdul-Jabbar a dog and saying of the aging Lou Hudson, "If Hudson were a horse, we'd have to take him out and shoot him."

After three seasons West fled, vowing never to return.

In 1979, Cooke sold the Lakers, Kings, and the Forum to Jerry Buss, a flashy L.A. real estate developer.

Buss hired Jack McKinney, the top assistant to Jack Ramsay of the division-rival Blazers.

Everyone was optimistic. The Lakers had just gotten Michigan State sophomore Magic Johnson with the first pick in the draft. Indeed, a new era was coming, but there would be twists in the road they couldn't imagine.

Accidental Tourist

*Friendly. Articulate. Very good loyal-type
human being. Pro-Laker.*

*Admittedly, I don't spend a lot of time with the
color man on the radio.*

—JERRY BUSS'S FIRST IMPRESSIONS
OF PAT RILEY

■

*Ten years ago, Pat carried the bags of West and Goodrich. In
1982, he's the coach of the West. The way he's going, in 10
years he'll probably be President of the United States.*

—CELTIC COACH BILL FITCH
AT THE '82 ALL-STAR GAME

On a peaceful Thursday morning, Laker Coach Jack McKinney got on his son's bicycle in Palos Verdes to play tennis with his best friend and assistant coach, Paul Westhead.

Instead he pedaled into an unwanted niche in NBA history.

The tennis courts were a mile and a half away at Westhead's condominium complex. The neighborhood was quiet and scenic with bluffs overlooking the Pacific. The streets were wide and lightly traveled. But going down a hill, McKinney lost control of his bike and flew over the handlebars. He couldn't use his hands to break his fall and he wasn't wearing a helmet.

He was found unconscious and taken by ambulance to a nearby hospital. He had suffered a severe concussion and fractures of the cheekbone and elbow. By the next day, his vital signs had stabilized and he could say his name. By Sunday, he could recognize Westhead, whom Claire McKinney had smuggled in as McKinney's brother.

It was a scary time for the principals and a bewildering one for the Lakers.

McKinney's prognosis was open-ended; doctors said he needed a lot of rest but didn't know how much. There was whispered speculation about brain damage.

McKinney's team was off to a running start, literally. The Lakers were 10–4 and fast breaking as never before.

It was easy to see Magic Johnson was special. For the first time since Abdul-Jabbar played with Oscar Robertson, he had a teammate who could run a game at whatever pace was needed, get him the ball exactly when and where he wanted it, and take over himself when necessary.

Johnson was 6–9 and 220 pounds, power-forward size, and not loath to wade in among the big guys. He was effervescent; on opening night in San Diego where Abdul-Jabbar had tossed in a game-winning hook, Johnson jumped into his arms, startling the hoary Kareem.

Suddenly, the Lakers had to turn this powerhouse over to a young assistant who'd been in the NBA 26 days.

Westhead had once been a rising star in Eastern college coaching, a Renaissance man type with a master's degree in English literature who'd taught Shakespeare on the college level. He read voraciously and widely; his wife, Cassie, said he always had two or three books going at the same time.

He had done well at Philadelphia's LaSalle College where he had shown he was adventurous in basketball, too.

Bored with Eastern slow-down ball, he started leaving a player at the offensive end, daring opponents to go five-on-four. If they missed, LaSalle would throw the ball to the other end for a layup (in theory, anyway). It offended purists as circus stuff. When McKinney offered Westhead a chance to move to the big show as an assistant coach, there was little objection at LaSalle.

In Los Angeles, Westhead was an unknown, even among Laker players and officials, but there was nothing to do but let him take over. The day after McKinney's fall, the Lakers, playing Denver in the Forum, were shaky but Jamaal Wilkes hit a 20-footer to force overtime and they won, 126–122.

So Westhead was allowed to keep going.

"I did it for myself for about six games," Westhead says, "and during that time, it was more like I was a substitute teacher. The management would say, 'Well, Houston and Chicago and when you get back from that trip, check in with us and we'll talk.'

"So after six games, they said, 'Well, things are going pretty well, we'd like you to stay.'

"And I said, 'I need somebody.' "

That was fine with the front office, which was wondering how to help him out, or more precisely, shore him up. The thought was that he'd bring in an NBA veteran. Laker officials thought of Elgin Baylor who was in private business but available.

Westhead, a man of his own mind as they'd learn, hit them with a candidate out of left field: Pat Riley.

If the idea wasn't preposterous to West and Sharman who knew Riley, it was a letdown to Buss. To the new owner, Riley was a nice guy whom he'd inherited with the furniture.

"I had talked on one of the road trips to Pat," Westhead says. "I asked him, 'Would you like to come work as an assistant?' And he was, I would say, pleased that I thought of him but uncertain whether he should do it or not. In the meantime, he went back and consulted with Chick Hearn.

"What was going on that Riles didn't know about, I suggested to Jerry Buss that Pat Riley be my assistant.

"And in typical Jerry Buss fashion, he said, 'You should think about that.'

"Over the years I've had my ups and downs with the Lakers, obviously. I've learned to respect Jerry Buss more in hindsight than I did when I was in the thick of things.

"But I realize that was one of his tricks whenever he didn't think what you wanted to do was the right thing. He rarely would say, 'No, I think that's a bad idea.' He'd say, 'I think you should think that over.'

"So sure enough, we go on another road trip and I come back maybe one week later. And Riles said, 'I'd like to do it with you.'

"Now I've got the one half but I don't have the other. And I went back to Jerry Buss and he said, 'Well, what do you want to do with this?'

"And I said, 'Pat Riley.'

"And he said, 'Well, it's your decision.'

"And I said yes and he said O.K. But it was not an instantaneous, Oh what a great choice I'm glad you thought of it and we had that in mind but you beat us to the punch kind of thing.

"I think they had some people in mind and I don't know what they were thinking. Obviously, I had coached six games by then and Riles had zippo. [Laughing] We were like the Blues Brothers. So I can understand their apprehension, not just about me but not having someone with a wealth of experience."

If the move alarmed Buss, it wasn't off the wall in the loosely structured NBA of the '70s. Players still moved into coaching with no experience, sometimes from the announcer's booth like Philadelphia's respected Billy Cunningham. Pete Newell, Riley's old GM from San Diego, spoke to Buss and gave Riley a nice recommendation.

But all Westhead really knew about Riley was that he liked him.

"I had no clue," Westhead says. "Up until that time, we were just two of the eighteen guys on a trip. [Laughing] And assistant coaches kind of gravitate to assistant TV commentators. So we were kind of like the two assistants."

So why exactly did he want Riley?

"Just someone to hang out with," Westhead says, laughing again. "I mean, it's *lonely* when you're by yourself.

"Clearly at that time, it was a very interim post. At that moment, we were just waiting for the days, weeks, maybe a few months before Jack McKinney would return. I had no apprehensions: How is whoever I hire going to do? He could be with me, just kind of hanging out, so it wasn't a big deal."

■|

To Riley, it was a big enough deal.

It had never occurred to him this might be an opportunity for him. He hadn't thought much about coaching since his lost beach days. He'd be giving up a real job for a temporary one and leaving Hearn in the lurch. Chick would have to find someone else and Riley might not be able to get his job back in a month.

Riley consulted Chris. She didn't think it was such a great idea.

Riley consulted Hearn who wanted to think about it.

"Paul, unbeknownst to me, asked Riles to be his assistant," Hearn says. "Riles came to me and said, 'I've been asked to do this, what do you think?'

"I said, 'Let me think about it overnight.'

"I thought about it. I thought about his dad. I thought about Ad Rupp. I thought about his contribution in the NBA. I thought about his work habits and everything I knew about him. I really measured him.

"I finally said the next day, 'I think you can do it.'

"And he said, 'What if I don't make it?'

"I said, 'I'll give you a written contract. You can come back in the booth any time you want.' And that sold him."

"Maybe he saw something in me that I didn't see," Riley said. "All I know is that if Chick hadn't advised me to take the job, I wouldn't have done it....

"As each day passed, the more I thought about it, the more excited I got. Finally, I reached the point where I figured I'd better tell Paul I wanted the job before he hired somebody else. This was a chance in a lifetime for me. There just aren't that many coaching jobs available in the NBA and I knew as an ex-player that with the great influx of college coaches in the league, there would be fewer and fewer openings for somebody like me.

"Along in there, we lost three in a row and everybody who'd said take it was starting to stay away.

"So I said, what the hell. I dove."

If Riley was a hard sell to the front office, he was fine with the players. The last thing they wanted was someone who'd start telling them how to do stuff.

"When McKinney got hurt," says Norman Nixon, "we realized we had a team that might be capable of winning the championship and we actually lobbied for somebody that we knew wouldn't come in and try to over-coach us." We lobbied for Westhead to keep the job and Riley to be the assistant. We could feel it very early, that this was a team that was going to be very special so we didn't want somebody like a—I'm not going to call a name—coming in there and trying to just overpower our playing abilities."

Eight days after he was offered the job, Riley came downstairs from the booth, sat on the bench, and watched the Lakers beat Kansas City in the Forum.

O.K., he was an assistant coach. Now what?

■

In the beginning, he tiptoed around a lot.

"To be honest, let's say the first few weeks on the job, he was just kind of hanging out," Westhead says.

"Pat's first couple of months with me, he was very standoffish. I think he felt awkward at first. As a matter of fact, I know he did. Awkward because the players he's now an assistant coach with are his peers, guys like Jamaal Wilkes and Kareem.

"It's very hard to say, 'Kareem, I think you ought to drop step this way.' Pat very smartly went slow and just observed.

"As the season wore on, I began to give him more things to do and he responded. The next thing you know, the clipboard's out and he really got into it."

Realizing he could do this coach stuff, Riley began preparing himself to run his own team. He became a regular on the clinic circuit, rare for an NBA guy at the time.

"I remember," Pete Newell says, "Bobby Knight and I had these two-man clinics. We'd have them on a Friday night and then all day Saturday. We had one all the way out by Orange County Airport, I remember. Pat came. He was an assistant then.

"We went Friday night 'til about 10. The next morning, we started around 8:30 and there's Pat. And I know he went home. He got home about midnight and he must've gotten up about 5 in the morning.

Knight, a latter-day Rupp, was passionate, defense-oriented, and an old-fashioned, high-decibel tyrant. He might have had his problems in the NBA where players were older, richer, more powerful, and harder to intimidate but at Indiana University he was a great artist.

Knight was everything Riley would be one day, except Riley would be the pro version, smoothing the waters rather than trying to part them.

They became friends. When Riley coached the Laker entry in the summer league, he used Knight's techniques for everything, leaving out only the screaming.

▮

They were off.

The Lakers never missed a beat, blitzing to a 60–22 record, 50–18 under Westhead.

"The players measured both of us," Riley said later. "Both our personalities were in tune with how they felt they wanted to be approached: Paul, the quiet, authoritarian one; me, the former player, friendly with them. It made for good chemistry."

The Lakers cruised into the Finals against the Sixers.

They split the first two games in Los Angeles. As the series moved east, word leaked that Buss had decided Westhead would be his coach next season. McKinney was out.

Anxious to return, McKinney had been pestering Buss for months. Buss held him off on advice of the doctors but something else was going on, too.

Westhead had emerged as a hot prospect. If the Lakers brought McKinney back, another NBA team was sure to come after Westhead. How many bright, young, Shakespeare-quoting assistant coaches were there who had already won a title?

Laker players told Buss they wanted Westhead. Buss needed only a way to soft-soap McKinney out of town. Before he figured out a way to announce it, the story broke in a Philadelphia newspaper; McKinney who'd set up a championship team, whose only mistake had been falling off a bicycle, found out from his son who saw it on TV.

The Lakers and 76ers split Games 3 and 4.

Back in the Forum, the Lakers won Game 5 to take a 3–2 lead but lost Abdul-Jabbar who sprained an ankle.

Heading back to Philadelphia for Game 6, Westhead opted for shock theater: He was going to have Johnson jump center as if to tell the 76ers this was a lark. No matter what happened, the Lakers could still go home for Game 7 when Abdul-Jabbar would be ready.

Johnson then rocked the NBA, scoring 42 points with 15 rebounds and seven assists. The Lakers won the championship right there.

In the tumultuous post-game celebration, a giddy Buss called Westhead "the best coach in the world." Four days later he signed him to a four-year, $1.1 million contract.

At the press conference Buss, determined not to criticize McKinney, said he'd chosen Westhead because he wanted a coach "I can run and chum with and have a beer with."

To make it up to McKinney, Buss quietly persuaded his business partner, Frank Mariani, who owned the Indiana Pacers, to hire him.

McKinney and Westhead were estranged for a year, though they later reconciled.

Not that anybody thought much about it, but Riley was an interim assistant coach no longer.

Humble as he was, at least he was permanent.

∎❘

Their first season had been a cakewalk. Their second, fate starting collecting dues.

The Lakers were beset by every imaginable problem: jealousy, bad luck, injury.

The chemistry problems started at the top with the strained relationship between Abdul-Jabbar and Johnson. Three weeks into the season, Johnson tore up his knee, underwent surgery, and missed 45 games.

The Lakers went 54–28, second in the Pacific Division to the Suns.

Westhead, a players' coach as a rookie, turned into a coach, period, and became more pointed in his comments.

Players began grumbling privately that Westhead was junking McKinney's system by making them look for Abdul-Jabbar first rather than last.

Westhead's erudition, once thought amusing, was now deemed kooky. Once, with the Lakers getting walloped, he told them a parable at halftime about being adrift in a boat and needing everybody's hand on the rope. It ran long and the players couldn't warm up before the second half.

"Here we are," grumbled Nixon, "down by 18 and he's in some damn boat with no oars."

Some of the players decided he'd forgotten who'd made whom.

The season became an ordeal. Riley felt the pressure so keenly by the spring, he spent five weeks in a neck brace.

Johnson returned late in the season. Everyone in the Forum got "The Magic is Back" buttons but the rest of the Lakers had long since grown tired of hearing about it. Before the playoffs, Nixon, talking to a writer about the sacrifices he'd had to make for Johnson, added: "Anyway, fifteen years from now everyone will have forgotten Magic."

The story ran the day the first series opened. That night the Lakers were upset in the Forum by the Houston Rockets, a 40–42 team in the regular season.

The three-game miniseries moved to Houston where an angry Johnson lashed back.

"If Norm Nixon feels that strongly about having the ball, we'll get him a ball, put his name on it and he can keep it under his arm during the game," he said.

If a resentment or two bubbled in Nixon's brain pan, he and Johnson were also buddies who regularly toured the discos together. Before Game 2 the next night, Nixon went up to Johnson to try to explain. Johnson listened, without changing his stern expression.

Amazingly, the Lakers won. Then, seemingly back in control with Game 3 at the Forum, they fell to squabbling among themselves once more.

"I walked into our locker room five minutes before the final game of the series," wrote Riley in *Show Time*. "What I saw when the door swung open, was a total breakdown of the team.

"Magic stood on one side, pleading, 'I didn't say any of those things in the paper.'

"A couple of players faced him from the other side of the room. They yelled back vehemently, 'If it wasn't true, they wouldn't have printed it!'

"Some of the rookies were actually trembling. Kareem Abdul-Jabbar and Jamaal Wilkes looked over the scene with pained, distant expressions, as if to say, 'I can't believe the shit I'm hearing!'"

The Lakers played like the divided team they were. They trailed, 87–86, in the closing seconds when Johnson, who'd already missed 13 of 15 shots, broke a play designed to go to Abdul-Jabbar and threw up a running 10-foot air ball. The curtain crashed down on the Lakers.

Just to show bygones weren't bygones, Laker players didn't vote Riley a playoff share.

It was a meltdown and it wasn't over yet.

That summer Buss gave Johnson a "lifetime" contract, $25 million over twenty-five years. There was already no question of who Buss's favorite was; he and Magic sometimes went clubbing together.

The offended veterans skidded to a stop on Buss's doorstep like cartoon Roadrunners: Abdul-Jabbar, Wilkes, Nixon. They wanted their deals re-done, too, and ultimately got them.

Everyone in the organization, it seemed, was now complaining about Westhead: players, officials who felt he was intruding on their turf. Despite what Buss had said, he and Westhead had never been social friends. Westhead was a religious family man, not likely to be running and chumming with his fast-lane boss.

Little more than a year after Buss had proclaimed him the best coach on the planet, there were hints of impatience.

"Is Westhead a genius?" asked Buss that summer. "We'll find out. He asked me to get the talent. He wanted it this way. Now we'll find out what he can do."

The outside world had no idea about the turmoil. *Sports Illustrated* set up a photo shoot for its pre-season issue with the Laker players in a classroom, wedged into old-fashioned wooden desks with lift tops and inkwells, with Westhead, dressed as a teacher, lecturing them with a pointer. The players hated it.

At the opening of camp, Westhead punctuated his remarks with a famous quote from Victor Frankel, a concentration camp survivor: "That which does not kill me makes me stronger."

Westhead insisted later he had no inkling of the storm gathering around him but everyone else did; the consensus was that if he survived, he'd be very strong, indeed.

Westhead plunged back in, damning torpedoes and half-measures.

He put in new plays for Abdul-Jabbar, intending to establish a more dependable half-court game and then go back to running. His players, who'd long resisted any move in that direction, made no secret of their distaste for the new offense.

The Lakers started 0–2.

After the second loss, in Portland, Riley joined several writers in Champions, the bar in the Marriott Hotel. The writers were used to a candid Riles who'd trust them with inside information, but this time when they asked him what was going on with the offense and Westhead, he got mad.

"I used to be able to sit down with you guys and have a drink," Riley snapped. "I didn't come here to be grilled."

The Lakers lost by 26 points at San Antonio and dropped to 2–4. When asked about it, Johnson said: "Ask the coach."

At dawn the next morning, Riley was spotted sitting alone by the hotel pool, poring over the playbook as if looking for a missing clue.

Three lackluster wins failed to cheer anyone. Before the next game on a Sunday night at the Forum, Buss called Sharman and West in and said he was ready to fire Westhead. They convinced him to wait while they looked around. There was a discussion of possible candidates to replace Westhead. The leader was Al Bianchi, a Suns assistant.

The Lakers won their fourth in a row that night.

They beat the Jazz to take their fifth three nights later in Salt Lake City, but during a timeout Westhead snapped at Johnson to get into the huddle. Afterward, Westhead pulled Johnson aside for a meeting in an equipment room and told him he'd messed up late in the game because he hadn't been paying attention. The meeting lasted less than a minute and cleared no air.

Westhead then talked to writers about the game. He was asked again about players' criticism of his offense.

Said Westhead, cryptic as ever: "The almond tree bears its fruit in silence."

Johnson went to the dressing room, dispensed with routine questions and fired the shot heard 'round the NBA: he wanted to be traded immediately.

"We don't see eye to eye on a lot of things," he said of Westhead. "Me and him don't see eye to eye. It's time for me to go."

Other Laker players who'd criticized Westhead privately, withheld comment, happy to let Johnson carry the ball.

Said Nixon, grinning: "Leave me out of this one."

Late that night, an angry Riley walked into the bar at the team's hotel, grumbling about the effrontery of the modern-day player. Bill Bertka, the veteran Jazz assistant, told him the affair would blow over but Riley wasn't sure. He and Westhead were a team, indivisible; for all Riley knew, they were indivisibly on their way out.

He was half right.

The next day, two years and eleven days after McKinney fell off his bicycle, Buss sawed the almond tree off at the ground.

Laker officials have insisted ever since that Johnson didn't get Westhead fired, and indeed, there was more to the story. Westhead had almost been axed the game before. Johnson had only said what most of his teammates were thinking. Only Abdul-Jabbar cared enough about Westhead to call him afterward.

But Johnson went off that Wednesday night, a press conference was called Thursday morning, and Westhead was fired that afternoon. Perhaps Johnson had only gored an already mortally wounded Westhead but any distinction was lost in the furor.

Suddenly the world saw Johnson as a willful brat and set about spanking him.

7-Up announced it would let his endorsement contract run out. Writers thundered. The *Los Angeles Times* ran a special Letters to the Editor section, most denouncing Johnson ("His next contract should be with Gerber's baby food") and Buss.

Almost unnoticed, the Lakers set about determining the line of succession.

■|

Buss wanted West.

The owner, a Hugh Hefner-style playboy who wore his shirts open to the sternum and showed off scrapbooks with pictures of the girls he dated, had idolized West as a fan and tried to get him to stay on as coach when he bought the team.

West declined. He'd sooner jump into a pile of snakes before a dressing room.

West had moved to the front office, first as consultant, then GM. On this turbulent Thursday morning, Buss called West to his home, Pickfair, the mansion built by Douglas Fairbanks and Mary Pickford, to ask him to take the reins during this crisis. As far as Buss was concerned, Riley was just an assistant. He could come or go, as West preferred.

"Jerry had just finished coaching," Buss says, "and I thought he had done a terrific job. I begged him to be coach again. He refused, flat out. I really made an effort to get him as a coach. He wouldn't do it."

West wanted Riley. Buss came up with what he thought was a compromise.

If he had to accept Riley, he'd get West to work with him as co-coach.

West would run the offense, which was what Buss really cared about; that was what got the fans screaming and attracted the beautiful people. Riley could coach the defense, which Buss considered a mandatory trip to the other end of the floor before they could run another fast break.

Since West was West and Riley was only Riley, Buss knew who'd be in charge.

"I have hired people before with no [pro] coaching experience," Buss says. "As a matter of fact, everybody I hired had no [pro] coaching experience. But they had more assistant coaching or college coaching or some type of coaching experience than Pat had had.

"I did have trepidation. Jerry felt very strongly he [Riley] would make a good coach. I trust Jerry very much, obviously. All I wanted was some assurance Jerry would work with him and make sure we were going in the right direction.

"I asked Jerry if he would help design an offense, to continue the kind of thing McKinney had set up. This was really why Westhead was fired, because he deviated from that original offense. A lot of people said it was because Magic said something. The decision to fire Paul had actually been made two days before Magic said anything. Our frustration came first. His came second.

"I asked Jerry if he would get us back to that offense, if he would work with the offense, etcetera, etcetera—and go so far, could I call him an offensive coach?

"And I thought he had pretty much agreed to that."

Actually, West was thinking in more conventional terms.

He thought he'd only agreed to help Riley which he assumed meant they'd talk about how to set up the offense.

Riley didn't know what to think. He'd just been asked to step into the head coach job over the body of his fallen friend, which was weird enough to start with.

"Both Paul and I went in to the office to work," he said later. "We knew there was a problem. There are psychodramas going on all the time with players. They usually remain inside. We thought it would blow over. It always did. Then I got a call about 11:30 P.M., as soon as I got home. They said to come to Buss's house. When I got to the press conference, I was numb and stunned. You take a look at all the faces. It looked like a funeral."

█▌

It was about to turn into a circus.

A room full of reporters waited in the Forum press lounge, eager for the lowdown on Magic's coup d'état. The hysteria was such that the spectacle they were about to witness would barely register: Buss trying to name West coach; West deftly lateraling the job to Riley right in front of everyone; Riley defending Westhead and accusing Buss of overreacting.

If Riley had just become another short-timer, it would have been merely bizarre, but he would become more. A great career was about to be born amid more comedy than irony.

Questions about other issues—notably Johnson's part in Westhead's firing—have been omitted. The rest is as it happened.

BUSS (*stepping to the podium*): We have appointed Jerry West as offensive captain for the Lakers. His duties will begin immediately. Pat Riley will stay with the Lakers as coach.

QUESTION: Doctor, offensive coach, does that mean head coach?

BUSS (*pausing for a drag of his cigarette*): I did not specifically make someone head coach and someone else assistant coach. That was not accidental. I did it the way I announced on purpose. I feel that Pat is very capable of running the Laker team. However, I feel that we need a new offensive coach. I asked Jerry if he'd take that job and fortunately, because of his relationship with Pat, I feel the two of them will coach this team together, with Jerry being in charge of the offense in particular.

Q: Jerry, there'll be a game tomorrow night. The game will end. Will two coaches come out to talk to us? Or will they choose which one it's going to be from game to game?

BUSS (*grinning*): We discussed that. In that I'm really making this change to change the offense, and since Jerry West will be in charge of that offense, he will be the one who you will question. (*Smiling*) You can, however, talk to Pat whenever you want, as well.

Q: Jerry, who picks the starting lineup?

BUSS (*grinning uneasily as he senses this thing isn't flying*): Who picks the starting lineup? In basketball, that's typically the coach.

Q: Which one of these two?

BUSS: Oh, which one of these two? (*Grinning over his shoulder at West and Riley behind him*) Uh, I think there are some things along the line, not only the starting lineups but other considerations as well—uh, potential trades, etcetera, etcetera—that Pat and Jerry are going to have to sit down and work out what their relative responsibilities are. Fortunately, we're dealing with a situation of two men who have worked together on and off for years and years and therefore I've decided to leave that up to them, the division of duties.

Q: What will Jerry do as far as actually changing the offense? (*Buss starts to answer.*) Let Jerry talk.

BUSS: That's certainly fine with me. (*to West*) Do you wish to say what your long-range plans are going to be right away?

∎

Indeed he did.
West had just learned he was going to run the offense, talk to the press after games, and, perhaps, choose the lineup. Additionally, he and Riley were going to decide between them who'd handle duties like making trades, which, until a few moments ago, had been his sole prerogative as general manager.
Yes, West had something he wanted to say.

∎

WEST: First of all, I'd like to clear up one thing. I'm going to be working for Pat Riley.

Q: With or for, Jerry?

WEST: With and for. And I think my responsibility is to him because I feel in my heart that he is the head coach. And hopefully my position here won't be a long-range position.

Q: Pat, will you take questions?

RILEY: Sure.

Q: Pat, what are your reactions?

RILEY: Well, Rich, I haven't had a whole lot of time to give it much thought and I'm reacting rather emotionally to this thing because it's not a very fun day for me, nor is it for Paul. So until we can really sit down, Jerry and myself, and discuss some of the things we can do to improve the incentive of the team, then I don't think I can really discuss that philosophy right now.

Q: Have you talked about any assistants?

RILEY (*laughing*): Have I talked about any assistants? I just want lunch.

Q: Do you see any major problems with the team?

RILEY: I'll be very honest with you. I'm speaking from an assistant coach's point of view and in my support for Paul. I think that there are problems that happen to every pro club. It could be the Dodgers, the Angels, or the Rams. Teams struggle early in the season. We gave them a fresh start with some offensive changes that weren't radical. It was only 20 percent of our total offensive concept. We kept 80 percent of our offense from the last two years. I think there was some overreaction. The players were about to work their way out of that. However, it may have gone deeper than that.

Q: Overreaction on whose part?

RILEY: Well, overreaction on the part that I feel that the offense couldn't have been worked out. I feel it would have. I know the players' pride and the fact they want to win would have dictated that. But you know, that's not the reality. The reality is what's happening right now. I can't do anything about what happened last week.

Q: It seems like the coaches are sort of contradicting the owner in some ways.

RILEY: I'm not contradicting anybody. I'm telling you how I feel. And I feel very confident that this is a very good basketball team and that sometimes it takes a left hook to get 'em going again. And I think we have all been dealt that kind of blow.

■|

Q: In your eyes, will you be making the decisions?

RILEY: From what I understand, I will be.... From my under-standing, I will be making the majority of the decisions.

Q: Are you interim head coach, head coach, co-coach, senior head coach?

RILEY (*turning to Buss behind him*): I don't know. I'm sure this is an interim basis but it hasn't been clarified yet.

Q: Are you going to keep combing your hair (which he had recently begun slicking back) in a funny way?

All laugh.

Q: Dr. Buss, are you hesitant to name a permanent head coach and when do you intend to do that, if ever?

BUSS: When the decision was made that Paul would no longer coach, the next question is, 'O.K., who will the coach be?' My reaction is Jerry West was the most qualified person out there, in my opinion, to do that job. When I discussed it with him, he felt the current arrangement as we've described it was the most workable.... That's simply the way I left it at that point.

◼

Amid the farce, something unexpected was happening.

Riley was growing up before everyone's eyes.

Buss, never at ease before crowds, was nervous. West was glum. Riley, the lifelong caddy who'd gotten an interim promotion by default, looked like the guest of honor at a birthday party.

If Riley was bewildered at the day's twists and turns, it never showed. He wouldn't give Westhead up to the mob, even suggesting Buss had overreacted. He expressed confidence in himself and directed everyone's attention to the future.

A lot of things would be said about Riley in this new career: He was the luckiest man in basketball; he was a valet for his players; he was a parrot for his wife's psychological insights and a servant to her ambition.

Actually, he was a natural.

If he was laid back in all other areas of life, he was a hard-driving, no-nonsense SOB when it came to basketball. It was a people job and he was a people person. It was a communicator's job and he was poetic. Most of all, he had a presence. People listened to him. He looked like he belonged up there.

For years, no one had taken him seriously. Everyone liked him but no one noticed the presence or sensed the potential. It was an object lesson in the requisites of charisma: Without an opportunity, Riley was anonymous; given a position of power, he began to radiate. He would make many more strides but none larger than this quantum leap from anonymity.

Years later, the press conference would be remembered as a classic, like a Mack Sennett comedy. Riley would recall saying, "If no one else wants it, I'll take it." This would have been a great line, except he didn't quite get it out.

For the moment though, the Riley story was lost in the Magic Buss controversy.

A headline in the next morning's *Los Angeles Times* read: "West and Riley Inherit a Paradox: a Team in Disarray... on a 5-Game Winning Streak."

Abdul-Jabbar, informed of the move personally by Buss, said he didn't like it.

"Maybe Paul wasn't the coach we needed," he said. "I didn't necessarily feel that way. Some people did...

"Personally, I think Paul was trying to make the adjustments that were necessary. Obviously, he didn't make them fast enough for everybody."

Riley had one day to put it all back together.

Between breakfast and supper Thursday, he'd gone from assistant coach to co-coach to head coach and he had a game coming Friday night. Westhead's pyre was big enough for one more if things didn't turn around fast.

Riley started getting ready for his debut. And getting ready. And getting ready.

"My first pre-game speech," he said, "I had forty-five pages of notes for a ten-minute speech."

An ordinary game against the Spurs became a marquee event. Everyone wanted to see how the Laker brats responded. The Laker crowd booed Johnson.

Offensive Coach West sat on the bench. True to his word, he let Riley do the coaching and confined himself to making suggestions like an assistant.

Johnson scored 20 points with 16 assists and 10 rebounds as the Lakers set the Forum rocking, blowing out the Spurs, 136–116.

"That's the kind of basketball I like to watch," Buss said afterward. "I think everyone was high emotionally. But let's give it ten or twelve games before we draw any conclusions."

A relieved Riley was asked what he'd told his players.

"Wing it, just like me," he said.

■

It was honeymoon time again.

Their coach was an old friend who'd been an NBA player and remembered how they felt. The players had to prove they weren't coach-killers, or at least that they didn't require more than one a year.

"We had a team that could really play together," West says. "It was an easier transition for Pat because he didn't inherit a bad team.

"They were going to be on their best behavior.... It was like a crusade for those players, not to hear about themselves getting someone else fired.

"And it worked out for all parties. He really prospered and grew as a coach. Coaches have to start somewhere."

As a coach's starter set, the Lakers had huge advantages but obvious dangers.

On Riley's first team, five of the twelve players had been all-stars. They were great stars, with personalities to match.

Abdul-Jabbar, 34, was no longer at the top of his game but he was close enough. Intelligent and intellectual, he could also be distant and forbidding. He had mellowed recently, with his new girlfriend, Cheryl Pistono, getting much of the credit, but everyone, Laker players and coaches alike, still approached him warily.

Johnson, a colt at 22—his teammates named him "Buck," short for "Young buck"—was just the opposite, sunny and gregarious, but he'd just shown he could dig his heels in, too. He was careful to defer to Abdul-Jabbar, the team captain and officially its No. 1 star but as Buss's special favorite, Johnson was already the franchise's centerpiece.

Nixon, who'd have been a star on a lot of other teams, was lost in this galaxy. A greyhound who could handle the ball and a great spot-up shooter, too, he was a fan favorite but after Johnson arrived, no one made a fuss about Nixon. It was always that way with Norman, and though Johnson was his friend, it gnawed at him.

With Johnson and Nixon was a third musketeer, 24-year-old Michael Cooper, a dark-horse No. 3 pick from New Mexico. Long and lean at 6–6, he was a tremendous athlete and dunker and his slams on lobs, called "Coop-a-Loops," delighted the crowd. He was high-strung and insecure, a kamikaze who'd go through a wall for a good word.

The Lakers had more stars than you could count: Jamaal Wilkes, a three-time all-star; Bob McAdoo, a five-time all-star who came off the bench. They were the thoroughbreds of the NBA, the league's fastest, baddest collection of athletes.

The problem was, they knew it.

Some of them thought a coach was a necessary evil. Others didn't think it was so necessary.

"A little of that was there," says Nixon. "That's why I say, look at the team.

"I watch tapes, it was amazing watching that team play, how quick we scored on people, the kind of passes. The ball'd never hit the floor. Bam, bam, bam, layup! Magic tip one in, Kareem, McAdoo comes off the bench. Just the foot speed!

"We knew in our heads, we had a whole thing, we tried to break teams. We tried to make them hit the wall. Because we knew couldn't nobody keep up. That's why teams could stay with us for two quarters, three quarters and we'd reach a point where we'd score 16 straight points and the game would be over.

"You'd see the teams, they'd go 'Fuck, we can't run with these guys.' And we'd blow 'em out and we'd go to the bench and get oxygen 'cause we were dying, too. But we knew we could take teams. We tried to push that rock on 'em all the time and tried to make 'em quit....

"It wasn't a matter of how ready Riles was. We, again, didn't want anybody who could come in and change the systems that we had.

"The best coaches leave the players alone. The years I was there, Riley knew how to get us in shape and he put the systems in.

"And man, he just let us play."

∎|

West was back in his office before he knew it.

The Lakers won 11 of 13. They forgot about pounding it in to Abdul-Jabbar unless they were in trouble. Their offensive average jumped from 108 to 119.

By January 15, Riley was 20–6 and the Lakers led their conference, making him the West coach for the All-Star Game.

"If we had gone 2–12, I'm sure they would have had somebody else here now," Riley said. "But it didn't work out that way and I'm happy as hell."

In early February, the going got bumpy.

The Lakers went 1–3 and Buss called in his interim coach. As Westhead could have told Riley, they didn't cut you a lot of slack in Lakerdom.

"I thought he was perhaps listening to too many people," Buss says. "And I told him, 'Pat, if you're going to coach the Lakers, coach them. You're the coach. Go with what you think is best.'

"He seemed to be too tentative, just in talking to him, watching him. I thought perhaps some of that tentativeness came from me, from what I had said or did or my body language, whatever. And I just wanted to assure him that was not true any longer, that I wanted him just to take the reins and go for it."

He hadn't proven anything yet. They were all watching him.

"He *was* intimidated. Kareem intimidated people. You've got this big guy who you know you've got to get along with somehow. Because it seemed like it was hard for Kareem to respect him in the beginning 'cause of the age gap. Kareem was right there with him in age. I think he [Riley] was like, 'How am I going to win this guy over?'

"He took charge but careful at the same time. With us, you had to come in and be assertive. You had to take charge because, you know, you're talking about a lot of veterans at that time who were looking at him, like, 'O.K., are we gonna run over him? Or is he going to be the man?' You've got Kareem, Jamaal, all those guys.

"You're taking over a team, you've got some players…[laughing] and you've got some egos…so you know, he's got to come in and say, 'O.K., how am I going to get them to play, 'cause they've got the talent?'

"It was hard for him to crack the whip in the beginning like he did later on because you don't want to rub anybody the wrong way."

▮▮

But Riley couldn't stay out of everyone's way forever.

All teams have their schisms and the Lakers had theirs. Young players coalesced around Johnson who was more their age and more fun, too.

Johnson was careful to defer to Abdul-Jabbar, but they had only a professional relationship and wouldn't become friends for several years.

With Abdul-Jabbar injured, the Lakers won six in a row, fast-breaking to their hearts' content. The young players started to say when Kareem was gone, you'd see the real Magic show. The Los Angeles *Herald Examiner*'s Rich Levin wrote a story, quoting one of them anonymously.

That was too much.

New or not, Riley wasn't going to accept Lakers talking to writers about internal problems or personalities or, come to think of it, anything. The boy who'd grown up feeling so protective of his own troubled family became a coach who wanted to make a surrogate family of his team, with players protecting one another. Talking to any outsider, much less a reporter, about a family member was unacceptable.

Riley called a team meeting post haste, demanding the author of the quotes identify himself. No one did.

Another point had been made, one he'd hammer home the rest of his career.

Actually, the quotes had come from Johnson.

"It wasn't really a friction," Johnson says. "See, I understood I had to temper my game down. Now that's fine. Whatever it took to win, that's what I was all about.

"He [Levin] was referring to Larry Bird, his game and mine. I said, 'I could do everything Larry's doing but I can't. You won't see the real Magic 'til Kareem retires.'

"I think Rich took it like it was said. But other people took it different, like we were in a scuffle. We never were. I knew when I came here, this was Kareem's team. And that was fine with me. I always made sure I took care of him, running the plays through him, knowing that he was our leader and my turn was going to come.

"So we had no problem."

Whatever problems they had or didn't have now would be contained from now on. A velvet curtain descended around the Lakers.

Until now, they'd been a veritable river to the press, but a new age was dawning. They would always be quotable and gracious but insiders would be in and outsiders would be out.

■|

Riley worried but the Lakers soared.

He stayed up all night watching video tape, compiling page after page of things to tell his players, then found himself with too little time to tell them half of it. He began having stomach problems and began pounding the Maalox.

Riley's humility was manifest.

He felt funny being called Coach. Coach was for a grownup, like Rupp or John Wooden or his father. It would be several seasons before he got used to the sound of it. Until then, he asked people to call him Riles.

His players were glad to oblige. He told them this was their team. They believed him.

"We made a deal with him," Nixon says. "We actually had a meeting. We said, 'Riley, shorten the practices and we're going to give you everything that we've got. We'll give you everything for an hour and 15 minutes. Nobody's going to walk around. We're going to push the ball every time, we're going to pick each other up full court every time.' And we actually made the deal."

There were lots of deals, and accommodations, for a while.

Checking into their hotel in Manhattan in early March, Riley told Nixon to get to bed early.

"It's a free country," said Nixon.

They both laughed.

The Lakers then lost back-to-back games to the Knicks and Nets. Riley canceled an off-day in Philadelphia and scheduled a practice. The usual suspects grumbled where writers could hear them but the incident passed.

A March slump dropped their record since January 1 to 18–13 and Riley began to actually pull on the reins.

Practices got longer, off-days fewer. The Lakers responded, winning 15 of their final 19.

After a late-season victory at Portland, Nixon walked up to Riley in Champions, the same bar where Riley had snapped at the writers in the strung-out days of November. Now Nixon pulled Riley aside and congratulated him for the moves he'd made that night. Riley glowed.

The Lakers were a legitimate powerhouse now. They hit the playoffs flying, sweeping the Suns and Spurs, 4–0.

Buss caught the fever. At the team's hotel in San Antonio, he acknowledged his early doubts about Riley ("My reaction was like, being from Missouri, you know") but announced his coach was now permanent.

They drew the 76ers again in the finals and dispatched them 4–2, for the championship.

Riley, soaked in champagne, embraced Chris in the dressing room, their lives suddenly replete with blessings that would have been unimaginable at the season's start.

"It seems like a millennium since I took over," he said. "Yeah, a millennium. I've got brain drain now, mush brain. I dug down for everything I could find. I need four months to rest up."

Somewhere, sometime was here and now. He'd finally found a place to make that stand.

CHAPTER SIX

The Hardest Working Man in Showtime

If you go back in history to the Crusades, he would be like King Richard or somebody. I think the job focuses his attention almost completely. He'll have a few words to say if he runs into you. He's always cordial. He's always polite. But he's kind of a man on a mission.

—DAVID WOHL, LAKER ASSISTANT

I want the players to be loose. I want them to have fun. I want them to use the court as an arena to express themselves. But on the other hand, I don't want them to be flip. I don't want to be good old Riles to the players, the guy they could treat as an old shoe.

—PAT RILEY

He was an NBA coach now, with a two-year, $450,000 contract and a job to do, the dimensions of which he'd only glimpsed.

The consensus, inside the biz and out, was that he was the luckiest man in basketball. Denver's Larry Brown told colleagues it was a sorry day for the profession when a broadcaster could walk away with a title.

Laker coaches were always hearing that they were nothing, and their players were everything.

"All the comments you heard at coaches' meetings, 'You know Pat's got Magic, he's got these guys, he's got this guy,' " says Dave Wohl, Riley's assistant for three seasons in the mid-'80s.

"I felt that one thing he really did that many coaches weren't able to do—and this might have been Westhead's downfall—Pat didn't try to overcoach the team during games.

"He did a lot of preparation. You know, tinker with the offense, but within the framework of knowing what he had in Earvin, Kareem, James [Worthy] and all the guys. He never tried to say, 'Look, these guys are getting all the glory, I'm a good coach, I've got to show them I'm a great coach, I'm not getting enough recognition.'

"A lot of coaches could not have dealt ego-wise with that, where year after year you have the best team and nobody thinks you're a particularly good coach. It had to be kind of galling."

For Riley, it was exhilarating.

Flat on his rear end a few years before, he had a highly developed sense of modesty and it wasn't just the usual act for the press. He'd been handed the keys to paradise and knew it.

He got Laker tickets for the beach gang all the time. One night Altie and Idell Cohen came, with Teddy Grossman.

"Thank God, they won," says Altie, "because if they lost, you didn't want to be around him or Chris after the game.

"We went into the lounge. Chick Hearn was acting as bartender. Riley was behind the bar with him. Teddy and I and Idell and Chris were sitting in front of the bar.

"Teddy said, 'Hey, Riley, Altie said you're the best coach in the country.'

"And Riley said, 'Did you say that?'

"And I said, 'Yeah, I did.'

"He said, 'I'll tell you something right now. I'm not saying I'm a great coach or a good coach but if I am, there are two words that can explain it. What do you think they are?'

"My wife said 'drive' and 'fairness.' Everyone came up with some.

"And it finally came to Riles and he said, 'Magic' and 'Johnson.' "And Chick said, 'Amen, Riles!' "

∎

Great as the Lakers were, it wasn't like they were the only power around.

The 76ers, who'd been good enough to make the finals in two of the last three seasons, had just acquired Moses Malone. The Celtics, a long-time Laker nemeses, their rivalry redoubled by Johnson and Bird, had won a title in 1981 and were gearing up, too.

Red Auerbach, who'd built a franchise by snookering fellow owners out of players like Bob Cousy, Bill Russell, John Havlicek, Dave Cowens, and Bird, was at it again, snaring Robert Parish and draft rights to Kevin McHale from the Warriors, and Dennis Johnson from Phoenix.

The East was loaded. The Celtics (63) and Sixers (58) had won more games than the Lakers (57) in Riley's first year.

The West, meanwhile, was a Laker lake.

They made the NBA finals in Riley's first four seasons, dominating the Western finals, 16–4.

The only thing the Lakers had to fear was themselves. It wasn't an idle threat. Their volatile social arrangement prevailed.

Abdul-Jabbar was distant.

Nixon couldn't decide whether he loved Johnson or resented him. Norman was convinced the organization (read: West, with whom he'd clashed when he'd been coach) was laying for him; and just because he was paranoid, it didn't mean they weren't out to get him, either. The Lakers put a private detective on his tail to check out drug rumors, a project that blew up in their faces. Nixon spotted the tail and the story wound up in the newspapers. The rumors were never substantiated.

They were still adding talent, though. With the No. 1 pick in the '82 draft, they got North Carolina's James Worthy, heir apparent to the aging Wilkes, a 6–9 "small" forward with a devastating post game who could run the floor like a deer and finish like Julius Erving himself, a perfect player for a fast-breaking team.

The Lakers went 58–24 in Riley's first full season and tore through the West in the playoffs, but injuries got them.

Worthy broke a bone in his left leg. The injury-prone McAdoo played only 47 games and missed two in the finals. Nixon partially separated his left shoulder in Game 1, and went out with a sprained left knee in Game 3.

The Sixers closed them out, 4–0.

At least in Los Angeles, everyone understood. They'd been injured. No champion had repeated since 1969. They'd made the finals.

There was no hint of displeasure with the coach, nor would there be when the next season ended traumatically. Riley had settled in. He was a perfect fit. The players liked him. The press ate out of his hands.

This job that had been juggled for years was now, indisputably, his.

■

Riley was developing, too.

If he wasn't ready to jerk too hard or redesign the game plan, he could ask, and he had the weight to ensure, that his players were as serious as he was, that they prepared as conscientiously, gave as much.

The players found themselves following along after him without question and trotting to keep up.

He suffered his way through the season. He went back to smoking, bumming cigarettes before games, at halftime, before talking to the press when it was over. Stress tightened his back and neck up. He found an acupuncturist in Santa Monica who helped; she could count on seeing him any time they lost two in a row.

"It's interesting to see a guy go from a player to a coach," said Jamaal Wilkes. "After about two years, it's like they never were players.

"Pat isn't as relaxed as he was last year. He's still relaxed but not like before. Because we won the championship last year and because of the players we have, there's a lot of pressure on him. No matter what we do, it doesn't seem good enough."

Riley had brought in Bill Bertka, the Jazz assistant who'd consoled him on the eve of Westhead's firing, in his first season. By the time Wohl joined the staff in the fall of 1983, the Lakers had become demon workers, belying their free-spirited reputation.

"I thought we practiced extremely hard," Wohl says. "I thought we practiced long.

"Practices were rarely cut down as the season went on. Pat had an interesting theory on this. He felt a lot of players' regimen was built over an 82-game season and if you backed off and made things easier, they would tend to respond less. That if you made things harder—for instance, in the three years I was there, I don't think he ever gave Magic a day off and Earvin worked very hard.

"But Pat's theory was, 'If I give Earvin a day off, he's going to believe he needs a day off. There are days he's going to begin to feel somewhat sorry for himself if he's tired or there's been too big a burden. So what he's going to do is, those games he won't bring his best. Not that he doesn't want to but he'll allow his body and his mind to convince him that he can't bring his best.' "

■

Riley, himself, worked around the clock.

His players had to respect that, even an older guy like Abdul-Jabbar for whom energy was finite, who wasn't going to leave his best on some practice floor or a game in Cleveland in March.

Riley's life had become coaching: screening hours of videotape, filling out one of those light blue cards he had specially made up with tomorrow's practice schedule, rehearsing his remarks to his players, reading to find new sources of inspiration.

He loved breaking the job down into a million pieces and examining them all and reexamining them all until every contingency had been covered.

Of course, to make room for his new passion he had to cut back on a few things, like the rest of his life.

He looked like he spent hours in fitting rooms. Actually, he hated to shop and ordered everything. He had one style of everything so he wouldn't have to think about it.

"I don't like fads," he said. "I get the same thing every time.

"To me, it's about efficiency. I never think about what I'm going to wear. I take a shower, pick out a suit, throw on socks, shoes, and a shirt and I'm out the door in three minutes. I have a frame that's easy to fit."

And if he gained five pounds?

"I never do," he said.

Likewise, his famous slicked-back neo-Lee hairdo was efficient. He said he was tired of taking all that time to blow-dry it. He had run the gamut: crew cut, DA, flattop, Ivy League, mop top, shoulder-length-or-longer, mustache, beard, but this look was him.

His trim figure suggested that he spent the other hours of his life in health clubs. Actually, he didn't work out during the season. He couldn't squeeze it in.

It was a joke on his staff. One of his assistants once bemoaned the fact that he lived on salads, ran daily, and gained weight while Riley sat by the pool, ate burgers for lunch, and looked "like a fucking Adonis."

During the season, the Rileys' social life was always on hold. Their friends knew he was too busy.

Summers were completely different. Riley dropped out of sight; Laker staffers who'd seen him daily for nine months wouldn't get a glimpse of him. The players' only contact would be the annual letter he wrote each of them.

Pat and Chris might take a week off after the old season or before the new one to lay on a beach somewhere. Otherwise, they traveled according to Pat's speaking schedule; he had become a regular on the motivational speech circuit and it was starting to mean real money.

Speaking had grown out of coaching. Riley read voluminously, looking for lines to inspire his players. He quoted everyone from Anthony A. Aardvark to Zarathustra: Shakespeare, Sun-Tsu, John Wooden, Wayne Dyer, Joseph Campbell. He read biographies of great men, looking for the key to their achievement.

He put together tapes to show the players, with great moments in Laker history, set to music.

"All the time," says Bertka, "I used to say, 'You're going to make me cry now.' I used to cry like hell."

All of a sudden, Riley had a new vocabulary: "making a statement...message games...comfort zone...toxic envy...work ethic."

They were catchphrases in his addresses to his players and that flowed from his conversations with Chris.

His new career was really their joint venture. Chris, who'd fought for her own career, had begun cutting back her counseling practice. His career became hers.

"Our dialogues and discussions are psychologically oriented," said the NBA's first New Age coach. "For instance, how to get a player to play harder or to create a situation where they will respond."

He talked about bonding and nurturing and a lot of other things that hadn't been previously discussed in NBA dressing rooms.

His following grew. He'd always come off as a man's man but now his appeal crossed over genders. Women adored him. He was so *sensitive*.

Of course, it was still early in his career. The players weren't crazy about appearing as patients on his couch and felt free to say so.

"To tell you the truth, every now and then I listen," said Cooper. "But it gets repetitious. The thing is, that stuff doesn't do anything for me. I don't need it."

"I personally don't need any of that," said Abdul-Jabbar. "It all seems obvious to me. I've been here a long time and I know all about the ups and downs. I've heard it all before."

❚

Riley had always been orderly; only now he was more so.

"Every day he would have his two-hour plan of practice written on his blue card and put in his back pocket and it never failed," Wohl says. "He almost wanted to choreograph his entire day. I thought that was a key to his success. He knew what he wanted to do every minute of the day, whether it was practice or when he went home. There were not a lot of moments, I felt, he would let his guard down.

"One thing with Pat, every move he does is calculated. Pat is not a spontaneous person. He may do something in a game that may seem spontaneous, a substitution here, a substitution there. He's not a hunch coach. If he's done something, it's because it was written down on a little pad that he spent three hours on the day of a game. A little like a chess player: 'O.K., if late in the game, with three minutes left, he does X, I can do Y or Z.' "

If you played for Riley, you worked hard.

If you worked with him, Heaven help you.

"I think he burns hotter than any other coach," Wohl says. "I think he becomes more tunnel visioned with it. I think his family situation is set up to allow him to do that. His wife certainly understands that kind of commitment.

"The thing is, when you're with Pat, you have the same kind of commitment. And I don't know if it was just Pat. I think it was the Laker organization.

"I know I did things as an assistant there, because of the quest you're on to win a title, that usually you don't have to do other places.

"I won't tell you who the coach was but when I left in 1985 (to coach the Nets), I got a call from another assistant coach in the league, asking me about the Laker job." Veteran assistant, been around a long time, been with a playoff team.

"He said to me, 'I'm interested in the job. I want you to tell me a little about it.'

"He said, 'Do you have to do this?'

"I said, 'Yeah, you've got to do this.'

"He said, 'What about that?'

"I said, 'Yeah, you do that.' And I said, 'Also, one of the other things, you'll have to do this…and this.'

"He said, 'You've got to do that, too?'

"I said, 'Yeah, and then you have to do this and this and this report and you'll have to go….'

"And the longer I went on with the responsibilities, the less interested he became in the job because he didn't have the commitment to do that. To him that was going to be too much work….

"I'll never forget the toughness of the people—one day we were there and Kupchak, McAdoo, and Rambis all go up for an offensive rebound near the end of practice, and they split Mitch's eye open. It takes 41 stitches. He's sitting under the basket with a compress on it, bleeding and everything.

"Pat begrudgingly stops practice and brings it to a halt—we've been going about two hours—and everybody walks by Kupchak and just looks at him. And Rambis finally goes, 'We're lifting weights now, don't be late.' Kupchak's bleeding.

"I mean, there was a toughness about this crew that went from the coaches through the players. And I think a lot of that had to do with the tone set at the top.

"Pat—I think the other thing that allowed him to be the way he was, he had the backing from above. Jerry West backed him. They would have a lot of disagreements but they were good friends. They arrived at things from a different approach but they were in basic agreement on what the team needed to do to win.

"Jerry would back Pat with the players and players knew you couldn't go around Pat and get to Jerry and have some relief.

"They knew from the top, from Jerry Buss on down, it was all in line. There was nowhere to go. I think that really allowed Pat to blossom because he knew he had support."

■I

Most important, they were family.

They weren't really, of course. They were professionals, assembled with a specific goal. If it wasn't attained, some of them would be waived or traded. Some wouldn't be back in any circumstance and a year from now, the holdovers would be losing touch with the ones who were gone.

But while they were together, they shared highs and lows. They knew each others' families and watched each others' kids toddle up to greet Daddy at the airport.

"I've had discussion with other coaches," wrote Riley in *Show Time*, "and some of them say, 'Oh, you've got to keep the wives out of it. Get the wives away from the team.'

"I tell them, 'What do you mean? The wives have more impact on their husbands than I can....'

"Managers like that recognize the power of the family but only in a negative way. They are afraid of it. They see it as something unmanageable, something that will bring chaos. They need to take a different attitude: respect the family connections that orbit around your team and try to keep them positive. Those connections are always going to be there. We all need people to love in our lives. The crux is that the love and the life have to work together. They have to be one set of interrelated forces.

"You have to be aware because the wives and families can become the team's allies or they can become the greatest Peripheral Opponents in the world."

Lots of coaches talked about family for pragmatic reasons, to keep their players from blabbing everything to the press, but none took it as literally and as seriously as Riley.

Basketball had been his refuge from that austere household in Schenectady. His coaches had been figures of respect, if not obvious surrogate fathers like Walt Przybylo. His teammates had been brothers, to whom he was fiercely loyal.

Now Riley had his own team and he intended to make it the one he'd always wanted to play on, the one where there was no backbiting, where everyone always protected everyone else, where everyone nurtured each other. Denied that experience growing up, he'd never stop trying to create it on his teams.

And it worked.

"Riley is the reason we became a family," Johnson says. "We were some guys who had talent and wanted to win but little things could creep in to divide us. Somebody get a little money, everybody else is mad.

"He came in and he changed us. He said, 'Look, we got to take care of each other and not let things outside the family,' as he called it, 'upset the family.' From now on, nobody could go in the papers and talk about each other. You come in here and we straighten it out in here.

"He started giving parties. It just became contagious. Guys just started giving parties, team dinners. I always gave the first one of the year and then Riley would always give the Christmas one. Coop gave the annual one after the Celtic game. Like he wanted, that's what we became, a family.

"Kareem didn't come one time and he [Riley] went off the next day: 'You know these guys, they go out of their way and give this party, they expect everybody to be there, the wives cooking all day and I expect everybody to be there.'

[Laughing] "And from then on, everybody said, 'I better not miss one of those team parties.'

"And that's what happened. If you just came and show up for ten minutes, that's just showing a guy respect.' "

Of course, there were still grievances. These were supposed to be hashed out internally in team meetings, however heated.

"We were playing bad once," says Johnson, "and the starters were getting off to bad starts. So he [Riley] said, 'O.K., I'll go down the line. What's wrong with you? What's wrong with the team?'

"So he got to Bob McAdoo and McAdoo said, 'You really want to know what's wrong?'

"And he said, 'Yeah.'

"He said, 'I'm going to tell you what's wrong. It's other guys on this damn team that can play! The problem is, if the starters aren't getting the job done, sit their butts down!'

"He [McAdoo] just went down the line: Kareem's not rebounding, I'm not being an assertive leader like I was before. Mouths just like dropped. 'Buck ain't getting it done, we got Michael Cooper! You got all these guys sitting here—myself, James Worthy. Hey, sit their butts down! Then I bet they'll start playing better!'

"It was like a trip but he was right."

There was one more thing that would have to be done in the name of chemistry: Nixon was going to have to go.

Norman's numbers were declining and the front office was suspicious of his free-wheeling lifestyle. In the summer of 1983, he was traded to the San Diego Clippers for rookie Byron Scott.

The deal was a bombshell, unpopular with Laker fans and players alike. At a farewell party, the Three Musketeers, Nixon, Johnson, and Cooper, went into the men's room and hugged each other and wept.

Johnson and Cooper then cold-shouldered Scott for months, barely talking to him until he showed he could take it, keep his mouth shut, and play the game.

By December, they were warming up to the kid and the Musketeers re-formed. For six years, it'd be Johnson, Cooper, and Scott.

■|

Now, about those Celtics.

Celtics had been torturing Lakers, it seemed, through history. Boston was generally the best in the East. The Lakers were usually best in the West. They'd met seven times in the finals; the Lakers were 0–7.

Celtics rubbed it in, too. Auerbach lit up victory cigars on the bench. The Celtics bragged of their "tradition" and "mystique" and regarded opponents as vandals in their cathedral.

The worst thing was, they always backed it up.

In 1969, Russell's last season, the aging Celts fell to fourth place in the regular season but got back into the finals against the Lakers. For the first time though, the Lakers would have home-court advantage.

Sure enough, the series went seven games. Cooke had balloons penned up in the ceiling for the celebration but the Celtics pulled a monumental upset. The Lakers fell to petty wrangling between Chamberlain, who took himself out of the game with a sore knee, and Coach Bill Van Breda Kolff who refused to put him back in.

Johnson became a Laker and Bird a Celtic in 1979, months after their meeting in the NCAA finals had become TV's highest-rated basketball game. They would later become friends, but then they were true rivals who disliked each other and measured themselves by the other.

They promised to kick the Laker–Celtic thing to new heights but until the spring of 1984, they hadn't yet met in the NBA finals.

"The showdown, finally," Johnson says. "So *yeah!*"

"All year long it had been a Laker–Boston rivalry," says Cooper. "People had been talking about that. Pat being part of that early— relationship is what I call it—you want to overcome that."

Actually, none of Riley's teams had ever met the Celtics in post-season but to be a Laker was to know the litany: Frank Selvy's miss in 1962, Don Nelson's shot that bounced in off the back of the rim in '69, the balloons, etc.

To be a Laker was to hunger to humble the Celtics. This was an infuriatingly worthy team with the trash-talking Bird, the acerbic McHale, the chirpy Danny Ainge, and the motor-mouthed Cedric Maxwell and M. L. Carr.

They had won 62 games to the Lakers' 54. The Celtics were a running team, too, but they couldn't run with the Laker greyhounds as the Lakers were about to demonstrate.

The series opened in Boston where the Lakers set the tone, winning, 115–109.

They led Game 2 in the final minute, 113–111, when James Worthy misunderstood Riley and called time out after rebounding a missed free throw. On the in-bounds play, Worthy then made a casual pass in the backcourt that was stolen by Gerald Henderson, who went in for a tying layup. The Celtics won in overtime, 124–121.

Back in the Forum, the Lakers bombed the Celtics, 137–104. Bird, asked what the Celtics needed to turn things around, replied: "Twelve heart transplants."

They found a more practical alternative: one tonsillectomy.

In Game 4, McHale put a chokehold on Kurt Rambis going in for a breakaway layup. The benches emptied. Cooper and Henderson wrestled. Bird and Abdul-Jabbar had to be separated.

The Lakers thought the Celtics had thrown down the gauntlet. In a move they'd regret, they picked it up.

Riley, whose job it was to keep a cool head, was swept up in the moment with everyone else.

The Lakers led, 76–70, when McHale hit Rambis. They led, 113–108 with :56 left—the fourth game in which they'd led in the last minute—but the Celtics rallied, helped by Johnson who let the shot clock run down in a key possession. Boston won in overtime, 129–125, after Johnson missed two free throws at 123–123. The series the Lakers figured should already be over was tied, 2–2.

Riley called the McHale play "thuggery" and went from there.

"I think what Boston did was the equivalent of two gang warlords meeting the night before a rumble and deciding the weapons," he said. "They both say bare fists and one of them shows up with zip guns....What they did is they came into our territory, a neutral zone out there and decided to use zip guns. Weapons that we didn't plan on because this is a game of basketball."

"As the series went on, you could see the change in him [Riley]," Cooper said, "as far as what he said to us in different parts of the game.

"When the incident with Kurt went down where they put the chokehold on him, he came up with this concept of 'No more layups.'

"He became adamant about it. He was feverish in practice. Nothing like a craziness but it was just a desire, a will to win. The only way he could do that was to let his inner feelings come out to us because obviously he couldn't get out there and play. But he could let us feel and the feeling became power in a sense."

The problem was, the Lakers had nothing to gain by standing and fighting. The Celtics had already won by luring them into the engagement.

"That turned the whole series around," says Johnson. "They knew they were in trouble. We knew they were in trouble.

"But they outsmarted us with that play. That took us out mentally. Instead of playing our game, we played their game. We stopped running."

They went back to Boston for Game 5. In the stifling 97-degree heat of the unair-conditioned Boston Garden, the 37-year-old Abdul-Jabbar and his younger teammates wilted. Kareem missed 18 of his 25 shots and the Celtics cruised, 121–103.

Riley called it "the most bizarre game of my career. Surreal. If I ever felt I was in hell, that was it."

The Lakers won Game 6 in the Forum, 119–108. The gentlemanly Worthy wiped out Maxwell on a layup, knocking him into the basket support.

"I'll tell you what, they play that way the whole series and nobody says anything about it," said Worthy. "So I don't want to hear about it.

"That's the way they play. We can play that way."

Things were getting out of control. A Laker fan threw a beer in M. L. Carr's face as he sat on the bench.

"After what happened to ML, the Lakers better wear hard hats on the bench instead of oxygen masks," sneered Bird. "Our fans can do anything."

■|

From a *Los Angeles Times* story before Game 7:

> Pat Riley has a dream.
>
> The Lakers are playing the Celtics in the seventh game in Boston Garden. He's wearing a white tuxedo, staring across court at a girl in the front row wearing an avocado-green dress.
>
> The game comes down to the final seconds. A Laker throws up a last shot.
>
> Does it go in?
>
> Who wins?
>
> He never finds out.

Riley told his dream to anyone who'd listen. He was a writers' favorite in those days, patient with their questions, colorful with his answers, and gracious with his time. Sometimes he'd send writers letters, thanking them for their part in the season.

For big occasions, he'd share his dreams.

He actually thought about wearing a tuxedo for the game but decided it would look like grandstanding. A white jacket was brought to the Boston Garden for him, just in case.

The city of Boston was wild. There had been pranks galore during the series, including a fire alarm that went off at 3 A.M. in the Lakers' hotel.

Bird claimed Commissioner David Stern had said he wanted the series to go seven games because "the NBA needs the money."

Riley said Bird was showing "signs of cracking up," adding: "Maybe we all are."

Just to put it all in perspective, Riley explained the cultural roots of the rivalry.

"Boston is a city of hard-working blue-collar people," he said, "a mentality similar to the team because you become like the city you play in. We are footloose, fancy-free, a glitz and glamour team. You put those players on another team they wouldn't try to hurt anyone. But you put them down there in Boston Garden with those flags [championship banners] and you either play that way for the Boston Celtics or you don't play at all. You are a product of your environment."

Products of a more temperate environment, the Lakers brought two portable air conditioners to the game, extra dry uniforms to swap for sweaty ones, canisters of oxygen, and an intravenous unit.

The temperature dropped into the 80s and the Celtics won, 111-102. Now the Lakers were 0–8.

Johnson went down fumbling. The Lakers were within 105–102 late in the game when Magic, bringing the ball up on a fast break, had it stolen by Dennis Johnson.

"The whole series was a disaster for me," Johnson says. "I let the clock run out in Game 2. We go back there for Game 7, another crucial play, I was coming down, I had James open, I could have gotten it to him but DJ took it from me."

Accepting the Larry O'Brien Trophy from Stern on national TV, Auerbach sneered "What ever happened to that Laker *dynasty* I've been hearing so much about?"

Chris and her parents were jostled after the game. Fans rocked the Lakers' bus. A window was broken on a press bus.

The Lakers had to spend the night in Boston. Johnson stayed up with his buddies, Isiah Thomas and Mark Aguirre. When he got home, he locked himself into his new mansion in Bel Air for three days, refusing even to talk to his mother on the telephone.

Michael Cooper stayed up talking with his wife, Wanda. When friends knocked on the door, Wanda told them Michael preferred to be alone.

The Rileys stayed up with the Bertkas. They sent out for beer and hors d'oeuvres. Pat tried to sleep but couldn't. He later called it "the longest night of my life."

Riley mooned around for weeks, second-guessing every move he'd made in the series.

"After we choked," he said afterward, "we never thought we'd live through the summer."

"You looked at Pat afterward," said Dave Wohl, "and, I mean, it looked like he had not eaten for three days, had not slept. I mean, you were looking at a person who was ravaged by the loss. We all were but because it was more on his head, I think he took it harder."

West looked like a man who'd seen a ghost, as he had.

"It was a loss that should never have happened," West says. "It was probably the worst loss in Laker franchise history. We should have won in four straight games. It just made me crazy. It was just unforgivable. But I've been through all that before and I know what that's like, to lose when you don't want to lose."

That was what it had meant to be a Laker. Glamorous or not, they were still second-best and unless they came to grips with this Celtic thing, would always be.

"It hurt so bad," Johnson says. "We hurt. All of us hurt. It was just heart-breaking. He [Riley] was through. He was a crazy man. Just like all of us. We knew we were better than them and to lose to them!

"But when we got out of there, we learned a valuable lesson. Only the strong survive and that's something we didn't know until then. Talent just don't get it. We realized it's not all about talent and that's the first time the Lakers ever encountered that, someone stronger-minded.

"So we said, 'O.K., we got to be stronger.' "

That was just what happened, too. The Lakers would get back into the finals against the Celtics and show up that old mystique for what it was.

"And I think," says Michael Cooper, "then is when the real Coach Riley came out."

The Green Monster

*I had to educate my players who the Celtics were. One day
in practice, I asked if anyone knew. Finally Kareem raised his
hand. He said the Celtics were a warring race of Danes
who invaded Ireland. I had to explain that they were
also a cunning, secretive race.*

We had to learn to overcome the mythology of the Celtics.

—Pat Riley

An entire franchise winced at its image in the mirror.

The Lakers had believed themselves uniquely blessed. Now that "soft Lakers" stuff was on everyone's lips and it made them crazy.

That image went back a long way. In the early West–Baylor era, the Lakers, the class of the West, had never had a center who could play against Bill Russell. Now they had the venerable Abdul-Jabbar, no banger, at center and the horn-rimmed, undersized, modestly-talented Kurt Rambis at power forward.

The Lakers actually had good size with their 6–9 small forward and 6–9 point guard, but you are what you do and they'd finished second best. They'd have to sit still for everything anyone said: they were soft, western, southern Californian, etc.

"A crock of shit," Riley told Scott Ostler and Steve Springer for their book, *Winnin' Times*.

"...I don't think there's any doubt that southern California and Hollywood and L.A. are considered to be filled with people who are soft and have no values and couldn't work a day in their lives, that everything out here is a free ride.

"Our road to success has always been a struggle, hasn't been easy but they don't want to agree with that. They don't want to hear it. They think you're on a magic carpet or something, being lifted up by the bright lights of Los Angeles."

▮

Johnson, emerging finally from his home, did a commercial with Bird for Converse that summer. They discovered, to their surprise, they actually liked each other.

The Lakers and Celtics were about to move into a new phase of friendly rivalry but it would be no less intense.

The Lakers could always summon up someone in green to make their blood boil: Carr taunting them on the free throw line, telling them they didn't have the heart to make these; Maxwell giving them the choke sign; McHale's never-to-be-forgotten tackle; Auerbach's mere existence.

For Riley, who even hated to see his players fraternizing, there could be nothing friendly about any rivalry, but this one was war.

The Celtics were Huns to him, "classless," ill-mannered, capable of anything from setting off the fire alarm at their hotel to spying on them at practice.

"He became obsessed with getting over that Boston mystique," Cooper says. "It was then that the change started to come.

"Kareem at that time was talking about retiring, not being able to go any more. I think he got caught up in it.

"The papers were saying Pat Riley wouldn't be a great coach without Kareem and Magic. I think everybody got caught up with different things and in the process, a change started happening and it was a great change.

"Because he started, not nailing down the screws, but making us more precise, making us own up to our own possibilities."

Riley always sent each player a long letter in the summer, talking about their play last season and what he expected in the upcoming one. This summer, the players could have written their own letters. No one had to ask what their goal was.

In camp in Palm Springs, Riley made the no-layup edict of the preceding spring permanent. Even in practice, players had to bump anyone going to the basket.

There were no significant changes in personnel. The Lakers knew they were good enough, if only they had character enough.

Nine months before it would mean anything, they began rooting for the Celtics to win the East. Nothing would do but a championship won against the Celtics.

▮

Riley's two-year, $450,000 deal was up. Now represented by Ed Hookstratten, a heavyweight West Coast lawyer, he worked the exhibition season without a contract. He signed for three years and $900,000 shortly before the season.

"It's not very close to what I wanted," Riley said, "but it's very good."

The negotiations had been low-key but dragged on for several months. Riley had no thought of leaving. He was a southern Californian through and through and only a raving idiot would walk away from this setup, to say nothing of his desire to redeem himself against the Celtics. But he was also an emerging star and he stuck to his guns until Buss moved nearer his figure.

Buss cared only about getting over the top. Riley glowed with a holy fire and it warmed everyone around him.

That summer, trainer Jack Curran retired. For Riley, a trainer was also a traveling secretary and aide-de-camp. He wanted to get someone young, sharp, and, of course, highly industrious.

Someone recommended Gary Vitti, a former baseball trainer working in Portland, Ore. Vitti had no intention of living on the road with an NBA team but accepted the invitation to fly to Los Angeles.

"I met with Pat for about two hours," Vitti says. "I kinda talked to Pat in a way that, 'Hey look, I've got a job, I'm not looking for a job. I've got a state-of-the-art facility I'm building up in Portland, a half-million dollar facility.'

"Pat's attitude was like, 'That's really great, what you're doing but look at it this way: everything that you're doing there you can do here with the greatest athletes in the world.'

"I had been in the pros a little bit but Pat was the most progressive guy that I had ever met as far as sports medicine goes from the coaching ranks, as far as flexibility and strength training and nutrition and all those things that I was interested in.

"He told me, 'Look, we got beat by the Celtics and I've got carte blanche. I can do anything I want to get a championship. And these are the things I want to do.'

"I came here not really wanting the job. I left *really* wanting the job and that was because of Pat and his attitude."

■|

Pat's attitude was ferocious as well as contagious.

"Looking back, I think he's one of the best coaches I've ever seen," says Dave Wohl. There are strengths and weaknesses to every coach. I thought sometimes he didn't allow the players to enjoy practices.

"There was a time once when Earvin came up to me and Bill Bertka. I think it was in '85, we were in first, playing good and Earvin said, 'Riles is just, you know, he's not letting us have any fun.'

"So Bill and I go into Pat and kind of bring this up. We said, 'Pat, I just want to point out to you that we've had some guys just mention some things, for whatever it's worth, they talked about how they're not having any fun.

"And I remember Pat was really upset because to him, practice didn't need to involve fun. It was to go to work to get better.

"And I can remember, he came in the next day and pulled up a chair at midcourt. It was funny because he couldn't take it lightly. He couldn't say, 'All right, look, you guys don't think we're having fun, maybe I'm a little too hard and we'll have a little more fun,' or something like that. Or he didn't even have to say anything, just let it happen.

"He sat down and he said, 'I understand you guys think we need to be a little more facetious at practice.'

"And nobody said anything.

"And he said, 'From now on, we're going to have ten minutes of facetious time.'

"Bert and I were looking at each other and rolling our eyes, like, 'No, this is not working out the way we thought....'

"I remember in the playoffs one time, Magic's knee had begun to hurt him a little bit. He came out once without a wrap on it and Pat goes, 'Gary, wrap Magic's knee.'

"And Gary goes, 'It feels O.K., he says it feels O.K.'

"Pat said, 'Gary, I want a wrap on it.'

"Gary looks at me. I said, 'Look, put any kind of wrap on it. Put a cellophane wrap on it. It doesn't matter, just let him feel good by seeing a wrap.

"And Earvin kind of rolled his eyes and he and Vitti went in and his knee was wrapped and it was O.K.

"Pat would get into these paranoid things where he could see demons all around, trying to distract his team. And in a way, it was a key to his success. I think the players, one thing they admired about him, was his focus. You knew there was a commitment beyond what any coach seemed to be doing. It was a commitment that he was willing to, like, walk on hot coals to be the best and to be at the top of the ladder, at the top of the mountain when the smoke cleared.

"And he suffered for it. There were really emotional highs and lows."

They all suffered for it together.

"There were times I looked at him," Magic Johnson says, "and knew he hadn't slept for days. That helped motivate me."

∎

The season worked out exactly as they had hoped.

The Lakers mopped up the Pacific Division with a 62–20 record, 20 games better than second-place Portland.

The Celtics went 63–19 and finished five ahead of the 76ers in the Atlantic.

The Lakers ripped through the West in the playoffs, routing the Suns, Blazers, and Nuggets, 10–2.

The Celtics dispatched the Cavaliers, Pistons, and 76ers, 10–3.

The Lakers had their rematch.

Riley, publicly, was low-key or no-key. He wasn't going to let his players start talking about what happened last season, and the humiliation they felt, and their desire to bite the Celtics in the throat.

Of course, the press would ask. They just weren't going to respond. The great spin doctor was born.

"I understand that history has to be chronicled again," Riley said, "but I don't want to dwell on anything but the positive. Opening up any lock-box about what happened or why would be counter-productive.

"I've cautioned the team about that. It was an experience lived. It was a good one and a bad one. This is a very simple process—either winning or being in a miserable state of mind.

"Why go back and open up a can of worms? Let's just get on with it."

If they needed some new worms, the Celtics would be happy to oblige.

On Memorial Day, under the Celtic championship banners, on the storied parquet floor where the Lakers had melted a year before, they ventured out in Game 1 to seek their revenge.

It was a disaster.

The Celtics shot a withering 61 percent, ran up a 30-point lead by halftime and won, 146–114 in what became known as the Memorial Day Massacre.

It was devastating, humiliating, and more to the point, only 72 hours before they'd be back out there again. Riley had to think of something fast.

It was his own Post-Memorial Day Massacre.

"His first violent blowup," says Michael Cooper.

"I think what happened at that point, he started reliving '84 again. 'Oh, this is going to happen again—No! I'm not going to let it happen!' "

Riley called a meeting at the hotel for the next morning. The players trooped in solemnly. Everyone noticed that Abdul-Jabbar, who usually sat in the back, took a seat in the front row, right in front of the video screen. Not that anyone had distinguished himself but Kareem had had a miserable Game 1, letting Robert Parish run the floor for several uncontested dunks.

The room went dark. It was Showtime of a different sort.

"It was just like a 30-minute video," Cooper says. "but he sat there and replayed it. Every time you fucked up, he'd rewind it five times. You just sat there and saw yourself fucking up five times.

"It literally stayed on Kareem. And he'd say, 'Cap, look at how this guy is beating you down the floor!'

"I thought the guy [Riley] had literally gone crazy, just totally lost it 'cause he wasn't maniacal, he was *silent*. And those are some of the worst people you can deal with. I said, 'Oh man....'

"I was waiting for Kareem to say, 'Hey Riles, fuck this, let's get on.' But he never said anything. He'd just shake his head and he continued to watch.

"And he went on down the line—Kareem, Magic. He went through all the starters. He went systematically to everybody.

"Once the video was over—like I told you, sometimes the craziest person is the silent person—the guy stood up, he put the thing [remote] down and he proceeded to go off on us verbally. Tried to put his fist through the back of the chalkboard. The chalk went flying. People who were sitting up front looked like they were at the movies when it gets scary. Things were happening!"

Both of Riley's assistants, Bertka and Wohl, remember Riley as measured and calm in that meeting.

But the players remember him as furious.

"He was a master at letting it sink in," Johnson says. "He was a master at going back, getting himself together, writing what he was going to say the next day—and how he was going to blast our butts. I'm serious. He was a master at that.

"He had blown up before but not individually. And not at Kareem.

"He came out and he started: '*You guys call yourselves the Three Musketeers? You guys ain't crap!*'—He was talking about the guards—'*DJ's kicking your ass, Buck! Danny Ainge is just intimidating you, Byron!*'

"Down the line. He just made you feel like you were this tall.

"And Kareem! He got to Kareem, just called him every name in the book! *You're supposed to be our captain, our fucking leader! You don't even show to play! This is the world championship! They just took it to you! And what makes it worse, Greg Kite came in and did it to you!*

"He was just going on and on: *You guys! I thought you learned something last year! You didn't learn crap! You weren't ready to play!*

"On and on and on.

That's all right, you're going to get to this damn gym and things are gonna change, I tell you what!

And what makes things worse, Buck, you foul DJ and then you pick his ass up! We're down 40 points! If one man picks up a Celtic, $500 fine! If there's one layup—one layup!—another fine! No box out, another $500!

"He was just going on and on and we had to sit there and take it.

"I mean, we didn't do nothing right. He was just showing them shooting wide open jumpers, layups, dunks in our faces. Then he showed us being nice, picking the guys up. I mean, the meeting lasted, seemed like six hours. It was probably about 45 minutes.

"He was right in Kareem's face and that was the first time he got on the Big Fella. Everybody was just waiting to see what's gonna happen! 'Cause he made him feel like he was a backup center. He rode him good, and I'm not lyin', for ten minutes. At least! All by himself!

"O.K., we had the meeting, then we went to practice.

"He wouldn't really talk to us the whole practice. He would talk at us but not to us. He was showing us, 'Hey, uh uh, this is the way I want it.' And any mistake, 'Stop, O.K., run!' And everybody had to run.

"He was so mad, I mean, I was scared to talk to him and usually I talk to him.

"I tell you what, it was the greatest coaching strategy that I've ever seen. Because we came out the next night and we were ready. Kareem was ready. You know what I'm saying?"

■

Two interminable days later, they filed onto their bus to Boston Garden. Abdul-Jabbar asked if his father, Big Al, could ride along.

Abdul-Jabbar was 37 and people had been trying to retire him for years. He'd always been able to show them but he'd never been as on the spot as he was now.

Riley had a hard-and-fast rule that only players and staff were allowed on the bus but when he saw the imploring look in Abdul-Jabbar's eyes, he relented.

"He was about to face one of the biggest tests of his career," Riley wrote in *Show Time*. "It was important to be with his father....

"Here were these two men sitting there. One big and the other a giant. I knew they had their share of father-and-son difficulty in earlier years. But that day they were feeling the importance of their mutual bond."

Riley started thinking of Lee.

Minutes before the game, he threw away the speech he'd written and started talking about his father, his struggles, and the last thing he had told his youngest son: make a stand and kick some butt.

"I talked about all the voices we've heard from those who cared about us in the past, coaches, mothers, fathers, teachers," Riley wrote. "I said, 'What I want you to do now is close your eyes. Rewind the tape. Listen. When your back is against the wall, that's the time to recall those voices.' "

"We were," Vitti says, "into, like, this father thing."

The impassioned sons ran out onto the parquet and began rewriting the basketball history of the '80s.

Abdul-Jabbar scored 30 points with 17 rebounds, eight assists, and three blocks. The Lakers led by 18 at the half and held on to win, 109–102.

"Kareem went to work," says Johnson. "And I'm going to tell you, you know when Kareem's in it, when he bends down real low when he posts up and he *stays* low. He doesn't stand straight up like he does when he's tired or whatever. He stays down *low*.

"He doesn't let anybody come down that middle. He was hitting people coming down the lane. I mean, he was just ready. Oh man...."

"We would slam guys down—*Yeah!* Leave 'em down there!"

Game 3 back at the Forum was a Laker rout, 136–111, with Abdul-Jabbar going for 26 points and 14 rebounds. The Lakers, still flexing their muscles, out-rebounded the Celtics by 12. Johnny Most, the Celtic broadcaster whose flair for descriptive play-by-play varied with the threat to the dynasty, called Rambis and Kupchak "something that crawled out of the sewer."

Afterward, the laid-back Celtic Coach, K. C. Jones, accused the Lakers of cheap shots, a compliment if Riley had ever heard one.

The Celtics had a trick or two left and produced one in Game 4, Dennis Johnson's 19-foot game-winner at the buzzer.

There was so much pushing, shoving, and woofing that NBA vice president Scotty Stirling brought Riley and Jones together before Game 5 to warn them to get their players under control.

Jones didn't even mention the warning to his players.

Riley was asked later why the league was intervening this year after having stayed out of it in 1984.

"We don't wear green uniforms," he said, grinning. "Is that what you're looking for?

"Point out I say all this with a smile on my face. If the league can't take a joke, the hell with 'em."

The series was being played with the new 2–3–2 format, rather than the old 2–2–1–1–1, eliminating one cross-country trip for both teams. The new format would also give the team that had won fewer games the pivotal Game 5 on its own floor, and Auerbach had complained bitterly about it.

Just to underscore Auerbach's point, the Lakers won Game 5 in the Forum, 120–111.

The Lakers were going back to Boston Garden with two chances to exorcise a demon.

■|

Welcome back to Boston, home of the 3 A.M. fire alarm and such Celtic skullduggery as only Riley could imagine.

"He could get as paranoid as anyone," says Wohl. "I remember the last practice before Game 6. The Celtics go on and practice first. The media talks to them and we go on.

"There's a Gatorade container over there. So Pat sees it and he says, 'Gary, what's in that?'

"And Gary goes, 'Just some leftover Gatorade.'

"And he literally told Gary to go change it because he thought the Celtics might have spiked it with something.

"Gary comes up to me and says, 'Do I really have to change this?'

"And I go, 'Yeah, you better go change it.' "

The Celtics had built their dynasty by winning Game 7 at home and the Lakers knew they'd better not get them in another one. They were going to hit the Celtics with everything they had right away, try to run them into the floor.

And that's what happened.

It was 55–55 at the half but the Lakers surged ahead in the third period and won going away in the fourth. The Garden, bedlam under normal circumstances, fell silent. At the end, as Johnson and Abdul-Jabbar embraced in front of the Laker bench, the Celtic fans applauded politely.

The Lakers won, 111–100.

Players showered the tiny visitors' dressing room they hated so much with champagne. Abdul-Jabbar, who'd averaged 28 points, 10 rebounds, and six assists since Game 1, called it the highlight of his career. So did Johnson.

For Riley, it wasn't even a question. Only now could he begin to hint at what he'd gone through.

"Everything is purged," he said. "Now they can't mock us and humiliate us, which is what they did last year...."

"Let somebody else feel that pain for 10 months."

All the questions had been answered. They had character. He was a big-time coach.

"When we won it," Cooper says, "that was the happiest I've seen Coach Riley in my life."

∎

The Lakers' golden era seemed to be upon them.

They had chemistry coming out of their ears. Johnson and Abdul-Jabbar were becoming real friends after years of mere coexistence. Scott fit smoothly into the role Nixon had struggled with. Cooper was a great reserve, a defensive stopper who could spell Johnson at the point, Scott at shooting guard, or Worthy at small forward. Worthy was ideal, a small-town man too reserved to resent the attention going to Johnson or Abdul-Jabbar or, recently, Riley.

Riley had become a force. If his players grumbled at his taskmaster practices, they respected him and felt warmly toward him. The press doted on him; he spoke their language, too.

But events have a rhythm of their own. The Lakers were getting older, too, and there were younger, stronger men who wanted what they had.

But for the moment, the Lakers could look in the mirror and smile. Somewhere, all their coaches, mothers, fathers, and teachers were smiling with them.

CHAPTER EIGHT

Pat Riley, Superstar

or

The Mousse Is Loose

It came out of nowhere. We won the championship and he always handled everything well and all of a sudden, he was the most marketable coach. He didn't let himself become bigger than the team, but it just happened. Boom, success! It was just there! You talk about camera presence, it's Riley.

—MAGIC JOHNSON

It is time to separate ourselves from the pack and become the only ones who do what we do. Unique. That is the essence of Showtime.

The future is now, fellas.

—RILEY'S LETTER TO HIS PLAYERS
AFTER GUARANTEEING THEY'D REPEAT

By the mid-'80s, with the Dodgers and Raiders stumbling, the Lakers had become the hot ticket. They had style and glamor. Movie stars flocked to the Forum, following the charter celebs, Jack Nicholson and Dyan Cannon, until there were so many of them hovering around, writers couldn't interview a player until Rob Lowe or Don Johnson was done offering his congratulations.

Unlike other cities, there was nothing desperate about Laker fans' passion. Los Angeles had no civic inferiority complex that its teams were expected to redress. It was just the opposite, a theme evident on New Year's Day when the local poet laureate, Jim Murray of the *Times*, prayed in his Rose Bowl column for bad weather lest more Midwesterners watching on TV decide to emigrate.

Most Laker fans were recent emigrants themselves, people who were still hanging on to old loyalties from New York or Chicago where local teams were like members of the family. In this golden land, a basketball team was just a basketball team and if it fell on hard times, there were always the mountains, the beaches, etc.

When the Lakers won, L.A. was happy. When they lost, it understood. It would have been unthinkable for Laker fans to chant "Beat Boston!" to some other team the way Boston fans chanted "Beat L.A.!" to the 76ers in the 1982 Eastern finals when it became clear the Celtics would lose Game 7.

L.A. fans weren't in it for blood, but entertainment. Win or lose, they arrived late and left early. They had a lot of freeway to cover.

Press coverage was measured. Since a strike crippled the *Herald-Examiner* in the '60s, the area was dominated by a single newspaper, the *Los Angeles Times*, which had a daily news magazine format. There were no newspaper circulation wars in the East Coast sense. Everyone had less of an edge.

This was Pat Riley's L.A. It was paradise.

▌▌

But how was he going to keep everyone from nodding off?

It had been 16 years since an NBA team had won back-to-back titles. Whether it was parity, expansion, travel, multiyear contracts, or the moon in the seventh house and Jupiter aligned with Mars, it was fact.

NBA veterans knew if they won a title, no one could rightfully demand anything of them the following season.

To Riley, hungering for more, this was anathema. In four seasons, he'd been in the finals four times. The Lakers had won two, figured they should have won a third, and were too injured to compete in the fourth. They had just rid themselves of their Celtic curse.

"In 1985, Pat was really ready to roll," says assistant coach Bill Bertka. "We started out in Palm Springs. Cap [Abdul-Jabbar] made the statement at our opening tipoff meeting in training camp, 'How can we top last year?'

Said Riley later: "It was the truth but right then I knew we were in trouble."

It was a different cast. The Lakers had cut Wilkes and chose not to pick up McAdoo's expensive option, Mac's scoring average having declined annually as his injuries increased. West acquired a long-sought enforcer, Maurice Lucas, who still had a snarl or two left. With the 23rd pick in the draft, West snared A. C. Green, a Bible-toting gladiator out of Oregon State.

The Lakers bolted to a 24–3 start, won the Pacific by an NBA-record 22 games and swept the Spurs in the opening round of the playoffs by 31 points a game. According to the hype, the Lakers were on the threshhold of becoming the greatest team, etc.

Three weeks later, after a stunning loss to the young Rockets in the Western finals, the Lakers were written off as dead.

The Rockets were in the second season of their "Twin Tower" lineup, with the 7–4 Ralph Sampson and 7–0 Hakeem (then Akeem) Olajuwon. The Lakers had to play the 6–8 Rambis on Sampson and the aging Abdul-Jabbar on Olajuwon. Usually the mere sight of the Towers was enough to inspire Abdul-Jabbar. He had a history of big numbers against them but now he wore down, unable to keep the relentless, bounding Hakeem off the boards.

The Rockets lost Game 1 at the Forum but won Game 2 when Rocket guards Lewis Lloyd and Mitchell Wiggins, whom the Lakers allowed to shoot, went 17 for 32.

In Houston, Olajuwon scored 40 and 35 in romps in Games 3 and 4. The Rockets out-rebounded the Lakers by an average of 10 per game.

They finished the Lakers off in Game 5 in the Forum on Sampson's game-ending corkscrew volleyball tap of an in-bounds pass. Michael Cooper fell on his back in the free throw lane and lay there, spread-eagled with his hands on his head in disbelief.

Everyone tripped blithely off the bandwagon. This Twin Tower thing was considered the new basketball of the future.

Among the converts were the Lakers.

"I think we've peaked," said James Worthy. "We've played the very best we could play. Maybe the way we were isn't good enough any longer. It's like going to the bank, using your automatic teller card, and there's no money in there."

"I don't want to sound like I'm trying to coach," said Magic Johnson, "but we need somebody big, that's all. Sometimes you need some youth. Maybe that's it."

Even Riley conceded what seemed to be obvious.

"Obviously, what the Rockets have must be matched so we can get size and fresh legs to support Kareem," he said. "We've been one step ahead of the posse. Now it's even."

All the Lakers had to do now was locate a talented big guy and steal him.

They found 6–10 Roy Tarpley, a rookie from Michigan who'd been drafted by Dallas. They agreed to send Worthy to the Mavericks for Tarpley and Johnson's buddy, Aguirre. Only West resisted, so bitterly that Buss called Mavs owner Don Carter to ask if he could back out. Otherwise, Buss said, he was afraid he was going to lose his GM.

Carter said O.K., unknowingly saving the Laker franchise. Within three years, the sulky Aguirre would be on the bench in Detroit and Tarpley would be in a detox program.

Riley had to start getting ready to make do with what he had.

The plan he came up with sounded like an old-fashioned homily, one of those bromides one tries in the absence of actual resources: the year of the Career Best Effort.

Riley had always kept his arcane statistics, an index comprised of everything: points, rebounds, rebounds pursued, dives on the floor, defensive helps, etc. "If he wanted to get at Magic for a game," said Cooper, "like Earvin might have played 300 the last three games, he'd say 'Well, look Earvin, [Michael] Jordan the last game played 700. Bird played 800 the last three games. Here you are at 300.' "

Afterward, Johnson, who hated being told he was deficient in anything, would usually go out and lay a large number on whichever team came next.

That summer Riley wrote his annual letters to his players, asking them to raise their games to career heights.

In a pre-camp retreat with Bertka and Pfund in Santa Barbara, he decided to revamp the offense. If they couldn't get bigger, they'd go back to their game, speed. Johnson would become the first option in the offense, Abdul-Jabbar the second.

The defensive scheme would change, too, to deal with teams attacking them inside. Although it went unnoticed, the Lakers were becoming a better defensive team every season under Riley. Their offensive average was sliding annually but they gave up fewer points annually too.

Not that Riley had any confidence any of this was enough.

"Maybe we've gotten all we can out of this team," he said in August. "Maybe this team has suffered a core burnout. That possibility has to be faced.

"Fans are going to have to have patience. After all the years of success, we may not be a championship team in the future. We'll be a quality team that might win 45–50 games a year after Kareem leaves but we are probably not going to reach the finals all the time. Getting to the Western Conference finals might be a good year for us. People are going to have to understand that."

Virtually the same Laker team reported back to Palm Springs. Lucas, who'd failed to enforce anything against the Twin Towers, was let go. A. C. Green, the second-year forward, began to get more time at power forward, a development that pained only Kurt Rambis and the Rambis Youth, his fans who used to wear horn-rimmed glasses like his. But Green was younger, faster, stronger, more skilled, and willing to do the dirty work, too.

Laker players and coaches still hoped out loud for a 7-footer to ride to the rescue, but West disabused them of their illusion.

"I told him," West said, "I said 'Pat, I don't know if that's possible. Maybe moving personnel around, doing things a little bit differently, maybe that'll help. I don't know if I can find another player that will fit those qualifications and can play at the level we need to play.' "

Riley started implementing his changes.

He wasn't going to say anything the way Westhead had, just blend in the new plays gradually. The first day's practice was so bad, he considered junking the whole thing right there. Bertka talked him out of it.

Everything depended on Abdul-Jabbar's reaction to being deemphasized. Several days into camp, Kareem walked up to Riley and said casually he liked the changes. Riley breathed a sigh.

The Lakers went 65–17. Johnson, who'd never averaged more than 19 points a game, jumped to 24 and won his first MVP.

Seven Lakers averaged double figures including Green and Mychal Thompson, the backup center West got off San Antonio's bench at mid-season.

Then they began a fearsome march through the playoffs.

They started with a 128–95 blowout of the Nuggets, after which Denver Coach Doug Moe who had estimated his chances before the series as "fucking zero," announced: "I'm going home tonight. We wouldn't show up Saturday if the league would let us. Are you kidding?"

Moe kept it up. After a Game 2 victory, Riley sniffed: "We worked hard for seven months to get here. When we get to the playoffs, we take it seriously. I expect our opponents to feel the same way."

Riley's opponents had enough problems without having to listen to his lectures about their attitude.

"I agree with a statement I read somewhere that maybe Pat needs a little humility and should coach the Clippers for a year, instead of all the talent he's got," said Nuggets president Vince Boryla. "Take his Ouija boards and motion offense and fancy clothes and hair and spend a year in the Sports Arena instead of the Forum."

Proving Moe had been right all along, the Lakers flattened the Nuggets, 140–103, to conclude the sweep.

Golden State came next. The Lakers hit the Warriors with a 49-point third quarter in Game 1 and ran away, after which the feisty George Karl announced: "I'll be honest with you, I have to think we can win this series."

By Game 3 in Oakland, which the Lakers won by a tidy 133–108, Karl was reconsidering.

"We played a team," he said, "that might have been unbeatable."

The Warriors went down in five. The Sonics fell in four in the Western finals.

The Lakers got Boston once more in the finals but this time the Celtics were clearly outgunned.

While the Lakers had waltzed to the finals, the Celtics had battled the Pistons through a seven-game series, winning only after Bird's steal of Isiah Thomas's in-bounds pass in Game 5. McHale was playing with a broken foot. The Lakers zoomed to a 21-point lead at halftime in Game 1 and won Game 2 by 19.

Back in Boston, the Celtics won Game 3, averting the sweep.

Then came Game 4, the last great Laker–Celtic shootout.

With :12 left, Bird hit a three-pointer to put the Celts up, 106–105.

With :02 left, Johnson hit his "junior, junior skyhook" over McHale and Robert Parish to put the Lakers up, 107–106.

At the buzzer, Bird missed a jumper out of the corner in front of the Laker bench that was dead-on but bounced off the back rim.

Perhaps for old times' sake, Red Auerbach chased referee Earl Strom to his dressing room and pounded on the door to complain.

The Celtics won Game 5 in Boston but the Lakers closed them out easily in Game 6 at the Forum.

The team that had been considering revamping itself nine months before had gone 17–3 in post-season. The Lakers won their fourth title in the '80s, separating themselves forever from the Celtics who had but three. In a backhand compliment to the Lakers, Celtic coach K. C. Jones congratulated his players on "an amazing job just getting to the sixth game."

It was Riley's finest moment. But he was only warming up.

While his players were throwing champagne on each other, he waited until the first person asked that tired old question about next season.

Quoth Riley: "We will repeat. I guarantee it."

Characteristically, he'd been thinking about that statement for weeks, going over the words again and again until he had it down perfectly.

Of course, repeating wasn't anything that was guaranteeable. It could count only as a standard that the team could be held to. Riley had served notice on twelve Lakers: they hadn't done nothing yet.

"You hear all these qualifications," Riley said later, "all these reasons why it can't be done. Winning teams have been guilty of talking themselves into losing. And I believe you are what comes out of your mouth.

"The pot at the end is greatness. By now the players have all had their walk in the lights. But now they have a chance to be a great team. Not a flash in the pan like the '71–'72 Lakers, but a team like the Celtics because of what they did over ten years."

The players didn't know whether to laugh or cry.

"I thought it was a little premature," said Abdul-Jabbar later.

"I hadn't even taken a sip of champagne," said Byron Scott.

"We didn't even get a chance to enjoy the one we'd won," said Michael Cooper.

In case anyone had missed it, Riley's guarantee had brought the Lakers to another watershed. Riley was openly manipulating his players now. He'd dared them in front of everyone.

Let's see how they'd handle *that*.

■

Suddenly, he was huge.

Riley's speaking career blossomed. He had built it from scratch, appearing for free as a player just because the Lakers asked him to, only to discover he liked to talk to groups and was good at it.

By the end of the decade, he was getting $20,000 for a motivational speech. When Riley attended a company's convention, he sat in on meetings, studied its assets, its goals, and its competition. Then he wove what he'd learned into a speech that would have its employees ready to run out into the street and start selling.

He wrote *Show Time*, a day-by-day chronicle of the '86–'87 season. It became a best-seller. And for anyone who'd missed it, the Riley Way was spelled out in two sentences that started chapter 1:

"There are two possible states of being in the NBA: winning and misery. Winning also breaks down into two categories: savoring victory and being too damn tired to savor victory."

It was time to savor.

It was an intoxicating time, and his pride of authorship showed. He was like a child, exhilarated at learning to talk, pointing out everything he saw and announcing a name for it: "I call it the disease of more…I call it toxic envy…peripheral opponent…statement game…hidden agenda."

Endorsement offers streamed in.

This is when director Robert Towne offered Riley the lead in *Tequila Sunrise*, which Riley declined, but loaned second-choice Kurt Russell some of his clothes to achieve that Riley look.

The Rileys and Townes were close friends. Towne found Riley "as sane as any obsessive man can be and as obsessive as any sane man can be."

The Rileys had other showbiz friends like Ed McMahon but few, indeed, given the galaxy of stars turning up nightly in the Forum. Pat didn't want to let himself get sucked into the tide of gladhanders.

"Chris and I socialize with only a few couples," he said. "I'm trying to clear the clutter out of my life."

The Lakers were his priority. With the two Jerrys, Buss and West, he formed a model management team.

Buss had pulled back from his day-to-day involvement in the early years. He had deep pockets, and abiding confidence in his general manager and coach.

West had found an outlet for his seething drive to succeed, becoming one of the NBA's most admired GMs.

West was at once beloved and driven, respected and tortured. He had a fractured kind of personality; at times his own celebrity seemed to mean nothing to him, nor did anyone else's, and he watched Riley's rocketlike ascent with as much skepticism as pride. "At least when I give a speech," he once said privately, "people know what I'm talking about."

People around the Forum used to say that West had always been what Riley wanted to be as a player and now Riley was what West wanted to be as an administrator. Each was aware of the other's foibles but they remained friends who respected each other. Riley didn't meddle upstairs and West didn't interfere in the dressing room.

By mid-decade, only Hubie Brown's Knicks and Mike Fratello's Hawks could challenge the Lakers as the NBA's hardest-working team.

Riley's practices were painstakingly planned to the smallest detail. He wanted his players' complete attention, not to mention the freedom to sick his veterans on a rookie to see what the kid had. He didn't want to see fights reported, either, and waged a never-ending battle with the public relations department over keeping the press out.

But except for set-piece tantrums that he planned every once in a while to wake everyone up, Riley rarely raised his voice.

He didn't have to. He exuded command. His players had become an all-business group.

They took practice seriously. Fights weren't unusual and session-long bitching back and forth was common, most often between Johnson and the combative A. C. Green. Lakers argued about the score of scrimmages, fouls, and anything else that came up.

They had esprit. They were proud to be Lakers and loath to admit anyone who hadn't proven himself to the brotherhood. They hazed rookies mercilessly, most notably Byron Scott who was cold-shouldered for half a season for the crime of getting traded for Norm Nixon. Scott never complained and, after winning his spurs, happily joined Johnson and Cooper in terrorizing any new guards on the lot.

Riley liked to keep them off balance, too.

He might give his players a day off if someone could hit a half-court shot. Or he might throw Rosenfeld, the publicist, out of the gym on a whim.

"Those '87 and '88 years, if we lost it wasn't because we weren't prepared," said Michael Cooper. "It wasn't because we weren't prepared mentally.

"It was because that team for that night was the better ball club. If a team wasn't ready to play, they were going to get beat that night, simply because Coach Riley went home, did all the necessary things, watched the video, watched what we did to that team the last time. And he had a damn game plan for [each of] those guys, if it was Michael Jordan, Twin Towers...."

∎

The easygoing Riles the reporters had known and loved was gone.

He was still pleasant, he was always professional, he was still a great talker. He had made himself a star by giving the writers such good stuff they were always quoting him. But things had changed.

Now it seemed he was never just talking, he was delivering some message—the appropriate words at the appropriate time to the appropriate people, as he put it. There was a degree of design in his comments and a degree of condescension, too, as when he told the *Times'* beat writer, Tommy Bonk, that he talked to him only as a way of reaching his players.

Bonk then went a week without quoting Riley who called him in for a truce.

Strains were inevitable. Riley had been one of the press guys but was no longer. He intended his team to be a close-knit family protecting itself against a hostile outside environment. He tried to control everything around it, including the press corps.

The process had begun soon after Riley took over. Within a year of becoming a coach, he was joking to the same writers he'd hung out with that they were "buzzards."

The press guys accepted it as kidding; Rich Levin of the *Herald-Examiner* went out and had "Buzzard" baseball caps made up for the scribes who wore them to see Riley who laughed in turn.

By mid-decade, the smiles were forced.

Riley had come up with the notion of the "peripheral opponent," of whom the press was understood to be No. 1. Of course, he smiled so the writers would understand they shouldn't take it personally, but they had to understand their place in the world. They ranked down there with agents and relatives calling for tickets as invasions of a Laker's privacy.

The press wasn't just a distraction but a threat. Riley, once so unpretentious, had become image conscious.

He'd gone back to smoking but hid it, lighting up only in private. Once as he puffed away after a close victory at Seattle, a writer cracked this had been a two-pack game. Riley told him not to dare write that. The writer decided that the line wasn't worth two weeks of the icy treatment.

If Riley lacked leverage with a writer, he'd withdraw completely. He not only declined to be interviewed for this book but said he would tell friends, who asked him if they should talk, that it was an "unauthorized biography." Chris called friends to urge them not to say anything. Pat's books, a diary of a season and a management primer, would be only lightly autobiographical.

Joe McDonnell, a radio reporter who remembered Riley as the rookie announcer humbly asking for feedback, interviewed him shortly after the '87 guarantee and was surprised to hear him go off on the press: The press was never going to let them forget it, etc.

Of course, it was Riley who'd set it up that way. Why else the guarantee?

He wanted the pressure on the players but not on him and was railing against the same press that he enlisted. He wanted it both ways. He had become like everyone else but more so.

"That," said McDonnell, "was when I knew he'd lost his perspective completely."

■

If you want to know where Riley's perspective went, his intensity ate it.

Riley's zeal grew and took on comic overtones.

In 1986, Wohl left to become coach of the Nets. Riley wanted a young replacement he could mold, someone loyal, someone single whom he wouldn't be keeping away from a family.

Bertka, who lived in Santa Barbara, recommended Randy Pfund, an assistant at a local school, Westmont College.

Riley put him on the list. Bertka gave Pfund some hints for the upcoming interview.

"He said, 'Pat likes decisive, strong people,'" Pfund says. "'When he asks you to diagram anything, make sure you don't make any light diagrams. Make bold, sweeping strokes.'"

"So when the time came, I went so hard, it like broke the chalk right in half. I thought, 'Well, that's what Bill told me to do.' "

Probably coincidentally, Riley hired Pfund.

There was no end to Riley's devotion to detail and it seemed no detail too trivial.

The Lakers began training in Honolulu. Riley, the devotee of the beach and going first class, loved it and sought ways to make it even better.

"It's the day before training camp," said trainer Gary Vitti. "We go over to the gym, we get the place clean, and everything is perfect. We're sitting around the pool and it's like the middle of the afternoon. It's like our last few hours before we go to two-a-days. When you're in those two-a-days, it feels like you're going to be there the rest of your life, you know.

"So we're sitting by the pool and you could just see him. I mean, he's so anxious to get it going. He's sitting by the pool and his blood pressure is going up and he's getting pumped. I mean, he had to find things to do.

"He goes, 'You know, I went over to the gym. Why don't you ask Rudy'—our equipment manager—'tell him to go down to the hardware store and tell him to get some orange paint and some bright new shiny bolts. I noticed there's a couple chips on the rim and the bolts are kinda tarnished. Let's get some nice shiny brand-new stuff out there.'

"It's like, you got to be kidding me! Klum Gym was built in like 1927. It's a quonset hut! It's a dump! It's got holes in the roof. It rains there every year, the roof is leaking and he thinks that by putting up a couple of bolts he's going to make this place into the Auburn Palace?"

As trainer, Vitti heard a lot of unusual suggestions.

In Pontiac for the '88 finals, the Lakers found themselves booked into the same hotel with the Monsters of Rock tour with groups like the Scorpions, Metallica, and Van Halen. Rob Lowe was there in his capacity as Laker fan. Groupies of all shapes and sizes roamed the premises, producing for Riley a vision of lobby hell.

Always interested in keeping his players together and where he could see them, Riley set up a lounge on the Lakers-only hotel floor with almost every manner of diversion a young man could want.

And yet something was missing.

"We set this room up and it's beautiful," Vitti said. "We've got this pool table, we've got big-screen TV, backgammon, cards, checkers, unbelievable amounts of food. You could go in there any time day or night, watch video, watch a game. It was like a social hall.

"And he comes in. I say, 'What do you think, Pat, everything O.K.?'

"He looks around and tells Billy Desser who was our video technician at the time, 'You know what would really finish this off and make it look nice is some nice pastel towels.'

"So Billy tells the management we need some pastel towels. [Laughing] Next thing you know, we get a bill for $800 for towels. I don't remember who went off, I think it was [assistant GM] Mitch Kupchak. He folded the towels, put 'em back in the box, gave 'em back to the hotel. Give me a break."

Then there were the limos.

At the 1988 All-Star Game in Chicago, Riley decided the three All-Star Lakers shouldn't be forced to ride buses like the other players.

"I wasn't there," Vitti said. "Josh [Rosenfeld, team publicist] was there. Pat tells Josh to order some limos. We're back in L.A. and all of a sudden, I get a message Jerry West wants to see us in his office.

"Jerry throws this bill at me and goes, 'What's this?' Like $1,500.

"I go, 'Gee, Jerry, I don't know. Looks like a bill for some limos.'

" 'These are limos for the All-Star Game!'

" 'Jerry,' I said, 'I wasn't even there. I didn't go to the All-Star Game. I was like in Palm Springs.'

"Josh says, 'Jerry, I ordered them, Pat told me to get some limos.'

"Josh didn't travel with us much at the time. So Jerry goes off on me! He says, *'If you ever order anything like this for your coach without getting it O.K.'d with me first, I'm gonna take it out of your check! Can you afford this? Do you think you can afford this?'*

"That was Pat. Pat used to tell me what his father said: 'If you go just a little bit more, you can go first class.' That was Pat's motto."

The husbands got limos and suites; the wives stayed home and watched on TV.

Riley's "peripheral opponents," an ever-growing group, now seemed to include spouses, to say nothing of girlfriends whom Riley called "excess baggage." All were prohibited from traveling with their husbands at playoff time.

However, not all of them complied with Riley's policy.

Wanda Cooper used to fly in and stay in another hotel. Michael would sneak out, spend the night with her, and sneak back into the team's hotel early the next morning.

Wanda said Riley kept her marriage exciting. She and Michael were like teenagers sneaking off so they could be together.

■

After Riley's 1987 guarantee, Johnson says, the Lakers were psyched to the gills. Magic remembers an early-season stretch of five days off where Riley had to shorten practice so the players wouldn't kill each other.

But the fervor wasn't universal.

Said Abdul-Jabbar of Riley's guarantee in an unguarded moment in camp: "That's easy for him to say. He doesn't have to play."

The Lakers got off to an 8–0 start but, in a sign of things to come, lost six of the next nine. The last one came at Milwaukee where Abdul-Jabbar's nine-season string of consecutive games in double figures was snapped.

Kareem was 40 and finally showing his age. He'd always paced himself but the end of this most insignificant of his records seemed to snap his resolve. Some nights now his pulse rate seemed to drop into single figures, to match his production.

In the last 65 games of the season, he scored in single figures twelve more times. His scoring average, 23 two years before, dropped to 15.

The Lakers compensated for Kareem's shortcomings. Scott averaged 22 points a game. The Lakers regrouped and finished 62–20.

Then came the playoff march from hell.

They swept the Spurs but the second-round series against the Utah Jazz turned into a fight to the death.

The young Jazz had a huge front line: 7–4, 290-pound Mark Eaton, 6–9, 260-pound Karl Malone with 6–11 Thurl Bailey coming off the bench.

The Lakers were vulnerable to size, especially when they couldn't open the game up, and the Jazz were good at keeping the pace slow. The Lakers had never played well before the rabid Jazz fans in the Salt Palace, a haunted house for them. It was the arena where Johnson had asked to be traded the season before. Riley had staged a memorable tantrum there, sweeping Cokes off a tray, which he proudly described in detail in *Show Time*.

Nevertheless, nobody expected the Jazz to give the Lakers a serious challenge. Jazz Coach Frank Layden, a wise-cracking

300-pound New York Irishman, punctuated his team's Game 1 loss with a standup comedy routine at the post-game press conference.

"I don't think we can beat the Lakers," Layden said. "If we can, I ought to be beatified."

Try crucified. Fans in Salt Lake City complained about his give-up attitude, Jazz owner Larry Miller among them. Layden was obliged to apologize.

By way of retribution, the Jazz jerked the Lakers to earth in Game 2. The immovable Eaton, barely bothering to jump or barely able to, blocked seven shots by halftime. Riley started complaining about Utah's "blatant" zone defense.

Eaton, a one-time auto mechanic who'd been unable to make UCLA's traveling team, was becoming a Laker obsession. In Game 3 at the Salt Palace, he blocked six more shots and the Jazz won again. Abdul-Jabbar, who looked like a small forward next to him, went 3 for 14, making him 6 for 30 in the last two games.

The next day, Riley held a team meeting which Mychal Thompson characterized as "loud."

Then Riley held a press conference in the eighteenth-floor lounge of the team's hotel. Outlined against the blue-gray Wasatch Mountains, the man who once promised he'd never publicly embarrass a player skewered his three biggest: Abdul-Jabbar, Johnson, and Worthy.

"I've always said I've come with these guys and I'll go down with 'em," Riley said. "But I can't let other guys on the team down by going with people who aren't going to make an effort."

The next day, the deeply chastened Lakers started taking the ball inside on Eaton who got into foul trouble.

With the Jazz leading, 67–61, in the third quarter, Eaton drew his fourth and had to sit down. The Lakers promptly went on a 23–9 run and won, 113–100.

"The obituaries written for our top three guys," said Riley, "were a little premature."

Of course, Riley had written those obits, leaving the press to publish them. Nevertheless, the Laker players glared at writers and grumped through post-game interviews.

The next day the *Los Angeles Daily News*'s Doug Cress told Riley he was using the press as bogeymen.

"He said, 'You have your weapons and I have mine. And you are mine, sometimes,'" Cress says.

Back in the Forum, the Lakers eked out a win in Game 5, 111–109, but the Jazz came back to win Game 6 by 28 points, 108–80, at the Salt Palace. A fan broke out a banner that read: "The Opera Ain't Over Til the Fat Layden Sings."

Riley, furious at his players, said he was only unhappy they hadn't lost by more than the 28.

"I wish it was 50," he said. "I didn't want them to feel good about anything. I wanted it total."

The repeat that Riley had planned on hung in the balance. There was nothing more he could do but play out the hand.

Before Game 7, Layden, merry prankster to the end, handed Riley a huge comb with scenes of the Brigham Copper Mine, the Mormon Temple, Dinosaurland, and the Flaming Gorge on it.

Johnson then ended Utah's lark, scoring 23 points with 16 assists and nine rebounds as the Lakers won, 109–98. Two fans held up a banner that read: "OK Fatso, Start Singing."

"I don't think we're going to play a better basketball team in the playoffs," said a relieved Riley. "Somebody is going to have to come hard to beat that."

Somebody almost did.

Against Dallas in the Western finals, the Lakers struggled anew. They won the first two in the Forum but, just as they were starting to feel good about themselves again, lost twice at Dallas. The Mavs outrebounded them by margins of 8–8–19–3.

The Lakers won Game 5 in the Forum.

The Mavs beat them again in Game 6 in Dallas. Mark Aguirre, the Mavs' star forward, tried to visit his buddy, Johnson, in the Laker dressing room as he had after Game 4. Riley, tiring rapidly of good will, had the Laker publicist, Rosenfeld, bar him from entering.

"He came to the door and asked how Magic was doing," said Rosenfeld, "and I told him he was O.K. Then he left."

By now, Riley knew he didn't have a problem of malaise on his hands but of basketball.

"Look, we're not the same team we were a year ago," he said before Game 7. "That's obvious. We always had an edge then, a reason to win. Everything was perfect. The competition has gotten better and now, suddenly, we can't turn it on and off like we used to.

"If we get through this thing, they should send us all away. We'll go nodding into the sunset, drooling, looking for the men in the white jackets.

"I said this would be the most dramatic or traumatic year of our lives. It's been both already."

Riley, arriving at the Forum 3½ hours before Game 7, found Johnson already there with that look on his face. As he had against the Jazz, Magic bailed the Lakers out, scoring 24 points with nine rebounds and 11 assists in a 117–102 victory.

Then they went another seven games with the Pistons.

Just to let the Lakers know what they were in for, the battle-tested Bad Boys slapped them aside in Game 1 in the Forum, running up a 17-point lead by halftime.

The Lakers broke back, winning Game 2 in the Forum and Game 3 in the Pontiac Silverdome.

The Pistons won the next two in the Silverdome by 25 and 10 points respectively. In Game 5, Johnson and Isiah Thomas, best friends who exchanged kisses on the cheek before each game, exchanged heated words and shoves. The Lakers went back to the Forum down 3–2.

Game 6 pitted Thomas against the world. The Piston guard put on one of the great shows in NBA history, scoring 25 points in the third quarter despite spraining his right ankle badly, capping the burst by hopping into the corner on one leg and hitting a fadeaway 17-footer.

He went 44 minutes, scored 43 points, and the Pistons led, 101–98 lead in the last minute. But Scott hit a clutch 15-footer and on the final Laker possession, Bill Laimbeer was called for a ticky-tack foul against Abdul-Jabbar in the low post.

Abdul-Jabbar had struggled in this series, too. He was 3 for 14 from the floor in this game but walked to the line, made both free throws and the Lakers escaped, 103–102.

There was only one day before Game 7 and Thomas's ankle was too sore to walk on. Raider owner Al Davis, who frequently sat courtside, offered the use of the team's facility to help him treat it.

Before Game 7, Raider promotions director Mike Ornstein walked up to Chris Riley in the Forum.

"I said, 'Chris, good luck,' " Ornstein says.

"She said, 'Fuck you.' "

"I said, 'Excuse me?' "

"She said, 'You undermined my husband's chances. You helped that Isiah Thomas. You shouldn't have done that. Stay away from me.' "

Actually, the Raider trainers hadn't performed any miracles. Thomas's ankle was still sore. He limped 28 minutes on it and missed eight of his 12 shots. The Lakers led by 10 going into the fourth quarter, held off a late rally and, at long last, fell across the finish line, the NBA's first back-to-back champions in 19 seasons.

Afterward, Abdul-Jabbar playfully stuffed a towel in Riley's mouth, lest he guarantee anything else.

Never one to retire a good gag prematurely, Riley reprised it at the victory parade several days later, wearing a gag when he came to the microphone. He later sent pictures of it to friends.

Lasorda has one framed on his desk in Dodger Stadium. On it, Riley wrote:

To Tommy,

My dad would have never let me guarantee anything but he would have been just as proud of you, too.

■

Although few understood at the time, Riley had done something remarkable and it wasn't just to call attention to himself.

Until the '85 title, the Lakers had won on talent. Now as their talent faded, they required more and more organization.

Riley's adjustments had put them on a roll that carried through the '87 playoffs. In '88, he booted them through single-footedly. Otherwise, no back-to-back titles and they'd still be arguing in bars from Boston to Los Angeles who owned the '80s.

The '88 title was the maraschino cherry atop the whipping cream and no one did more to earn it than Riley.

"The 1987–88 team, I call that Pat's world championship," says Bill Bertka, "because his personal intensity when we went 7–7–7— he would not let 'em lose. He would *not* let 'em lose.

"And then to come back and dedicate himself to go for the third one, he was really driving."

"I thought, 'Shoot, you're playing for a legend,'" says Michael Cooper. "You have your Johnny Woodens, Ray Meyers, Red Auerbachs, Bill Sharmans. I think Coach Riley can be considered in a group with those guys."

Riley was a hell of a coach and Laker players had to deal with it. They'd watched him grow from a tyke into a multimedia colossus.

The Lives of
RILEY

A young man's progress through the hairstyles of the twentieth century: At Linton High School (upper left); As a San Diego Rocket, (note near blond look) (lower left); As a Laker with sideburns (upper right); As a Phoenix Sun with rock-star look (lower right).

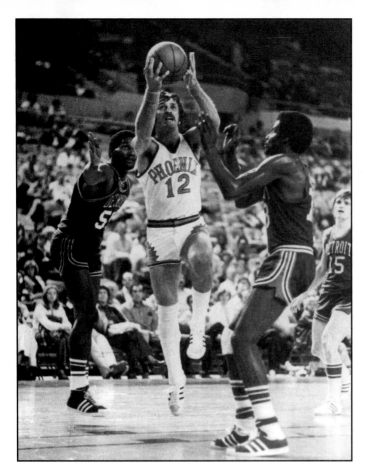

Making his last stand as a Phoenix Sun: teammate Paul Westphal called it his Sonny Bono period. (Photo courtesy of Phoenix Suns)

With Jim Gregory at State Beach in Santa Monica, 1976: Friends call them the Smith Brothers.

The sorcerer's apprentice: Assisting Paul Westhead (NBA Photos)

On his own: Riles takes charge. (Andrew D. Bernstein, NBA Photos)

Brothers in arms: With Magic Johnson in the Hall of the Mountain King, Boston Garden. (Andrew D. Bernstein, NBA Photos)

With Kareem at the Silverdome: Mutual respect survived, barely. (Andrew D. Bernstein, NBA Photos)

With Chris at the White House after beating the Celtics in 1985. (Andrew D. Bernstein, NBA Photos)

The famous gag shot: Making no promises at the 1989 victory parade. Riley liked this photo so much he sent copies to friends. (Nathaniel Butler, NBA Photos)

Will the real Gordon Gekko please stand up?: With Michael Douglas at the Forum. (Andrew D. Bernstein, NBA Photos)

Working for NBC: Looking forlorn in the studio. (Andrew D. Bernstein, NBA Photos)

Back in the biz: At the 1991 press conference announcing his hiring as Knicks coach. (Nathaniel Butler, NBA Photos)

With Bob Costas on location. (Joseph E. Lipinski, NBA Photos)

GAG CITY

The Knicks led by 12 going into the final period last night, but somehow, Pat Riley's crew finds itself one loss from elimination after the Pacers rally for a 93-86 victory in Game 5 at the Garden. Pacers' 20-1 run keyed comeback, and Reggie Miller lit it up for 25 fourth-quarter points, 39 overall. Pacers take 3-2 lead in Eastern Conference Final series, and can wrap it up tomorrow night in Indiana. **Coverage starts on Page 68**

LINDA CATAFFO/DAILY NEWS

ISLES' AL ARBOUR STEPS DOWN — P. 77

When you're up, you're up, when you're down, you're down, and when you are in New York you're either one or the other. After being named Coach of the Year in 1993, savaged by the tabloids after the game 5 loss to the Pacers in the 1994 playoffs.

Cooper had always been close to Riley and considered him a friend. But he wasn't the same Riley anymore.

It couldn't be, not after the years of humiliation and this sudden, dizzying ride. The Greeks had a word for it—*hubris*—and, indeed, it was as if the gods, themselves, had set out to seduce Riley.

How could he fail to swell with pride at the things he'd done, the distance he'd covered in so few years?

What was he to think when some CEO welcomed him as a peer and shelled out $20,000 for an appearance? That was a lot of money for a pep talk but then, what was a captain of industry but a starstruck little boy who'd grown up and assumed control of a corporate budget?

Did it occur to Riley maybe it wasn't the Laker players any more, it was him? Well, it *was* him.

He'd squeezed two more titles out of a team that was supposed to be washed up: the first by redesigning everything they did; the second almost by an act of sheer will.

The problem was, his players still thought it was them.

"That came in '87 when we won the championship against the Celtics," says Cooper. "I think at that point in time, he felt that he, rather than we, were the reason that we were winning, if you understand what I'm saying.

"We were winning because of his philosophy. We were winning because it was his techniques or theory of practice. Everything was because of what he did.

" 'Eighty-seven came, we win the championship and then the biggest statement of his career that I think actually changed him. Right after we win, he says 'We *will* repeat.' We're going, 'Shit, this guy crazy? Think we can?'

"At that particular time, we believed almost everything Coach Riley said because we were successful. If he said, 'Hey, play defense this way,' I kind of went along with that because we'd been successful playing defense like that.

"So in '87, it was, 'Hey, this guy thinks we can, we can.' "

"We won in '88 and I think that's where he says, 'Shit! I am the shit!' He believed it. And I think that's when the so-called parting of the Red Sea happened.

"Because when a coach gets to that point and he brings a team up to that point, obviously you're going to have a collision."

CHAPTER NINE

The First Lady of Showtime

Chris was nothing but generous and loving to myself and my family....She was like the First Lady. She took the role very seriously as the coach's wife. She was not in the background. She was very much in the foreground.

And regardless of what anybody says good or bad about her, her intentions were always good....I don't care what anybody says, that's what she tried to do. I don't know how they came out but I know that she wanted nothing more than for the Lakers to be successful.

—LAKER TRAINER GARY VITTI

Like Hillary Rodham Clinton, Chris Rodstrom Riley would become the active partner of a successful husband and would be admired, misunderstood, and, by some, resented.

When Chris's psychological training showed up in Pat's vocabulary, people whispered he was her puppet.

When she manifested an ambition to match his, people said she was pushy.

When she asked the front office for little touches that resembled his own array of compulsions, Laker officials considered it meddling.

Chris was in deep but Pat liked it that way. "The career of Lakers coach," he wrote in *Show Time*, "is a shared experience."

They were engaged in something more ambitious, they were trying to run a team like a family. If they could truly get everyone in it together, they'd be unbeatable.

■|

She looked like she had it all.

She was pretty, intelligent, and nice. The daughter of a Navy submariner and a Navy nurse, she grew up in San Diego where she was a high school cheerleader. She was a San Diego State coed majoring in psych when she met Riley on a beach. "This great-looking guy, definitely a hunk, asked me out," was the way she remembered it years later.

Riley, for his part, remembered Chris's "ankles, her tan, and her avocado-green polka-dot bikini."

So they went out.

"I got dressed up for a romantic dinner for two," Chris said. "...He picks me up in this yellow Corvette and announces we're going to the fights.

"We sat in the front row, blood all over the place. Obviously, he was not out to impress me. He was just out for a good time. Driving home he sang 'Cowboys to Girls' at the top of his lungs as if I wasn't there."

Nevertheless, she kept seeing him and discovered that under that jocko exterior was a nice guy. They were married in June 1970, and she embarked on a career as a player's wife.

That was all she was, too. Though he'd share his coaching career, he kept his playing career for himself.

He led the life. She waited at home, restlessly.

"I was bored silly," she said later. "My first years of marriage were the unhappiest of my life. Being Mrs. Pat Riley wasn't enough. We looked at our marriage and I said, 'O.K., I'm not going to be the cookie queen anymore.'"

Friends say she was devoted but torn between pleasing him and a having a career of her own, which he opposed. She wanted children badly but she and Pat never conceived.

In 1972, she returned to school and finished work on her bachelor's degree. Three years later, she got her master's at Cal State Northridge in marriage and family counseling.

"He made it about as hard for me as he could," Chris said. "He'd tell me, 'I know you want equality but I want you home. I love seeing you bring in the groceries.'

"It was the basis of a new relationship. He was a real man to deal with."

Two years later, she got her licence to practice, and he was out of work.

Friends thought their marriage had problems but when Pat went into his period of mourning for his lost career, Chris became his therapist and best friend as well as his wife. She went down to the beach with him, too, and some of his beach friends became her friends.

"She was a very good friend," says Idell Cohen, still living in Pacific Palisades with Altie, now running her own casting company. "Very caring, very loving, very supportive. We had an excellent relationship. She gave me a baby shower.

"She was absolutely beautiful, beauty beyond belief. Pat was not a sex symbol when we were friends. He was a nice-looking guy. She was the beauty, no question.

"He was tall, he was lean, he was handsome. But he had his nose done in Century City. Deviated septum—O.K., everybody tells you they have a deviated septum. They have it done because they can't breathe, that was part of it but it definitely changed his face. No question. I mean, he told me. I remember it....

"She was very beautiful—very, very beautiful. I mean, she was a truly beautiful girl and sweet besides. I think people don't know that. They think, 'She's pretty, she's probably wicked or bitchy.'

"But I think she had a power trip, no question about it in my mind. I think everybody likes celebrities and wants to be around them but I think it meant more to her than most people. Even though she had basic values of liking good people, warm people, sincere people, I think her big thing was to keep going up.

"This girl was going to make it. Her husband was sitting on the bench for a long time and it was important for her for him to get ahead. And she was going to push him. I mean, you hear about that wife thing. I really saw it in her. He was more laid-back. I didn't see him as a leader of men. I saw him as easygoing, laid-back, put himself on an equal par with everybody, didn't take a power trip. She did. I imagine that quality really took off when they became big time.

"I think she had so much influence over him. I think it was very important for him to make her happy but she wanted to please Pat. She was really into pleasing him. I mean, they were a twosome. Nobody got into that twosome. It seemed like they were as close as you can get."

■

Their sense of privacy was well developed. They were gracious hosts but they expected friends to call first.

"You didn't drop in on Riley," says Altie Cohen. "I remember, we dropped in one time and it [their behavior] was almost shocking. They didn't want to be disturbed. But if they knew you were coming, they were delightful and warm and hospitable. But it wasn't an open house there. You didn't drop in. They were private."

Chris once called their home, "a refuge, a place for replenishing. It's not a social place."

Until the mid-'80s, they lived in Brentwood, south of Sunset. Their house was set in foliage so dense it looked like a rain forest, thanks to the original owner, a landscape architect. The pool had a waterfall and a deck made of hand-fitted rock. Next to the deck, in place of the cabana Pat had leveled, was a separate office filled with video equipment.

If the end of his playing career drew them closer, the beginning of his coaching career accelerated the process.

At first, she didn't like the idea of coaching. But when he dove in, she did all she could to help him. His success became as important to her as it was to him. If that meant she was ambitious, O.K.

Ambition is a gender-differentiated trait, considered admirable in a man but unseemly in a woman, especially in a male-dominated world like professional sports.

People sometimes whispered Riley was a nice guy fronting for his wife's drive, but that did both Rileys a disservice. If Pat was mellow away from basketball, he was a killer at it; he had beaten up opponents from the playgrounds of Schenectady to the post-retirement pick-up games with the writers. He mugged the *Times*'s Scott Ostler so badly one day, Ostler wondered if there was something personal in it.

As a player, Riley's ambition had been circumscribed by his talent. As coach of a dominating team, there was nothing he couldn't aspire to. Chris's ambition only dovetailed with the gnawing hunger inside him.

It turned out there was a lot Chris could do to help. If she wanted to please Pat and do something satisfying, too, it all came together in his career.

To Pat, coaching was something you did 24 hours a day. There was always something he wanted to think about or talk about. A lot of it involved interpersonal dynamics, which Chris had studied. She became his sounding board and adviser.

They began giving team picnics. They were well received. Soon there was a Laker party circuit. Players' wives and steady girlfriends were institutionalized in a charity group called Forum Community Service, Inc.

More and more of Chris's time went into the Lakers. She lived and died over the team along with Pat, who shared all of his thoughts. During the 1984 Celtics series, she asked writers on the team flight back to Los Angeles if Pat should go public with his complaints about referee Darrell Garretson.

Pat did and was fined $10,000.

In 1985 the Rileys adopted their first child, James Patrick, and Chris gave up the counseling practice she'd worked so hard for. From then on, she was a full-time Laker wife and mother.

"Maybe it's old-fashioned," said Chris, "but I think in looking at most successful careers, one person has to nurture the relationship in order for it to work. There has to be a primary nurturer of a relationship and that's my role."

"Chris is very energetic," says Magic Johnson. "And she was very involved, especially with the wives and girlfriends.

"She was just a person who cared more than the average coach's wife. She always asked how your family was. She'd invite you over if you didn't have anywhere to go for Christmas. Riley took the game personally so she had a lot to deal with. He took his job home."

For years, it worked smoothly.

Inevitably, there were hurt feelings here and there. The Laker wives thought Chris considered herself first among equals because she was the coach's wife. Their wives' group had elected officers and they wanted those leaders to call the shots.

There were hints they thought Chris's den mother role a bit much. A story made the rounds of an argument with Cookie Kelly, Magic Johnson's fiancée.

"They were sitting in the Forum Club [before a game]," Johnson says. "She [Chris] said, 'Maybe you guys ought to leave a little earlier to go up to your seats.'

"Cookie wasn't offended. She just said maybe she should have said it in a different way. She was a little upset she said it in front of people. If you want to say it, pull her aside."

If those had been the only complaints, it would have come to nothing. The Lakers had something special and Chris was a big part of it.

But every year Pat turned the pressure up internally and externally and Chris followed along.

Chris began making suggestions to people in the publicity department about game notes or Pat's bio information. She was nice, she wasn't overbearing, she'd just mention that Pat thought such and such was a good idea.

In one cause célèbre, Chris approached Richard Krasnick, the young promotions director in charge of the music for time outs, and gave him a list the Rileys thought would be livelier—'60s Motown stuff.

She came back twice. Krasnick took no action. Finally Chris went to see Claire Rothman, the general manager of the Forum, who all but threw her out of her office.

A meeting was convened between Rothman, Jerry West, and two members of the P.R. department to discuss the Chris problem. The publicists were told, in blunt and obscene language, they did not have to accede to any of Chris's requests.

When the story leaked into print, Chris pulled back as if scalded and stopped doing interviews.

The Rileys adopted a second child, Elisabeth Marie, in 1988. They moved from their old house in Brentwood to a larger home with huge grounds in the ritzy neighborhood north of Sunset, then to Greenwich, Connecticut when Pat took the Knick job.

Chris remains involved. At Madison Square Garden, she sits at half-court across from the players' benches, next to the runway, a few rows up. She gets halftime statistics.

But publicly, she doesn't exist. Ken Auletta, profiling Pat for *Vanity Fair*, called the Greenwich house once and found himself talking to Chris who told him how much she'd heard about him.

Auletta suggested he'd like to talk to her, too.

Chris demurred, politely.

∎

Pat was a hit.

The world opened itself up to him and said, Take me. Once he'd been happy just to be working but now he wanted his side deals, too.

The summer after the Lakers beat the Celtics, his speaking fee went up to $15,000. (It was $20,000 by the time he left the Lakers.) He did, by his estimate, fifty appearances that year, two a week during the summer. His commercial agent, Mark Reede, said he had to get a list of men like Dick Enberg and Rick Pitino to handle Pat's overflow.

Not that Riley let much flow over.

"First of all, I don't think anybody could take four months off," he said. "It's unnatural. That's a forced vacation. I want to be busy.

"For many years, I said no to all this. But I think we all come to a time in our lives when we feel it's O.K. to step out. I've worked hard for this so why not take advantage of the opportunities?"

That summer he stepped out all the way to Europe where his shoe company, Reebok, was holding clinics in conjunction with its sponsorship of the Amnesty International rock tour, headlined by Bruce Springsteen and Sting.

Riley, who would have liked to bar all celebs from the Laker room, told everyone he'd made it a point not to hang around backstage. But he did meet Springsteen; he was thrilled when Bruce spoke first.

"I never went backstage," Riley said. "I refused to go into their locker rooms because that's their territory. I didn't want to impose on them.

"The only time I talked to Bruce was when I ran into him on an elevator. I was there with Chris and Bruce got on with five members of his entourage.

"He looked at me, smiled and said, 'Hi Pat....'

"So I said, 'They're right. You're as good as they say.'

"Until I saw what he brought to the show each night, I didn't think much of him. Mitch [Kupchak] was always telling me how good he was. I didn't go for rock music but he really inspired me."

Similarly, Riley discovered Amnesty International.

"I used to be like the great percentage of Americans," he said. "I read about what the Amins and Pinochets and other dictators were doing but it really didn't mean much to me. But as I became enlightened, it became obvious to me that I wasn't doing all that I could do to spread awareness."

He resolved to convince the Lakers and the NBA to dedicate one game a season to Amnesty. But they had lighter marketing motifs, nothing came of it, and Riley stopped talking about it. A few months later, a writer asked him about it. Forget it, said Riley.

He did a motivational video, a motivational book, and posed for a GQ cover. CBS was interested in him. He was a natural for TV and had experience to boot. He and Chris flew back to Schenectady and started a drug awareness program.

Riley's contract had a year left but Buss had promised it would be renegotiated. Riley wanted something like the $700,000 Larry Brown was making in San Antonio, the highest coaching salary in the business, and discreetly pushed for it.

Buss pushed back.

"I told him, I wanted to talk about my future with the team," Riley said. "And he said, 'Thank you very much but I don't want to get into that now.'

To which Riley said he'd replied, "I may not be going to Hawaii [the new Laker training site] after all."

Word leaked out that Buss was upset. At a summer league game, West told a writer that Riley's young assistant, Randy Pfund, might coach the Lakers next season.

"They appear to have amnesia," Riley told the *Santa Monica Outlook*'s Mitch Chortkoff. "They told me my contract would be extended in the summer before the final year. Now they're saying they only agreed to look into the situation.

"I've also been told not to bring an agent because Jerry Buss won't deal with one. So I've met with him myself."

With things out in the open, Buss quickly moved to smooth Riley's feelings. Riley didn't get Larry Brown's $700,000 but he got close enough.

"It's not what the other guy is getting," Riley said, "but I'm more than satisfied. I don't know if I should say this but Jerry is in a very giving mood this year, for everybody."

He was a star now and stars are allowed to jerk their bosses around. He had a new sense of himself; there were things he could do besides coaching.

He didn't need to keep putting his ass on the line year after year. The Lakers were getting older. Kareem was going into his last season. He saw that in a few years when Magic left, there'd be nothing left. Riley said he'd leave then too. He was *not* a lifer, one of those geezers who hangs around and takes whatever punishment the game dishes out because he has to.

He even wondered if it was time to leave now.

"A very romantic notion, the idea it was time to move on," he said in Honolulu that fall. "Intellectually in my head, I was thinking, 'You don't need this any more. You don't need it.'

"But I do. I didn't listen to what my head was saying but what my heart was saying.

"You know what happens to anybody who follows their heart all the time? They end up with heart disease. But I followed my heart. I always will."

■|

His players regarded this new phenomenon of a larger-than-life Riles with discreet horror.

Some of them could remember when Riley had been delivered to their doorstep like a foundling. Now his face was on billboards all over town and on best-seller lists. Only Magic Johnson had more endorsement income. A coach who was hotter commercially than his players was unprecedented in the NBA.

Morally, they had no complaint. They lived by a single rule— everyone's entitled to everything he can grab—but the NBA didn't run on morals. It ran on players.

For the record, they said it was O.K.

"There's nothing wrong with what he's doing," said Mychal Thompson. "As long as we remain together in this, it's all right.

"But I figured he'd be big. I'd have thought he'd be speaking to Morton Downey by now."

Actually, the guys didn't like it. Even Johnson, the Riley arch-loyalist, thought there was a double standard working.

"What happened was, he thought about himself before the team," Johnson says. "That's what happened.

"People could come in now and film the practice. People could shoot a commercial for him and set up stuff but they couldn't set up for other guys. *That's* what the difference was.

"Guys didn't like that. And that's what turned some of the guys against him."

Riley's stardom was a curious one. The old rap, that he was the luckiest man in the game, would never go away. No matter what he achieved as a Laker, his players got the credit.

Even in Riley's GQ cover story that fall, his biggest star turn to date, skepticism bubbled up, and from Laker sources.

Wrote GQ's Diane Shah:

...Privately, the Lakers, like all egocentric athletes do, tend to downplay a coach's contributions to their success.

The winning attitude comes from them, they insist. The motivational stuff is a joke. "Those letters he sends out in August," note two people in the Laker hierarchy, "are tossed right into the garbage."

"In no way does the Lakers' success reflect on Riley," says someone close to the team. "Moe from the Three Stooges could coach this team. Xs-and-Os-wise, I mean, if all else fails, throw it into Kareem, right?

"No, Riley's greatest asset is that he doesn't coach. He lets the greatness of the team shine through."

∎

There was more greatness in there that he meant to let shine through, too.

If back-to-back championships were good, a third would be better. The quest for the "three-peat" was born.

Riley, the born-again capitalist, even trademarked the word (although he didn't coin it; Byron Scott did at the 1988 victory parade) so anyone using it on a T-shirt or a cap would have to pay him royalties.

Not that he wanted it known. When the *Los Angeles Times*'s Scott Ostler wrote about it, Riley told him sternly he shouldn't have.

If anyone suspected Riley was interested in winning for the sake of the money, they didn't know Riley. For him, anything he hadn't won was like Everest. It was there.

"That's what he used to say in practice," says Michael Cooper. " 'Hey, we did this twice. Why can't we do it again?'

"That's where the push came from. He started really pushing us. Practices started going just a little longer. We started running more.

"Coach Riley started wanting to isolate us, get us away from the media, which he called peripheral opponents. Get us away from the vultures. What we were supposed to do was work, work, work because we've got to perfect our game. And again, to me, that's not bad. I don't see anything wrong with it because it's all I've known."

Obsession abhors a vacuum and control is a never-ending crusade. Now, when the regular season was over, Riley would take them to Santa Barbara for a pre-playoff boot camp of two-a-day workouts, unheard of in the rest of the league. Riley had his players where he wanted them, away from their wives, families, agents, friends, distractions, and temptations. They were going to focus if he had to sever them from society altogether.

They rode along with it but the grumbling got louder.

"I saw it building up for years," Vitti says. "When people demand top performance from you in all walks of life, it's hard to live with those people. The tendency is for people to slack. He wouldn't let people slack.

"Sure, I'd hear things in the locker room, I'd see things. You know, it's up to the discretion of the trainer what to say, what not to say. Sometimes I may tell him something. I may not tell him something. I may tell him something and not attach anyone's name to it.

"He'd say, 'Who?'

"I'd say, 'I'm not *telling* you that. I'm just telling you this is what I'm hearing....'

"I would say Pat worked the same. It was just that his intensity grew. I mean, his intensity grew even more and more and more so that he became less tolerant of mistakes or letdowns or human error as time wore on. Almost to the point where it was intolerable.

"I think the pressure Pat put on himself manifested itself in that way. You know, it's hard for people to like someone who forces them to be the best they can be every, every, every second."

∎|

Riley pushed everyone to their limits. That was his secret. He pushed the 41-year-old Abdul-Jabbar, too, even if it took a toll on their friendship.

This was Kareem's last season, which would be celebrated in every city in the league with a going-away ceremony, a testimonial of the respect that had accrued to this thorny public figure over his long career.

His relationship with Riley had dwindled to formal professionalism. Abdul-Jabbar liked the old Riley, they went back to high school together, but this high-powered carrot-and-stick version was something else.

The two men respected each other and there was never a confrontation, but Abdul-Jabbar told confidantes he "hated" Riley.

There was a tug-of-war in their dealings now.

Kareem's last two-year contract, signed before the 1987–88 season, stipulated he only had to practice once during two-a-day drills in training camp.

When camp opened the next fall at Palm Springs, he worked out in the morning and was nowhere to be seen in the afternoon.

Riley had Josh Rosenfeld call Kareem back at the hotel to tell him he still had to be there.

Abdul-Jabbar bit off several curse words and came over.

The same thing happened the next day....and the next....and every day for the two weeks they were there. Abdul-Jabbar wouldn't come over until Rosenfeld placed the call.

On the last day, Kareem picked up the phone and before Rosenfeld could say anything, said, "O.K., Josh, I'm leaving."

The next season, the Lakers' first in Honolulu, Riley announced a new practice schedule. They'd work out in the morning, break for a film session, then work out again. In effect, they'd be on the court two times but there was only one supersession. Everyone thought Riley had done it to keep Abdul-Jabbar there.

Their lack of communication became legend. Once, on the road, Abdul-Jabbar had a toothache and wanted to return home. Riley didn't want him to. Telephone calls flew back and forth, to Abdul-Jabbar's agent, Leonard Armato, to West, and back down the chain of command.

Riley and Abdul-Jabbar, who were in the same hotel, never talked to each other directly about it.

There was nothing personal in it for Riley. He had a deep appreciation for what Kareem had done for the Lakers, not to mention for him. If he didn't intend to compromise his team's readiness, Riley wanted to make sure Kareem got every bouquet the world cared to present and went out of his way to accommodate him.

The nightly pre-game ceremonies were a real distraction. Riley held still for it but he could only bend so far.

Abdul-Jabbar gave press conferences in every city and was often accompanied by his personal publicist, Loren Pullman, and his ghostwriter, Mignon McCarthy. Once, when Pullman was stranded at the team's hotel in the wilds of rural Ohio, Riley refused to let her ride the bus to the airport, even after Vitti pled her case, pointing out how helpful she had been.

The Laker farewell ceremony came last. Abdul-Jabbar's teammates and coaches presented him with a $150,000 Rolls Royce.

It was Riley's idea and he assessed each player his fair share. Riley's came to $30,000, the same as Johnson's.

∎

The train kept rolling.

The team that had limped through the 1988 playoffs snapped back.

Abdul-Jabbar was down to 23 minutes and 10 points a game but Johnson, taking the challenge personally, had his best assist season, his second-best rebound season, led the league in free throw percentage, and won his second MVP.

The Lakers won 57 games, second best to the Pistons who won 63.

The Pistons roared through the East in the post-season, beating the Celtics, 3–0, the Bucks, 4–0 and the Bulls, 4–2. The Lakers shut the West out, sweeping the Blazers, Sonics, and Suns with a combined record of 10–0.

The NBA finals promised to be a heavyweight battle. But on the eve of the opener, Scott tore his left hamstring in practice, sidelining him for the duration.

In the second half of Game 2, Johnson pulled a hamstring, too. He limped off the floor with tears running down his cheeks. Johnson tried to come back in Game 3 but it was no good. He lasted five minutes before having to ask out.

The quest for the "three-peat" ended that suddenly. The Pistons mopped the Lakers up in four games.

The Lakers were disciplined by now. They didn't wail where people could hear them but some of them blamed Riley's tough regimen.

"It was silly, to be honest with you," Scott said—a year after Riley resigned. "It was something we shouldn't have been doing. It was crazy.

"Rebound drill the day before the game. By the time you get to the finals, if you don't know how to box out and rebound, you're going to lose anyway. It was a physical-type practice. I could deal with the running and other stuff but that part of practice, we shouldn't have been doing.

"A lot of guys felt that way when we started. To end up having that happen confirmed everybody's feelings."

"Guys will say that," Johnson says. "But when you look at who we had to play—Detroit's strength was offensive rebounding and we weren't a very good rebounding team.

"You never know why that happened. Maybe it was fatigue. You don't know if it's that or not. I know some of the guys—I won't say a lot of them—some of them want to blame Riley for that.

"But Riley was a guy who was always going to practice whatever the strength of the opponent was. So it was no different. I don't know how the guys can be upset but that's their opinion."

There were questions now about the rest of the program and the Santa Barbara boot camp. Had the workouts worn down the two hamstrings?

"Nobody complained until it actually happened," Cooper says. "But you know when we did feel it—and I admit this, I went along with everybody else—mentally it was fatiguing to think so much basketball. We were given game reports, scouting reports. It was a lot of stuff. It was just pound, pound, pound.

"Practice had stopped being like what it used to be like. We kinda could come in and joke around a little bit.

"Now you come in and Coach Riley's standing there and you could see him thinking about the game. I don't want to say it lost its fun but it just wasn't the same kind of light air that you need, especially in an 82-game season.

"We used to bullshit still but when you see your coach really thinking, that gets you thinking and practice becomes a mind set. You get there and you gotta work, you gotta work.

"After a while, it's like, 'I'm dizzy from so much basketball.' And then I've gotta go home and study those reports and you'd come back the next day and it was almost like school. You had an exam.

"He put little messages at the end of the video or somewhere in the video to make sure people watched. There was a key word you had to know.

"He'd come in the next day and say, 'O.K., what's the key word?'

"And we'd look at each other. He wouldn't call anybody out but he knew who knew.

"And most of the time, Kareem didn't know. So after a while, Kareem started asking, 'Hey man, what's the key word?' "

School was out for Kareem. Riley and Magic were on their own.

Norman Bates

It's like a marriage. You're not going to fight with your lover because you're having sex and you're having a good time. But as the marriage goes on and goes on and you get used to each other, you get set in your ways and this and that.

—MICHAEL COOPER

∎

You can only whip the mule so much before the mule turns around and says I've had it.

—KURT RAMBIS

Of course, Riley had changed.

Only Riley would ever try to argue he hadn't. In the mid-'80s, the L.A. *Herald Examiner*'s Doug Krikorian, who could remember riding on a bus with him in the '70s and Riley joking his salary wouldn't buy Wilt Chamberlain's groceries, told Riley he had changed more than anyone he'd ever seen.

Riley, surprised, replied that he didn't think he had, he was the same guy with the same wife, the same house.

He would change a lot more in the years after that, as the Lakers would, too.

They grew older. He grew into his job like Harry Truman or Genghis Khan.

Not everyone liked the new Riley but all of them, admirers and detractors, agree: It was inevitable. No one could rise from circumstances as humble as his, catch the meteor's tail as he had, and stay the same.

"I think Pat *has* changed," says Jerry West. "I don't think there's any question he's changed."

"But, you know, the changes were based on his success and so, things had to change. I mean, here was a guy who did not come into the league a star. Here's a guy who got ahead because he worked so darn hard. And he coached a great team."

"Riles changed," Magic Johnson says. "With that much success and what was coming to him off the court, yeah, you have to change."

"He changed but so did we. He became a coach. Yeah, it happened. He became a coach and he thought his way was the way."

"Yeah, I think he changed a lot," says Kurt Rambis, "but hell, we all did.

"I was a rookie his rookie year and I know I wasn't the same person when I left as when I came in. He was kind of the guy I talked to, being an assistant coach. I remember talking to him in Palm Springs, just sitting by the pool. He was just kinda like one of the guys. And the more he coached, the more he got away from the players.

"He was so tunnel vision in what he wanted to do. You rarely saw the man laugh."

Never casual, Riley now lived and died the job.

Laker employees grew used to seeing him in the office on the morning after a loss, unshaven, looking gaunt, a shell of the dandy they'd see the night of the game. He made myriad demands of them. There were itineraries to be changed at a moment's notice and he was impatient if they couldn't get it done now. Sometimes they called him Norman Bates in the front office.

His players got a more restrained treatment but they felt the impact, too.

"He wore his losses," said Johnson. "I'm a guy who took mine home. I'd turn off all the lights—where he wore his on his face.

"And you knew what was coming. Some mornings at airports, he didn't speak to anybody. I don't think he could bring himself to say anything. And we knew all hell's gonna break loose at practice."

"I think Pat was tired," says Bill Bertka. "His last three years— when you go through a back-to-back championship and then for a third one, with his style of coaching and what he put into it, the emotional drain on him was incredible."

If they grumbled behind his back, they soldiered on.

It was just part of living with Riley. If few around the league seemed to notice, all the Lakers knew who was driving the organization now. In the front office, some of the grunts used to say the fun went out of it in the mid-'80s but they accepted it as the price of winning.

Of course, without Abdul-Jabbar, it would be harder but Riley always looked for a challenge.

So did Johnson. He was like Riley; whatever they'd done, someone would say they couldn't have done it without Kareem.

Of course, Johnson and Riley were rich, famous, and popular and might have just shrugged it off, but neither was wired that way. Each lived to show *every*one. It was more than a motivational technique in them, it was based on something deeper, a hunger.

"I wanted to [win without Abdul-Jabbar] bad," Johnson says. "And I thought that's something they [his teammates] wanted to do. 'Hey, let's show everybody!' That would have been great for me. I mean, I was excited."

If the Lakers had been hard-driving, they became harder-driving.

With only the undersized, 34-year-old Mychal Thompson at center, they rolled to an amazing 63–19 season, best in the NBA, four games better than the defending champion Pistons.

Johnson won his third MVP in four seasons, a neat accomplishment in a league with Michael Jordan. The old running, gunning Lakers were No. 7 in the league in team defense.

Of course, they were all but consumed in the process.

■|

Two leaders, one crusade.

Whether Riley knew it or not, or cared or not, he had long since ceased being a players' coach. He wasn't into compromises or half-measures or taking it to committee. Other coaches conducted game-long running dialogues with their assistants, but Laker assistants spoke when they were spoken to. It was Riley's show and he ran it with a dogged determination; his watchword was taking a stand, planting his feet, and kicking some butt.

Whether Johnson knew it or not, he and Riley were leaving the rest of the team behind.

"Magic became like Coach Riley, more intense," says Michael Cooper, Johnson's closest friend on the team.

"He [Johnson] was really pushing us in practice, telling us, 'Hey you got to do this better, you got to do that better.'"

In a sense, it was like they became mirrors of each other. They were after the same thing.

"Shootarounds turned from forty minutes to an hour and a half with a lot of video. It was mentally fatiguing more than anything else."

"Coach Riley had changed a little bit. He wasn't as open as he used to be. If you had a suggestion, he didn't take it wrong. He just didn't take it. He heard you. Then it was like, 'O.K., you gave it to me, fine, but we're going to do it this way.' Where in the past, he really would listen to you and kind of compromise with you.

"Just the aura he started putting out that year. You felt, don't invade his space today, not now, not the time.

"So, 'not now, not the time' turned into the whole season. We were kinda hesitant. We were looking at each other out on the court. It was the first time I can remember players making a mistake and glancing over at the bench for a second. We had never done that before."

Cooper's own role was disappearing before his eyes.

He was 34 and his high-jumping Coop-a-Loop days were behind him. If there were several unhappy Lakers, Cooper headed the list.

Riley was anything but callous about it. Only Johnson had been with him longer and only Johnson had been closer to him. But on the floor, this wasn't a family but a team and had to be run as such.

"What you have to understand," says Johnson, "Coop wasn't Coop any more.

"And it was hard for him to come to the reality of that. As much as I love him, I would never say anything bad about him, but sometimes players—it's hard to come to 'I'm not the same guy I used to be.'

"And Riley was trying his best to show him because he was close to Coop. He didn't want to hurt him.

" 'Cause he always used to come to me—'Buck, Coop can't do it any more, he can't shut guys down like he used to, I don't know what to do.' "

■

The pressure was getting to a lot of players. Some were going upstairs to complain to anyone who'd listen, right up to Buss.

At mid-season, West suggested to Johnson he back off, especially with rookie Vlade Divac, a rookie 7-foot Serbian. Divac was a ball-handling wizard but he wasn't as tough as the American big men, despite Johnson's forceful attempts to close the cultural gap.

"We had a mid-season meeting that I was pushing the guys too hard," Johnson says. "I said O.K., I had to back off.

"See, we didn't have that cushion any more. The guys failed to realize we couldn't just walk out there and say, 'O.K., now at the end of the game, we've got the big man still standing down there. We can just throw it into him and we're gonna win.'

"Riley knew it. I knew it. Things were gonna change. We knew we had to be pushed to the limit and we knew everybody was coming on.

"They [his teammates] didn't want to accept it—hey now we're almost on an even keel with these teams. It's not the Lakers and everybody else. Here they come now. Three seven-game series [in 1988] should show you that.

"They took it personally. They thought I was siding with Riley."

Getting Johnson off their back was the easy part.

What would it take to get Riley off? Intervention by West? By Buss? A U.N. peacekeeping force?

Later, Riley told confidantes his problem had stemmed from one disgruntled player, Cooper, going upstairs to complain to West, who had overreacted.

Cooper says he only went with the other two tri-captains, Johnson and James Worthy, at West's invitation.

In any event, there were several unhappy Lakers.

Riley never lost the whole team. He had allies: Johnson, Mychal Thompson, A. C. Green. The bench guys were no factor in any uprising. Backup center Mark McNamara said later if the Lakers thought that was a tumultuous season, they should have seen the other teams he'd played for.

But Riley was losing support from key players: Cooper; Scott who'd never been one of his favorites and vice versa; even the good soldier James Worthy, who was concerned that Riley was grinding his slender body into the dust.

West had never before let players use him to get around Riley. Now, alarmed at the rising chorus, he told Riley he wanted to go downstairs and meet with the team.

Riley didn't like it but had to take the meeting.

"I think the personalities finally clashed," Johnson says. "When things didn't go well that season, guys took their complaints to Jerry. Now for the first time, Jerry West's got to confront Riley."

West insists his only aim in calling a meeting was to mediate.

"I did it for him [Riley]," West says. "The team was so fragmented.

"The thing that concerns you, we pretty much had players that were in there to do what we wanted done. But when I have people come bickering to me, it's not my job to coddle those people. To me, I think a coach should know that.

"I told Pat that. There was a lot of complaining. I thought he should know. I thought that was something that helps you. I think you have to be honest in those situations. It was something to try to right the ship instead of having players bitch and complain."

They had the meeting. Everyone promised to work together.

▌▌

If their future lay ahead of them, they might have been able to ride it out.

There is no shortage of turmoil on pro teams. GMs come downstairs for meetings with grumbling players all the time, no matter what their coaches think. The Lakers were still adept at containing their problems. The story did leak—the *Los Angeles Times* reported it—but it lasted for one day, was hardly remarked upon and quickly forgotten.

But the Lakers weren't kids any more. No matter what they did this season, more changes lay ahead.

Meanwhile, Riley's options grew daily. NBC had just outbid the NBA's long-time network partner, CBS, for television rights so all the old broadcasters like Tommy Heinsohn were going to be gone. NBC was looking to make a splash with someone like Riley or Detroit's head coach Chuck Daly.

Daly was a late-blooming sharpie himself, a natty dresser, with a lot of personality. He and Riley both had TV experience. But as Daly, himself, would always acknowledge, he was a character actor next to Riley's matinee idol.

"I remember back in the middle of that season," then-assistant Randy Pfund says, "there was talk about, 'Will Pat stay? Is he going to retire? Would a change be good for this team?'

"The NBC thing—that stuff was swirling around. It had always swirled around."

It swirled around the Laker dressing room, too. Players talked about it too, some of them hopefully, most of them in terms of disbelief. But they talked about it.

Meanwhile, Riley's passion for "organization" continued to extend tentaclelike in all directions.

Concerned that the crowd sat and watched the Laker Girls' routines instead of cheering, he quietly enlisted a writer to address the "problem" and got them benched during fourth quarters.

When the Lakers began traveling by charter on the luxurious MGM Grand plane with its individual staterooms, he wanted players to sit in seats he designated. No one was going for that one.

"He's just like that," Johnson says. "What happened, he wanted to control everything.

"I think that's another mistake. He tried to control the whole arena. He wanted to control the locker room, the band, the Laker Girls. He just tried to control everything and he got away from what he was there to do."

▌▌

If the Laker team was a walking corpse, they still looked marvelous.

The season ended just as they'd hoped it would. They sewed up home-court advantage throughout the playoffs. NBA writers voted Riley his first Coach of the Year award.

In Portland, for a meaningless game the final weekend, Riley sat out three regulars. The Blazers were incensed. The NBA office slapped the Lakers with a $10,000 fine.

Since Riley had neglected to inform West, Buss, or anyone, the Laker front office didn't think it was such a hot idea, either. West fumed.

"Well, that was wrong," West says. "That *was* wrong.

"He should have let Jerry Buss make the decision on that because Jerry Buss had to pay the fine. That was wrong. I did not like that at all and I didn't think it was fair. I mean, I would have understood, as long as he gave the owner a chance. But that was wrong."

It wasn't the fine, which was small potatoes, a crummy 10K. Riley could go through that in room service in Santa Barbara where he took the team for the usual pre-playoff boot camp.

They polished off the Rockets but it wasn't the usual tidy 4–0 sweep. The Rockets won a game—the first Riley had lost in an opening round.

They moved on to the next round against the Suns, a long-time pigeon.

The Suns had a lot of firepower but a casual attitude toward defense. They'd just gone five games to get past Utah. They'd never won a playoff series against the Lakers.

They'd lost 21 games in a row in the Forum over nine seasons. Their coach, Cotton Fitzsimmons, had lost 37 in a row in the Forum with five different teams, dating back to a 1974 game that Riley had played in.

Thus it was no small surprise when the Suns came from six points down in the fourth quarter of Game 1 and won, 104–102.

Proving the earth was still round, the Lakers rose up to smite them, 124–100, in Game 2. The series moved to Phoenix where CBS had been given back-to-back games Saturday and Sunday, no favor to an old team playing on the road.

In Game 3, the Suns shot 60 percent and won going away, 117–103.

Everywhere Riley looked, he had problems. The Suns' Mark West, a journeyman center, was putting an end to the notion the Lakers could get away with Mychal Thompson. In Thompson's four starts in the series, West would average 15 points and 10 rebounds and shoot 75 percent.

Scott couldn't guard Kevin Johnson. While the Lakers chased KJ, Jeff Hornacek spotted up and killed them from the outside. Tom Chambers was hot, James Worthy was not.

With 18 hours to turn the tide, Riley called a meeting back at the hotel and brought down the thunder once more.

The coaches thought it was appropriate.

"He was pissed," says Bertka. "That was the one he vented his feelings toward the team and justifiably so. That's the meeting the players point to but to me it was a justified meeting."

"As Pat always did, he challenged the guys," says Pfund. "To me, it wasn't much different.

"Players want to talk about, 'Oh, everything blew up.' To me, he approached it like we always did. We challenged 'em when they needed to be challenged and worked 'em hard."

Riley spared Johnson who was putting up big numbers but he held everyone else up to the flame.

The players thought Riley had completely lost it. Before Game 4 the next afternoon, several of them called writers over in the dressing room to describe the outburst in detail.

"Riley always felt he had to hop me first to get to other guys," Johnson says. "He said, 'Buck, I got to get on you for something.'

"But that time he didn't. Here I am, putting up 40-something a night so wasn't too much he could hop me about. He jumped Orlando [Woolridge] pretty good and he wasn't used to getting it. He hit Byron real hard 'cause he wasn't making his shot.

"He singled me out the other way and that kinda killed everything—'*Only one guy playing good in this whole group and that's Buck!*'

"I was saying, 'Oh man....'

"It was over. We were through after that meeting. '*He got on me? I can't believe it!*' No way we could beat them.

"We started off the next game, went to Byron three straight times—missed. Couldn't get him into it. He complained he wasn't getting enough shots so we went to him.

"And he [Riley] just said, 'O.K., Buck, forget it! If they're not going to play, I'm going to run this same play every single time!' "

"And I changed one time and he got mad at me! '*I told you to shoot!*' "

Johnson scored 43 points but the rest of the Lakers combined to shoot 33 percent. Only Worthy and Magic got off more than 10 shots

143

but Worthy missed 16 of his 21. The Lakers fell with a resounding thud, 114–101.

There was a day off before Game 5—off for rest, recuperation…and irony.

That day the league announced Riley's coach-of-the-year selection. The Lakers held a press conference in his honor but it was more like a wake, with Riley playing the part of the departed.

"I am ready now to see if I can coach," he said, managing a grin.

West, introducing him, said how proud he was of Riley's record.

"What?" asked Riley, "533 wins or 1–3?"

The gloom was palpable. Riley smiled, said the right words, expressed his deep appreciation and so on but he was as low as he could go. Even such a stoic as he couldn't hide it.

"Jerry told me last week," Riley said, "so I've been carrying this ever since we got beat that very first game against Phoenix. I was thinking about all the history of the coaches of the year getting fired immediately after that…."

"I know there's always something you hear about, that they're tired of hearing the same old song. As long as you keep staying truthful and dealing with the present moment—I know I get accused of conjuring up all these motivational ploys and all this stuff—you can stay connected."

The truth couldn't save him now. The truth was, his team was split wide open.

The Lakers had a pre-game shootaround the next day. Johnson and Cooper almost came to blows.

"We got back here and guys were just upset," Johnson says. "Upset at me, upset at Riley because he said that. I was caught in it and some things were said. They were upset at me, especially Michael.

"A guy [reporter] had asked me, 'What do you have to do to win?'

"I said, 'More guys have to play better.'

"Michael said that morning at shootaround, 'What the hell are you doing? Going in the paper! Buck, I never thought you'd go in the paper!'

"I said, 'What are you talking about, Michael?'

" 'You went in the paper and said guys got to play well. You're pointing the finger!'

"I said, 'Michael, did I say that Michael Cooper has to play well? Did I say that Byron Scott has to play well? Did I say that Orlando Woolridge has to play well?'

"Michael was coming in and I was coming in. When a guy challenged me, you know, I had to come in and hold my ground. So yeah, it was getting to that point. He pissed me off."

That night the Lakers grabbed a 15-point lead in the first quarter. The Suns blew by them, almost contemptuously, outscoring them, 86–68, from then on, winning, 106–103.

What had been the Lakers was no more.

Riley had been pushing them for nine years. He had started as their buddy, evolved into their daddy, and finally, lost touch with them altogether. Finally, they'd had enough of him and they balked, just as they'd balked under Paul Westhead.

Family? By the end of the Phoenix series, they were barely a team.

"When Pat left," said a Laker player, "he didn't have a friend left in the locker room."

Not even Johnson?

"When Pat left," the player repeated, "he didn't have a friend left in the locker room."

■|

If the old order was passing, getting it to actually turn over was something else.

Riley didn't know what he wanted and asked for a few weeks to decide.

West, exasperated, said they had to start considering a replacement. He already had one picked out—Milwaukee assistant Mike Dunleavy—but Dunleavy had other opportunities.

"They were announcing Coach of the Year," West said, "and he [Riley] said to me before he went out, 'I don't know, I have misgivings.' And then he said he wanted to think about it for a while.

"Deep down in his own mind, I think he wanted to get away from it. The pressure of it is enormous after a long, wearing season. He told me, 'You better start looking for a new coach.' "

Riley and West, undeniably, were no longer the buddies they had been.

"I don't know if it deteriorated," West says. "but I don't think there was the closeness there at the end that I would have liked. But his life had changed a lot. But it wasn't something that was intolerable for me to deal with at all. Not at all."

Buss would make any decision on Riley. West insists he played no part in it and could have taken Riley back with no problem. This would have have made West a distinct minority in his own organization. Despite West's denial, the consensus is he didn't want Riley back any more than anyone else did.

"I don't think [West wanted him back]," says Johnson.

And Buss?

"Up to Jerry West," Johnson says. "I think Dr. Buss wanted him back but it was 'Whatever you think.'"

Buss was the last Riley man in the organization. Johnson, the second-to-last, still liked Riley but could no longer function as liaison between his coach and his eleven teammates.

"What happened was, he made more money, commercials, and things than players," Johnson says. "He became a national figure, bigger than some of the players. And then with the complaints—he just had to go.

"It wasn't any two ways about it. It was one way. He had to go. Not because he wasn't a good coach....He could never come back to that team and coach those guys."

■|

NBC sent word to Riley it was interested.

But Riley was a career Laker. Even if there wasn't enough left of him to pour into a thimble by the end of a season like this one, he still loved to coach.

Announcing? It was just O.K.

"It has nothing to do with NBC, HBO, Paramount Studios, or Disney World," Riley said. "I haven't talked to anybody. I would not make the decision based on other opportunities....

"I'm addicted to coaching."

He had two years left on his contract and his popularity among Laker fans was undiminished. Buss considered him a friend and had no appetite for firing him, but Buss was also aware of the players' grumbling and the combat fatigue in the front office. If Riley said he wanted to come back, the organization would look like a Civil War battleground.

Riley had always maintained he wasn't a lifer; his plan was to go another few seasons and retire when Johnson did, but the swiftness of the collapse caught him by surprise. The suggestion that the players had turned on him was an affront to everything he'd built for nine years.

Sometimes he wanted to accept the inevitable. Sometimes he wanted to come back to prove it wasn't so.

He met with Buss.

"I don't like to say, yes, there was [grumbling] because it would be too easy to take it out of context," Buss says.

"If you're asking me, did they grumble about Pat, yes or no? Yes. If you're asking me, was that more than you've heard other people grumble about their coaches, the answer is no.

"He came to me and said he had some unusual opportunities. He had an opportunity as an announcer. He had opportunities to produce some television shows. He just said, 'I've been doing this for a long time and I think before I just start in next year, I would like to think it over. Is this what I want to do for the next X years?'

"I said, 'Well, Pat, I used to be a college professor, then I was in real estate, and now I'm in sports so I'm a guy who's acquainted with career change. Go ahead and take some time off.' "

Riley went to Buss's home for lunch several times. Riley seemed to be waiting for Buss to ask him to return to the Lakers.

Buss never did.

Later Buss compared it to a conversation he'd had with one of his sons. The son had asked why Buss hadn't kicked his butt through college. Buss had answered that wasn't his way. If he hadn't done it for his own son, he wasn't going to do it for Riley.

What Buss was willing to do was pay off the rest of Riley's contract—and more.

Riley was due about $1.3 million over two seasons, but Buss had also promised him another extension. Buss said he'd keep the promise even if Riley didn't return. Buss offered a package that would pay him $2 million his first year in retirement.

"There are certain people that I feel have converted the Lakers from another basketball franchise to, in my estimation, *the* basketball franchise," Buss says. "And I've tried to say thank you in monetary terms.

"I know Magic's aware of that. I know Kareem's aware of that. I know James Worthy is aware of that. And Pat Riley is aware of it, as well."

What the heck. Riley decided to go.

"I know Jerry called me and said Pat was not going to coach anymore," West says.

[Laughing] "And it wasn't until after that, I found out he had made a…[laughing] wonderful…contract arrangement with him. I thought it was great."

Riley went to Johnson's house to break the news personally.

"It was already a sad day because it had just rained," Johnson says. "It was, like, dark.

"I said, 'Do you want to sit inside?'

"He said, 'No, let's go outside.'

"We went out there and he started talking. We started thinking about the season and what had happened in the playoffs.

"He just said it—'Buck, I think I'm going to retire.'

"He started crying. It was just wild. It was like I was losing my best friend. He started and I think we were both doing it.

"I learned a lot from him. There were some bad things that happened and I saw them. Probably more than anybody else, I could deal with it. I was his guy."

On June 11, 27 days after the Suns had eliminated the Lakers, Riley announced his resignation.

Although he'd later complain that everyone had forsaken the dream that had been the Lakers, the team did it right.

Riley's departure and Dunleavy's arrival were announced at a rare joint press conference. Everyone was gracious to everyone else. Riley was thanked in the most profuse terms. Riley offered Dunleavy his best wishes.

A rosy Hollywood glow hung over the affair like a mist. But the world keeps turning and mists blow away.

■I

The next day, in a rare burst of candor, Byron Scott called it "like a resurrection…like a raising from the dead."

But despite the drain of the last few years and the turmoil of the final days, little was said publicly. Even without Riley, Laker players held to the Riley code of silence.

Of course, the insiders knew the real story and accounts went around the league. The following spring, when Riley became a candidate for the Knick job, there was so much muttering from the West Coast, Knick president Dave Checketts decided he'd better ask Riley if he understood there'd been a problem and he'd been part of it.

Riley began getting questions about it from the press. In public, at least, he conceded nothing.

"I was there twenty years," he said, "twelve years coaching. There's nothing that I would ever have done differently. You know, people change, things change.

"I thought that last year after I left, they had to de-Rileyize the Lakers and they did. I was gone. Once I left, they had to get rid of me. They had to do that. That's the way organizations are. I mean, they had a new man who came in and they had to forget about all those other things. I expected that.

"I mean, there was so many things written that were inaccurate when I left. I made the break and I left on June 11. That's the statement that I made and that's the way it is.

"It was really embellished a lot. I harbor no ill feelings, contrary to what people think. None at all. It was a great run for me."

To *Vanity Fair*'s Ken Auletta, he went even further. "*They* changed," Riley said of his players. "I never changed."

Alliances in professional sports are temporary and based on self-interest, but Riley's attachment to the Lakers had been something else, romantic and unqualified. He wasn't a mercenary but a knight. He longed for his Round Table.

But he could no longer pretend that gracefully. It had finished. To intimates, he'd even talk about it.

"We had dinner the next year, in New York," Johnson says. "He said, 'Yeah, I know the guys couldn't stand me. And even you, Buck.'

[Laughing] "And I could never say that."

■|

It took more than two years before Riley publicly acknowledged the anguish of those final months, to NBC's Bob Costas.

"The thing I regret most about it is how it ended," Riley said. "I looked at that Laker team in the '80s as a team that was significant, that was unique, that did things no one ever did. And one of the things that we had there was the sense of being family and being solid....

"It ended a little bit bitter and it ended a little bit toxicly and to me, I regretted the fact that the team would not embrace protecting the '80s....We had a great run, we had a great time, let's preserve that by showing the respect for this organization, for that run, and for all the players that played there. And I don't think, for the most part, with how it was chronicled at the end, that it was left that way.

"I'm just talking about the team. When it comes down to it, it's really twelve players, three coaches. Really. Those are the people that go through it. I mean, management is very, very important but the ones that are on the floor, that are sweatin', that are going through the whole thing, the ups and downs, are the ones that have to preserve that time. And you preserve it by protecting each other, by taking care of each other.

"And I'm sure, 5 to 10 years from now, when we look back on that time, nobody's gonna remember that last year. But there'll be somebody who'll remember and will say, 'Well, they fragmented.'

"You know? 'They couldn't keep it together.'

"And once it's over with and it was good, you let it go and you move on and you just remember it for the good times.

"But that's what I wanted most out of that thing and I don't feel like it was that way."

∎

It was and it wasn't.

If the Lakers couldn't pretend Riley's days had ended happily, few could deny his importance.

"Pat's intention was to create this wonderland in sports, where we played together and we lived together as if we were a family," says Gary Vitti.

"And I think we were in a lot of ways. Sometimes in a family, a really strict family, the parents—you know what I mean?—they're kind of looked at by the children as kind of hard to live with. You know what I mean?

"But some of those children who come from really strict families wound up doing very well and have a really good work ethic. We were very successful. A lot of that had to do with Pat's *demanding* excellence. He demanded it."

Johnson, still close to Riley, calls him the difference between the Lakers and the Celtics, the reason the '80s were known as the Lakers' decade.

The Celtics won three titles in the '80s, two under easygoing K. C. Jones after they unseated their own hard case, Bill Fitch.

The Lakers won five, the last two with Riley driving them beyond expectations, their own and everyone else's.

When Riley went to New York, Michael Cooper applied for a job on his staff.

As legacies go, Riley could have done worse.

CHAPTER ELEVEN

Talking Head

Pat totally engulfed himself in this thing. Other guys are into music or cars. Pat was like, when he left here, instead of listening to music, he put in a motivational tape to get ready for the next practice.

Everybody was like, "TV? That ain't Pat! Pat will never survive that!"

And everybody thought he'd come back in a year.

And he did.

—Laker trainer Gary Vitti

B ack to the beach.

Of course, it was completely different from that lost summer of 1976. This time there were things to do, new challenges to be met, things to be learned.

He signed with NBC and set about relearning the craft. He began commissioning his own movie projects, doing lunches, taking meetings. He had scripts in development. He did appearances. He had a life.

Unfortunately, he didn't like it.

There wasn't anything wrong with it, exactly. The living was certainly comfortable, with homes in Brentwood and Malibu. The job was still lucrative; NBC was paying him $500,000 a year for little more than two days' work a week from Christmas to Easter. He didn't have to put in a five-day week until the NBA finals in June.

It was just so *easy.*

He threw himself into his new TV career. NBC had intended to use him as a color commentator at games but Riley persuaded the network to let him work from the studio. He'd done studio recently in a special for HBO and it had gone off smoothly.

NBC Sports president Dick Ebersol and executive producer Terry O'Neil said yes. They named the program "Showtime" in his honor. Riley turned the office behind his home into a mock-up of a studio to practice. An NBC exec later laughingly referred to it as "Riley's now-famous garage."

If heaping preparation upon preparation had served him well as a coach, it only turned up the pressure too high on him as a broadcaster. In the first telecast Riley looked as if he was glazed over, as if he'd spent three months asking himself, "What if I open my mouth and no words come out?"

If his first appearance was disappointing—everyone had always considered Riley a natural for TV though few actually had seen him work with Hearn in the '70s—it was only one show. Everyone had to start somewhere and they'd all had the jitters.

Riley understood, too. It was just, he was no longer…in command.

He wasn't sure where he fit into the world any more.

At his first assignment, the McDonald's Basketball Classic in Barcelona, friends kidded him that he might be barred from the Knicks' practice. Coach Stu Jackson said it was all right for Riley to watch but a security guard with an automatic weapon saw Riley's press credential and waved him behind the rope, with the rest of the media guys.

It was a couple of months into the season before Riley could make himself go to his first Laker game.

He didn't get out of the car. Instead, he turned around in the parking lot and drove home.

"You know," he said later, "it was sorta hard. I just felt at that particular time, it was better I didn't go, for myself and maybe for everybody else.

"Any time you're around something so long and you're so passionately involved in it and you're not there and you can't be part of it, it's sorta hard to go back and watch it for a while.

"You miss them, you want to be part of it but you made the decision to move on. That's what happens for a while. Happens to everybody."

Plainly, the Laker players didn't miss him.

If they weren't firing on him publicly, there was enough celebration of the new, relaxed atmosphere under Dunleavy to signal how they felt.

If Riley walked back into the dressing room, they might be polite. Or they might look at their shoes and mumble a greeting.

It was too much to risk. When Riley attended his first game, he waited until the players had gone onto the floor to warm up, then went into the dressing room to see Dunleavy, Bertka, Pfund, and Vitti.

∎∎

He still lived in Brentwood but now he worked in New York and commuted.

The networks were New York–based and influenced by New York sensibilities, not to mention New York critics. The critics weren't down on Riley, or up, or anything.

Mostly, they were bored.

"Understand something," says the *New York Post*'s acerbic Phil Mushnick, "NBC in the Ebersol–O'Neil days has worked almost exclusively off the star system which is a formula for failure.

"They didn't care if Pat Riley had any ability to be an insightful broadcaster. And almost by design, no coach right off the coaching box is going to come in and do that kind of job because he still regards himself as a member of that fraternity....

"Unless he had it in his head that he wanted to excel as a TV broadcaster—and by that I mean work to serve the audience first and foremost, damn the torpedoes, damn everybody he worked with and might one day work with again in basketball—if he had it in his head he wanted to overcome and supersede all that, he would have succeeded because he's clearly a bright guy, he's clearly got opinions, he's clearly got insights.

"You could almost sense the disappointment in himself as it was happening. It just wasn't happening.

"There was absolutely no feedback on Riley. His whole stay at NBC was a study in ineffectuality.

"Given the big luster trip he was coming off, you'd think it'd be a natural kind of continuum, that he'd come in and blow people away. By the end of his stint at NBC, I don't think anybody wrote anything. There was a curiosity factor. It wasn't impressive. It wasn't horrible but it wasn't impressive."

Riley told friends NBC wanted him to be more controversial but he didn't see himself as a buzzard or peripheral opponent. It just didn't feel right to criticize guys, however constructively or politely.

Riley's play-it-safe approach created tension in his relationship with fellow "Showtime" panelist Pete Vecsey, a sportswriter brought onto the show to provide fireworks after a career spent terrorizing players, coaches, and administrators in print.

Riley, the consummate insider, and Vecsey, the consummate outsider, had been on cordial terms as writer and coach but working together on the air was something else.

"When I was covering him, I gave him utmost respect as a coach," Vecsey says. "Almost to the point of being mildly in awe of him.

"When I contacted him, he'd get back to me. He'd say things I hadn't heard. Combined with what he was producing on the court, I thought this guy was sharp.

"I gave him utmost respect. He gave me none. He thinks writers are shit and coaches are the ultimate being."

The Lakers suspect that Riley was never serious about TV, that he parked himself with NBC for a year to await further developments, always intending to return to coaching.

However, it seemed that Riley had prepared for a life after coaching for so long, it's hard to believe he didn't want to give it a try.

But the tide of events was turning the other way.

Even as the season went on and Riley settled in at NBC, it became clear the Knicks would be looking for a coach soon and he'd be their No. 1 candidate. He knew if the money and the deal were right, he'd take it.

"After the studio show each week," he'd say later, "I'd walk out of NBC alone. I'd get in a cab alone. I'd take a flight back to California alone. Then the next weekend, I'd get on a flight to New York and come back alone.

"After you've been around a team for thirty years, it's hard being alone like that....

"I never wanted an easy life. I don't want an easy life. When I'm 60, I might want an easy life. I needed this. That wasn't enough. This is what I do. It's what I love to do.

"It actually was a great year for me because all those other things I thought I wanted to do—I realized how much I didn't want to do them.

"I tried to do them and I was just so damn bored. We had three movies that we were producing and we were doing television shows and we were writing books. We were fishing.

"We were doing all that stuff and I realized this is what it's all about."

■

If Riley needed the Knicks, the Knicks really needed him.

A franchise that had long known turmoil, the Knicks were becoming caricatures of themselves, about to go through their fifth coach in five seasons, along with their general manager and the president of Madison Square Garden, too.

For a few precious seasons almost too long ago to remember, they'd been the showpiece of the NBA, winning titles in 1970 and 1973 under Red Holzman. The names of those Knicks were still hallowed: Reed, Frazier, DeBusschere, Bradley, Barnett, Monroe, Lucas. They were a team distinguished by intelligence, unselfishness, ball motion, and, most of all, "Dee-fense," the chant of the Knick faithful.

New Yorkers embraced the Knicks. Madison Avenue fell all over them. The NBA, basking in unprecedented attention, proclaimed itself "the sport of the '70s."

What could have been more appropriate than the inner-city game of basketball reaching its highest point of evolution in the greatest city of all?

New Yorkers loved basketball. Even if some Canadian doctor had invented it in some YMCA in New England, and if some hayseeds in the Midwest went wild for it, this was still the cradle of the game: Harlem, the Rucker tournament, young Lew Alcindor on the sideline watching Wilt play on the asphalt, the playground legends Earl Manigault, Helicopter Knowings, Jumping Jackie Jackson plucking quarters off the top of the backboard, the Hawk, the Doc—New York!

New Yorkers had grown up with the game and studied its nuances. They took pride in their knowledge of its "subtleties," the word you only heard there.

"I think there's a basketball smugness about New York," says WFAN radio talk show host Mike Francesa. "As New York being the basketball mecca. As 'What do these guys know around the country?'"

"Kentucky and Indiana can have their college basketball. North Carolina can have their college basketball but as far as basketball, the city game, played the way the great Knick teams under Red Holzman played, with Sen. Bill Bradley and Frazier and Monroe and Reed and Dick Barnett, that kind of chic way to play, that smart, sophisticated way to play. New York has a patent on that.

"Oh yeah, I think New York thinks that."

New Yorkers had standards and the Knicks couldn't live up to them.

The 1970s dynasty dissolved. Willis Reed, who limped out to start Game 7 of the '70 finals with a hip shot full of painkillers, retired in 1974, having averaged 33 games in his final three seasons. The Knicks were out of the playoffs by 1976 and Holzman was out of a job. Walt Frazier, the toast of Manhattan, was traded to Cleveland in 1977.

Pro basketball came closer to folding than becoming the sport of the '70s. The rival American Basketball Association engaged in a bidding war with the NBA that turned the decade into the Age of Piracy. Players like Julius Erving signed any contract put in front of them and left the judicial system to sort things out. Owners raided the rival league and their own. The Knicks tried a naked power grab, signing Indiana's George McGinnis whose NBA rights belonged to the 76ers and were reversed by the NBA.

The NBA–ABA merger in 1976 resulted in a barely viable league. By the decade's end, there were reports of rampant drug use by players and several teams were about to fold, obliging the NBA

Players Association to agree to unprecedented reforms, a salary cap, and a substance abuse program with teeth.

The league rebounded nicely with the revival of the Laker–Celtic rivalry.

The Knicks rebounded only partially and intermittently.

There was a brief heyday early in the '80s with Hubie Brown and Bernard King and a false sunrise several years later with Rick Pitino and Patrick Ewing.

Mostly there was internal strife. The Knicks' corporate masters, Gulf + Western, then Paramount, were entertainment-biz showmen throwing big names to the crowd. Smitten by stardom, they had a weakness for arranging shotgun marriages between incompatible GMs and coaches.

Sonny Werblin, who'd made the Jets by signing Joe Namath, hired Hubie Brown—on Howard Cosell's recommendation—as coach and paired him with GM DeBusschere, resulting in a tug-of-war that lasted several years.

This, however, was a golden era compared to Richard Evans's hiring of Al Bianchi as GM and Pitino as coach.

Bianchi, whom the Lakers had considered to replace the fallen Jack McKinney in 1979, was a popular NBA hand who'd been around since the early days. Pitino was a rah-rah college coach who wanted to know why you couldn't win in the NBA by pressing and shooting three-pointers. Bianchi would have been glad to tell him had Pitino been interested in his boss's opinion, which he was not.

The Knicks won 24 games the season before Pitino arrived, 38 in his first, 52 in his second.

Meanwhile, Pitino, once described as "Larry Brown on training wheels," hinted he wasn't getting front office backing and was more at home in college basketball. Then he proved it, jumping to the University of Kentucky.

Bianchi replaced him with one of Pitino's assistant coaches, the inexperienced Stu Jackson, confiding privately they didn't need any more Pitino-style geniuses.

The Knicks swooned. Bianchi fired Jackson after one season plus 15 games, complaining Jackson had been calling Pitino for advice.

Muttered Bianchi to a writer: "That little cocksucker in Kentucky is running my team!"

By now, Bianchi's job was on the line. With only the rest of the season left on his own contract, he brought in his old head coach from

Phoenix, the gentlemanly John MacLeod. The GM and his coach weren't just lame ducks, they were stiff.

The Knicks went 39–43.

In the playoffs, the Bulls swept them, 3–0.

The last playoff game was in Madison Square Garden. The Knicks had a Patrick Ewing night and passed out seven-foot posters of him. Fans tore them up; several were made into paper airplanes and sailed down at the real Ewing.

■

Help was already on the way.

Paramount was going to sweep MSG out from top to bottom. Bianchi, MacLeod, and MSG president Jack Diller were axed. Another showbiz guy, Stanley Jaffe, producer of *Kramer vs. Kramer* and *Fatal Attraction*, was being brought in to head up the whole thing.

Jaffe hired Dave Checketts, a young executive from the league office, to run the Knicks. Jaffe and Checketts knew they needed the credibility of a big-name coach.

One and only one big name dominated their thinking: Riley.

Checketts invited Riley to lunch to gauge his interest. No specifics were mentioned but Riley could read between these lines with his eyes closed.

"I mean, that's how I am," Riley told PBS's Charlie Rose later.

"I'm this dreamer. I visualize everything. I've seen it every single day. Actually, a year before I got the job with the New York Knicks, I visualized that that was going to be my next job.

"I knew it was going to be my next job. I knew the job was open because it opened six times in five years.... And once the job opened again, maybe I could become a candidate for it.

"But I kept visualizing the opportunity as I was running up and down the beach in California. I was working for NBC. I kept visualizing talks I had with the team, talks I had with Patrick Ewing, Mark Jackson, Charles Oakley. I knew what I was going to say to them."

Short of joining the Bulls in case Phil Jackson fell off a bicycle, it would have been harder for Riley to find a better job.

The Knicks needed players but they had one of the game's great centers in Patrick Ewing. There was no downside risk to taking the job, the depths of this team having been fully explored by the previous coaches. Knick management would give Riley, not only carte blanche on the court but a say in personnel matters.

Best of all, it was New York.

Riley's first request was a $2 million annual salary, a book contract with Paramount's publishing house, Simon & Schuster, a mortgage-free house and a movie production deal.

The Knicks leaked the word they'd knocked him down to a more modest five-year, $6 million deal with no house, book, or movie deal. In fact, they went for a package of guaranteed speaking appearances, picked up part of his house, and threw in perks—like a limo—that brought him near $2 million a year, making him by far the game's highest-paid coach.

Still Riley held out.

He wanted assurance Ewing would stay on board. There were meetings and more meetings.

On May 31, Riley was in Manhattan's Regency Hotel under an assumed name to foil the news guys. Ewing and his agent, David Falk, were in a second floor suite at the Mark Hotel, seventeen blocks away. Checketts, shuttling back and forth between them, was getting nowhere and growing desperate.

Ewing wouldn't be pinned down. Finally Checketts called Riley's bluff, giving him a 4 P.M. deadline to decide.

Riley said yes.

"Eventually, I believe people go back to doing what they do best," Riley said at a press conference that afternoon. "I realize that I'm a coach.

"I don't believe I was as bad on TV as some of the first reviews said I was. But I guess my future was always going to be coaching."

It was official. He was a Knick and a lifer.

Chapter Twelve

Tough Town, Tough Team: May the Best Man Win

The TV lamps lit him up like a movie star and there was a mood in the room, a cynical one. Paramount Communications had not given us a basketball coach but some sort of a Warren Beatty facsimile.

—Mark Kriegel, *New York Post*

As honeymoons go, Riley and the Knicks had one of the shorter ones. Forget months or weeks. They could have timed it with a stopwatch.

It lasted a matter of minutes until Dave Checketts, having just hired Riley, told Patrick Ewing and his agent, David Falk, the good news.

Falk had been contending that Ewing was eligible for free agency, trying to force a trade. But Checketts had just bagged the elephant. He and Riley were starting fresh. Surely Patrick would be caught up in the excitement....

Ewing promptly disabused Checketts of his illusions. He was pursuing his claim to arbitration.

Ewing and Falk would campaign through the off-season, filing papers, hiring lawyers, enlisting the players' union, casting about for more creative avenues of escape while Riley and Checketts hunkered down, trying to ride out the storm.

Welcome to New York, indeed.

What the Knicks had lost over the years wasn't going to be salvaged in a day. Riley wasn't the first big-name coach they had brought in, only the latest. He was a West Coast guy and this was the East Coast. His Schenectady roots cut no ice. This was New York. Schenectady was some village upstate.

This wasn't L.A., a suburban sprawl dominated by a single newspaper with a daily magazine format. New York had four downtown papers, three of them tabloids that depended on headlines and newsstand sales. In L.A., a newsstand was a relic, like a jukebox at Johnny Rocket's. In New York, every hiccup was a story, every story an opportunity, and everyone lived in the crossfire.

The tabs were fighting each other for their very existence and cut no one any slack, as Riley would soon learn. He held an illegal practice New Year's Day. The league found out from the *Daily News*'s Peter Finney, who called up to inquire about it, and fined the Knicks $10,000. In L.A., no one would have ever noticed a New Year's Day practice, nor would anyone have cared.

Riley, unhappy at accounts of his Laker exit, was professionally correct but also nakedly contemptuous of the press, which he began calling "the animal that has to be fed every single day."

In New York, that required a lot of feeding, too.

If the tabs tended the flame of American populism, WFAN, the all-sports station, gave it its voice, making Vinny from Staten Island and Sam from the Bronx forces in the lives of the once high and mighty. Mets manager Bud Harrelson, a former fan favorite, gave up his pre-game show on the station when the feedback got hot and heavy. Met star/disappointment Bobby Bonilla, the New York native who had quickly broken his promise to keep smiling, said talk radio had changed his hometown.

Whatever befell Riley would receive saturation coverage before a passionate audience. They'd kiss his feet if he won and kneecap him if he lost, maybe both the same week.

It would be your basic Riley season, nine months of pushing the envelope, but with a different kind of team, not a champion or even a fading one. If he failed or was merely carried out by that Knick tide, everyone would say, "No Magic, no Kareem, what did you expect?" All Riley had built, all those footsteps he'd talked about filling, would wash away.

This was New York. Only the strong survived and not all of them, either.

■

If New Yorkers sympathized with the Knicks' predicament with Ewing, that was nice but irrelevant.

Riley didn't need sympathy. He needed Ewing.

Any trade would be at fire-sale rates and wouldn't return a star 7-footer. Few could appreciate the difference like Riley, who'd played with and without one.

The dispute revolved around a clause in Ewing's contract making him a restricted free agent if his pay fell below the top four in the league. Falk contended it had. Checketts had already offered Ewing a $33 million, six-year extension that would make him the world's highest-paid athlete but Ewing rejected it.

New York waited, impatiently, to see what would happen.

Ewing, pleasant but reclusive, was anything but a troublemaker. He was, instead, a mystery. He shunned publicity. In an era when major stars earned millions in endorsement income, he had no major outside deals. He granted interviews minimally. It wasn't personal with Patrick; he rarely consented to talk to the house announcers on the Madison Square Garden Network. He lived across the Hudson River in a condo in Fort Lee, N.J. When the season was over, he went "home" to Washington, D.C.

More to the point, whatever the Knicks needed, he couldn't deliver by himself.

In his six seasons, they were 221–271. His free throw shooting sagged late in games. He preferred perimeter jumpers to the pivot although he was uncannily accurate. He refused suggestions he attend Pete Newell's big man's camp in California to work on his post moves.

The desperate Bianchi had shopped Ewing the previous season. Other teams climbed over one another trying to steal him. At the All-Star Game in Charlotte, Clipper owner Donald Sterling told Knick president Jack Diller, "You have to talk to us first."

Sterling's offer didn't take long to get out since he made it on an NBA bus within earshot of several writers.

The shopping expedition came to nothing but did little to reassure Ewing. After Game 3 of the '91 sweep by the Bulls, he was asked if he intended to return. "I'll decide by the end of the month," he said.

Reporters watched as he dressed slowly, the last Knick to leave the dressing room—his way of saying good-bye?—and walked into the hall.

"Where to now, Patrick?" someone asked.

"Home to Washington," Ewing said, and then dropped out of sight for the next two months.

On June 21, three weeks after Riley was hired, Ewing filed for arbitration. Falk, supported by lawyers from the NBA Players Association, now argued the Knicks hadn't tendered a proper qualifying offer, making Patrick an unrestricted free agent.

On July 22, Ewing's case was heard in Manhattan's Omni Berkshire Hotel before Daniel Collins, an NYU law professor. It lasted seven hours and was attended by 21 people, 17 of them lawyers. Ewing, making his first public appearance since season's end, hurried by reporters and TV crews without comment.

On July 29, Collins announced his decision in favor of the Knicks.

Ewing, in a prepared release, said he was "very disappointed."

Riley was sitting it out in Los Angeles, running on the beach, thinking of what he wanted to say to Ewing.

On August 13, he went to Washington to meet Patrick face-to-face, but Patrick wasn't having any.

"He looked at me," Riley said later, "and said, 'Coach, why is it going to be any different with you? I had six other coaches tell me the same thing. They came in, they sat me down, [they said] it's gonna be different.'

"And I couldn't guarantee him anything. I told him about a dream I had. I don't know if it had any impact on him but he was sitting there with his wife, Rita, and I told them about this vision.... I don't know what street they go down. Is it Broadway? Is it Fifth Ave.? I saw the confetti coming out. I said, 'One day we're gonna have that here.' "

Ewing's response was to give Riley a list of teams he wanted to be traded to.

Had Ewing sat out of training camp, the Knicks would have had to consider trading him but, although Falk was keeping it to himself, that was farther than Patrick would go. Maybe this Riley guy could deliver. By September, the $33 million offer was back on the table and the two sides were talking.

On October 4, the players flew to Charleston, S.C., for the opening of camp, Ewing among them.

"New York is a great town," he said, "I started my career here and I definitely would like to finish it here. But I wanted the Knicks to do the right things to insure that we'd be an elite ball club."

Riley had his center.

That left the other four positions to figure out.

■

It was a tattered little band that gathered in Charleston to start the new regime.

Riley, harkening back to the Lakers' Hawaiian setting and intent on tutoring a new organization in class, thought about the Caribbean but settled on this antebellum jewel. Riley had more than a little L.A. left in him; he still kept his watch on West Coast time.

"I've had it that way for twenty years," he said. "I haven't changed it no matter where I've gone. Why should I?"

Other preparations recalled his Laker days, too, like curtains over all the windows in the gym for privacy.

This was Riley 101, the crash course.

Trainer Mike Saunders got instructions for team meetings (the placement of the podium and VCRs), and dinners (round tables seating four, white tablecloths, china, cloth napkins folded into triangles).

Riley decorated his office at Madison Square Garden in earth tones with small overhead lights for the little illumination he needed while watching videotape. There were no pictures or plaques. Insiders called it "the Batcave."

The Rileys had bought a big house in Greenwich, Conn., shipping 45,000 pounds of furniture from the West Coast. The Knicks would practice at the Purchase campus of the State University of New York, north of the city, where Riley had another Batcave, set up and decorated in the same colors and style as the one in the Garden.

On the Lakers, they'd have just said, "That's Riley." To new initiates, it looked bizarre.

To Knick players, reviled as underachievers and worse, it was more than just the new program. They'd been down so long, anything looked up to them, and this smooth-looking dude with all the rings looked like visiting royalty.

Check the record; they needed him more than he needed them.

There was Ewing, paying the price for being the star of a perennial disappointment.

There was Charles Oakley, the Oak in name and fact, a 6–9, 250-pounder, big-chested, big-hearted but limited offensively. When the Knicks lost, people were less likely to remark on Oakley's unselfishness than his scoring average. Oakley wasn't one to suffer in silence and with every season, moaned louder.

There was Xavier McDaniel, the ex-X-man. Once a terror weapon of a small forward at 6–8, 215, he was 28 and seemed to have reached that point when players wander out from the basket to avoid the rough stuff. The old X would give them a front line to fear but they'd have to see.

There was the point guard, Mark Jackson. Everybody knew the trouble he'd seen; he'd been making headlines of one sort or another for his four Knick seasons. Brooklyn-born, a star at St. John's, Jackson owned the city as rookie of the year in 1988. He was an all-star the following season, then took an express elevator to hell when his sponsor, Pitino, left. The Knicks started playing half-court basketball, exposing Jackson's weakness as a shooter. Bianchi didn't like him. He fought with Bianchi's coaches. The fans, who'd once delighted in his cocky antics, turned on him in a way only a fallen homeboy could have provoked.

Then there was Gerald Wilkens.

The younger brother of Atlanta's Dominique, Gerald was a good athlete but a poor shooter, which made him a bad complement to Jackson. When Gerald was right, he was a good defensive player, one of the guys who could make Jordan work.

When he was right? That was never going to do under Riley.

"He just wanted a whole different Gerald Wilkins," Wilkins said later. "He didn't want me to change just a little bit.

There were John Starks, an ex-grocery clerk who'd climbed out of the CBA to win a spot the year before, and Anthony Mason, a free agent who'd played in New Jersey, Portland, Venezuela, and Turkey. Starks was mercuric, but he could play and he was hungry. Mason was a 6–7, 250-pound pocket power forward with an awkward shot, flapping his shooting elbow as if intending to fly, but he'd put his body on people. He had the hunger, too.

If it didn't look like a championship team, it was something to work with.

But first, the Knick innocents had to learn what it was to work, Riley-style.

Veteran Lakers, who knew the drill, shuddered at the thought. Riley wanted to bring in his old Laker center, Mychal Thompson, but Thompson chose Italy, partly because he didn't want to go through the old regimen.

"I heard he practiced tough," Wilkins said, "but I didn't think it would be like that. His practices are long—long and hard. Everybody else's practices are either short and medium hard, or short and hard. Or if they're long, they're not really as hard as his practices…. He demanded a lot. I guess that's what I want to say.

"Practice started at 9:30. You look up, it's 10:30, 11:30, O.K., practice is getting ready to stop now, well, 12, not yet, 12:30. All of a sudden it's almost 1 o'clock. You know, we've been in there three hours. Those players have never done it. I don't think any players in the league have done it.

"You still don't like it. No matter how much you get accustomed to it, you still don't like it. No player would. You just deal with it. You'll win games, there's no question about that because you play so hard. But you never like to practice that way."

∎

Then there were the rules.

When Riley told Magic Johnson over dinner he realized he'd made mistakes in L.A., he apparently didn't think being too controlling had been one of them.

If his authority had been challenged in L.A., his answer in New York was more authority.

Riley would no longer be available to the press before games. Anyone who wanted to talk to him had to come to the morning shootaround. Knick players were also discouraged from talking to the media before games.

The press was barred not only from Knick charter flights but buses. The press wasn't just the newspaper writers but the announcers who were employees of Madison Square Garden. Included were Marv Albert, Riley's old NBC teammate, and Walt Frazier. Albert was as popular as any Knick player, so much so that the team had a night for him. Frazier was still a legend in New York. Now the Knick legends were off the Knick plane.

Practices were closed. Not only was the press barred, Riley didn't want any MSG people walking through the arena when the team worked.

"Is he a control freak?" asked Checketts. "I suppose he probably is. Does that bother me? No. He delivers."

"You know Pat's a superstar and you deal with him at a certain level but always toward the commitment of winning," said MSG president Bob Gutkowski. "Like top actors, there's always some things they want done in a certain way and you address that as best as possible.

"He has certain rules and regulations and we adhere to them. He likes the arena closed when he's practicing, there's no doubt about that….

"Yeah, I can walk through. But I wouldn't because I know that something like that would make him uncomfortable."

A new day was dawning in the NBA with Riley as its herald. It was no longer a bush league eking out a day-to-day existence but a high-powered marketing dervish. It was major league with the attendant hallmarks of fame: increasing opportunities, demands on one's time, scrutiny, pressure.

In the NBA, coach–reporter relations had traditionally been cordial. Neither side took itself too seriously, befitting a discourse held in the bowels of old arenas, in unadorned cement-brick hallways with pipes running across the ceiling and workmen barging through.

Now the stadiums were new and coaches, especially on good teams in big cities, began to resemble their control-minded NFL counterparts. Schedules became hardened, access limited. Now Riley's post-game interview, outside the Knick room in the Garden, was televised live by MSG cable. When his five minutes were up, Riley didn't hang out in the dressing room, as he had with the Lakers, but disappeared into the Batcave.

Old NBA people missed the one-for-all–all-for-one days when the play-by-play man might double as assistant GM as Chick Hearn had; when the color commentator might double as traveling secretary as Riley had; when a coach needing an assistant might turn to a member of the traveling party as Paul Westhead had with Riley.

Now the team chartered out after the game and the press went the next day. The coach and the media guys didn't have dinner together on off-nights on the road or go out for a beer, or know much about each other.

One of the men who missed the old days, not to mention the charter, was Frazier.

"That took a lot of sleep from me," Frazier says. "I mean, 1:30 in the morning, they're in their beds and I'm on the road.

"Why? Control. Just control. Because Riley wants to ostracize the team from the media, from everything....

"No, I don't [have a relationship with Riley]. Because I don't like—I'm just a regular guy. So you won four championships, so what?

"Pat made a lot of rules, even for the press. Practices were closed, they couldn't interview him before the game and certain times. So when I saw all that, I just said I couldn't be a part of that. I just like to be a regular guy.

"Not that I don't understand him because I'm sure he's like that with everybody. Not only me but Marv Albert, the guy who he worked with. He doesn't allow Marv on the plane. I'm sure Marv took it like I did. It's a slap in the face. I could see it if there's something negative we said about the team or something that happened on the plane.

"The other Knick teams, we had access to the players. When you travel with them, then you have a relationship with them. Whereas now, I never see the players, only at the games. So, it's different."

■|

The Riley era opened at Orlando against the third-year Magic. The Knicks lost.

The second game was at Miami against the fourth-year Heat. The Knicks lost again.

This was not the start Riley had envisioned; in a departure from form, he showed his dispeasure. The cool dude from L.A. was suddenly strung out in New York.

"No one should expect this team to win 60 games," he said after the Heat loss, "or else the writers are hypocritical, the way they lambasted this team last year."

Just in the nick of time, the Knicks got a win, in the home opener against the Bucks.

Their next game was November 7, 1991. A few hours before, Magic Johnson announced he was retiring because he'd learned he was HIV-positive. Riley got the news directly from Johnson who telephoned the half-dozen people he considered his best friends, Riley, Jordan, and Bird among them.

Riley was stunned. Johnson was a fixture in his constellation, like the North Star. Before that night's game against Orlando in the Garden, a friend from L.A. sat with him and for once, Riley didn't hide his feelings. It was like Louie Dampier watching Riley the day JFK was shot. Before the tipoff, Riley called the Knicks and Magic together on the court and led players and fans in prayer.

The Knicks won four in a row but spun out again as soon as they went on the road. With two days off in Houston, Riley held successive three-hour practices and snapped when asked about it.

"Do I ask you guys why you write for eight hours?" he told Knick beat writers. "Let me work, would you? Let me work!"

Only later did he acknowledge how tight he'd been.

"There was a time when we weren't doing very well and there was a lot of pressure and I sort of created a lot of pressure on myself," he said. "And as I was explaining the problem of the day, Chris said, 'You know Pat, every now and then just sort of.... you know, smile. Just smile. It warms you up and everybody up.'

"I'd never thought about it that way. I do believe there's something to that so at least once a day, I try to smile now.

"Even when I'm miserable."

The Knicks eased into first place in the Atlantic Division. With 15 days left in the season, they were five games up on the Celtics.

Then came 15 days to rock Riley's world.

April 4: The Knicks lost at Cleveland. Larry Bird sat out with back spasms as the second-place Celtics beat the Bulls in Boston Garden.

April 7: The Pistons made 14 of their first 17 shots in the Garden and won, 104–93, slicing the Knick lead to three.

The Knicks had to play the next night at Boston, where they'd lost 22 in a row.

Said Ewing: "We can't let doubt creep in."

Translation: It already had.

April 8: The Celtics beat the Knicks, 93–89.

Said Boston's king of irreverence, Kevin McHale: "There's always a chance. New York is going to have to cooperate. If they would all come down with a case of botulism, I think we'd stand a better chance."

Riley and Checketts met later that night for a drink. They talked about a couple of late calls that had particularly infuriated them. Riley had given the press his it-doesn't-do-any good-to-whine speech but now he started in again: It was always that way up here, etc. He went on and on, bitterly. Checketts was taken aback by the depth of his hatred of the Celtics.

April 12: The Knicks lost, 72–61, at Detroit, setting an NBA record for fewest points since the advent of the 24-second clock.

April 15: The Knicks led at Atlanta, 94–85, with 3:41 left but the Hawks scored the last 10 points and won, 95–94.

Riley, his shirt soaked, called it "probably one of the hardest losses I've ever been through."

The Celtics won at Detroit to tie for first. Having taken the season series from the Knicks, they had only to win their final game to become division champions.

In a final ignominy, the tabs had been playing the story inside, Knicks having collapsed before. But the *Daily News* finally put them on its back with a headline in type 2½ inches high: AN AWFUL GAG.

April 18: The Celtics routed Miami. Riley's worst nightmare had come true. His ancient enemy had bested him again after all these years.

■I

The Knicks flew into Milwaukee to play out the regular season like gloom personified.

Xavier McDaniel had had enough. He was still the missing piece in the puzzle but things were getting worse, not better. Riley talked to him from time to time but X, about to become a free agent and suspecting a financial angle in everything, refused to open up.

Riley began giving Mason more and more of X's minutes. In a 10-game span down the stretch, McDaniel had played a total of six minutes in fourth quarters.

"I initiated the contact," McDaniel says. "I called him and he said come on down [to Riley's hotel suite]...

"I told him, 'If I'm going to talk to you, then we're going to talk man to man, let's cut out all the bullshit.' That's what I felt too, when I would come to the meetings, it was, like, bullshit. You know, it wasn't real, weird.

"We got it all out in the air. Lots of things. He told me he didn't think I cared. Because on the court, I played and I played with high intensity, I don't take no bullshit from anybody. But once I get off the court, I could have a bad game and be talking to someone or joking. Where he felt that if I had a bad game, maybe I should go off by myself. What I do on the court doesn't necessarily affect me off the court. If Oakley is talking to me, then I'm going to talk to him. If Pat Ewing is talking to me—it goes with anyone.

"I told him I'm always hurt on the inside.

"He said, 'Well, show it.'

"I don't feel like I have to show it in front of everybody.

"He said, 'Well, some of the people think you don't care on the team.'

"I said, 'That's bullshit. Nobody can ever tell me that I don't care.' And I said, 'Matter of fact, you're the only coach ever fucking told me I don't care....'

"I just told him, 'Hey, personally, this is the way I am and you have to accept me for this. I have to accept the way you are.' I told him, 'I may not always like your practices but I show up and I just do it because it's my job.'

"He wanted to get me back to the way I was playing in Seattle. I just said, 'You have to put me back on the basketball court.' We cleared the air about everything that night and the last game, I played 35 minutes."

■❘

Not that the Knicks were going to be able to sit around and feel sorry for themselves before the playoffs.

Riley thought his mistake had been letting up on them after a West Coast trip in March. He decided to take them back to Charleston for a refresher course in intensity.

Not that they felt like going.

Down the stretch they'd begun complaining, off the record, of fatigue. Falk said privately Ewing was exhausted by the games, practices, and video sessions. Now they were getting an extra three-day trip tacked onto their schedule.

Jackson, asked if he wanted to go, said, "I think it helps to get away and concentrate on what we have to do in the playoffs."

Fibbing the day before Easter? a writer kidded him.

"Is it 12 o'clock yet?" asked Jackson.

No, said the writer.

"It helps then," said Jackson.

They flew back to South Carolina for four practices in three days. There were group video sessions and individual videos for homework featuring segments on each player's assignment. The scouting report included a breakdown from a consultant in Los Angeles working with a computer. Did they realize Bill Laimbeer put the ball on the floor four times in 69 shots? That 54 of Rodman's 70 shots were putbacks? That Joe Dumars hit 52 percent of his shots when he was open, 38 percent with a hand in his face, and drove left in crunch time?

They only had three days or Riley might have had them studying the Pistons' fingerprints.

"He's dangerous," said Jackson, "because his life is basketball."

Meanwhile, Piston Coach Chuck Daly worked his team at a routine pace: off Monday, one practice Tuesday, Wednesday, and Thursday, shootaround in New York before Friday's game. The *Daily News* ran a box, comparing Riley's ten hours to Daly's five. If the Knicks lost, players would complain and Riley's lyrical quotes wouldn't save him from the animal that had to be fed every single day. Given a bad outcome, it would dine on him.

A Knick loss looked like the smart bet, too.

Detroit had beaten them twice down the stretch. The aging Pistons were still savvy enough to deny the Knicks their first option—Ewing—and let someone else beat them. In a breach of protocol, Chicago Coach Phil Jackson announced: "We expect to play Detroit."

In Game 1, the Knicks flattened the Pistons, 109–75. Oakley held Rodman to four rebounds. Madison Square Garden didn't sell out.

In Game 2, the Pistons broke through to win, 89–88, on Isiah Thomas's 15-footer with :07 left. Again the Garden didn't sell out; attendance even fell from Game 1.

In Detroit, the Knicks looked right down the barrel.

With :27 left in Game 3, they trailed, 79–77, with Dumars, an 87 percent free throw shooter, on the line for two.

He missed both. With :13 left, Ewing tied it with a 12-footer and the Knicks won in overtime, 90–87.

"The gods," sighed Riley, "owed us one."

If gods were watching, they must have been tuned into another series because this one was no treat. Game 3 featured six technical fouls and one flagrant foul as the officials struggled to bring the canons of civilization to bear on these two wrestling bears. Once official Joe Crawford yelled at Riley: "Anybody that screws around any more is history!"

Daly complained afterward about Knick tactics. The coach of the Bad Boys calling the Knicks dirty?

"They were the former Bad Boys," snorted McDaniel. "We didn't do no more than what they did....

"Rodman couldn't get a rebound. He was getting around, what, 18? Pat played him, Oak played him, I played him and Mace [Mason] played him. We hit him every time we got an opportunity. Not dirty but when he came down the paint. And Rodman, he's a hard worker. He's relentless on the boards. But what each and everybody was saying, whoever's on him has to be the same way. He grab you, you grab him. He throw you down, you throw him down, too. If you're going on the floor, you take him with you. And that's what we did."

The rest of the series played to form. The Pistons won Game 4 in Detroit. The Knicks won Game 5 in the Garden.

Knick players, glimpsing their first daylight in a month, celebrated wildly. The Bulls were next but everyone recognized that for the mismatch it was.

Said McDaniel, who'd averaged 19 points and 10 rebounds: "After a series like this, we all proved we could go on American Gladiator with Ice and Nitro."

Of course, there was some disagreement.

Over Madison Square Garden's own air, Frazier got into an argument with play-by-play man Jim Karvellas.

FRAZIER: "This jubilation will end quickly when the Knicks focus on the Bulls because the Knicks have won *nothing*. This is a team they should've beaten."

KARVELLAS: Give them credit, Walt.

FRAZIER: For what?

KARVELLAS: For coming back…. Give them credit for winning the series, Walt.

FRAZIER: They should've won the series, they had the home court….

KARVELLAS: All right, Walt. That's your opinion, my man.

FRAZIER: Hey, that's everybody's opinion that *knows* the game…. First of all, they squander the division title. Now an inept Piston team takes them to the brink…. Look at the reality. Look at the big picture. The reality is they won 51 games. They won nothing. If they beat the Bulls, then they've done something.

KARVELLAS: All right, Walt. Thank you.

FRAZIER: That's my opinion. You have *your* opinion.

This was still New York.

■

Gutkowski, the MSG president, had a talk with Frazier the next day.

The problem was, Frazier's wasn't a minority opinion.

"I believe Pat Riley gave us a lot more than we deserved, with the talent we had," Gutkowski says. "He absolutely made the most of the situation.

"And yet it was always, 'Are they any good? Can they go far?' We didn't think we could beat Chicago. And coming down to the last week of the season, we blew first place when we'd been in first place for so long. You know, we blew it and there was a real negative feeling as far as that was concerned. There was a sense we wouldn't even beat Detroit. We didn't even sell out Detroit. I don't think New York accepted the team yet and that showed in the Detroit series."

Chicago?

Forget Chicago.

The Bulls were defending NBA champions, 18–2 in the last two post-seasons. They'd started this season 35–5 before leveling off to 67–15. They'd just swept the Heat with Michael Jordan averaging 45 points. While the Knicks were fighting for their lives, they were resting.

One man dreamed of winning and breathed life into it, making it real for twelve players.

The morning after the Piston series, the Knicks were back on the floor in Purchase, listening to Riley spit fire. The press got the tame version, which was warm enough: The Bulls were sneering at the Knicks; no one else was giving them a chance, either.

"Fine," said Riley, "slap 'em in the face. Hell with 'em. Really.

"We didn't work for seven and a half months just to win the first round and say, 'Well, O.K., that made our season.' That's bullshit. It really is. And anybody who has that kind of attitude on the team, I want them to stay home."

Usually, Riley had to stretch a point or the truth to claim an opponent didn't respect them but this time it was true, every word of it. The Bulls hadn't lost to a New York team in three seasons. When their greyhounds turned up their pressure defense, the Knick plowhorses were hard-pressed to hang onto the ball, much less run an offense. The Bulls owned New York.

Phil Jackson eyed Riley warily, perhaps explaining his bald prediction of a first-round Knick loss. And Jackson had the hammer, Michael Jordan.

The Knicks were going to have to go through Michael.

Riley took Wilkins and wound him up, and wound him up tighter, and aimed him at Jordan like a homing missile.

"He challenged me all year," Wilkins says. "He wanted me to be as tough as Michael even though my skills weren't as tough as Michael.

"At one point he told me in the locker room, he said to me, he said, 'You're afraid of Michael Jordan.' It threw me for a loop because I knew I was one of the players in this league who guarded Michael well. And he said to me, 'I think you're totally just *afraid* of Michael! I think you're terrified of Michael!' In front of *every*body! In front of the guys!

"I looked up, I couldn't believe he said that. But he said it. He just kept coming. He just kept coming. I got to a point where I couldn't take it any more. It was coming down to the wire. He was taking me for everything I had. The saddest part was I worked so hard and he got on me so much that I gave in. I finally gave in to what he wanted.

"It got to the point whether he wanted me to or not, that's what I was gonna do. Because I had established that in myself, that I was gonna be mean. I didn't care! I mean, I cussed everybody out. I got to a point, I didn't care. It opened up in me something that I couldn't open up myself and that's the ability to play hard and play tough.... Now when I step on a court, guys know that Gerald Wilkins is gonna get in your face. He ain't gonna back off. You might score but he's gonna keep coming and he's gonna keep coming."

Or in other words, Riley had his man.

The Bulls had been off for six days, the same down time that drove Riley crazy as when he was Laker coach and his team finished first. He knew how fast favorites could lose their edge, how vulnerable they could be if they were fat and happy and someone took it to them.

No one else knew. But they would soon.

■

Game 1 went through New York like an electric current: Knicks 94, Bulls 89.

Ewing had always had trouble with Bulls center Bill Cartwright, his ex-teammate. Now Riley let Patrick play on the wing, exposing the slower Cartwright. Ewing scored 34 points, including a running five-footer with :33 left to put the Knicks ahead to stay.

Back in New York, they watched the final minutes in homes and bars and on the big screens in the Garden where the Rangers had just finished playing. Stan Jaffe, watching in the MSG suite, had the TV feed put on the scoreboard and a few thousand hockey fans stuck around to cheer the Knicks.

In Game 2, Jordan struck a match to Wilkins and Starks, scoring 15 straight points in five minutes of the first quarter, but the Knicks hung in.

With 2:03 left, Ewing hit a 19-footer to cut it to 79–78.

Jordan was spent. Scottie Pippen was backing away from shots. The Bulls were dead in the water. If the Knicks went up, 2–0, going back to New York, there was no telling how far this could go—to the Eastern finals? The NBA finals? Riley's ticker-tape parade?

They only had to get the ball back.

Jordan tried to free himself on the right wing, drove to the top of the key, saw a double-team coming and passed to B. J. Armstrong. BJ, the 6-foot sixth man with the unlined face of a choirboy, was bottled up by Starks, 20 feet out with six seconds left on the shot clock.

Greg Anthony came over to help. Armstrong up-faked and Anthony jumped in the air, a mistake, allowing BJ to step through the double-team.

Armstrong took two bounces into the lane and hit a running 12-footer.

Moments later, the Bulls' waif hit another clutch shot, lobbing an 8-footer on the baseline over Ewing's outstretched arm. The Knicks had had them in their crosshairs but the Bulls would live to fight another day.

"I don't know if we've got them running scared," Wilkins said afterward, "but we've got them on their heels."

Said Jordan: "He's probably right."

The Bulls won Game 3 in the Garden, taking back their home-court advantage. The next day the Knicks arose again, out-rebounded the Bulls by 19 and won, 93–86.

Said Riley: "Our dreams are bigger than this."

This was toe-to-toe stuff and people were losing it. In Game 3, Mark Jackson argued with a referee. Phil Jackson yelled "Don't listen to him!" and Mark yelled "Fuck you, I'm just playing basketball!" and Phil replied "Fuck you!"

Phil Jackson was ejected in Game 4 and booed off the Garden court where he'd once been a favorite.

"I think they're licking their chops on Fifth Ave. (where the NBA had its offices)," he said.

"I don't like orchestration, it sounds fishy, but they do control who sends the referees. If it goes seven games, everybody will be really happy. Everybody will get the TV revenue and the ratings they want."

If an ex-Knick could turn Eastern Conspiracy theorist, then the founding father of "Showtime," who once decried thuggery annually, could turn into the Beastmaster.

At the next day's Knick practice, Riley read Jackson's comment with reporters surrounding him and minicams whirring. You could almost see him turning it over in his head, deciding how to use it.

"He's insulting us, basically," Riley said, deliberately. "I was part of six championship teams. I've been to the finals 13 times and I know what championship demeanor is all about. The fact that he's whining and whimpering about the officiating is an insult to how hard our guys are playing.

"He's not respecting the fact that this team is playing with as much heart as any team has ever played with. What championship teams are all about, they've got to take on all comers. They don't whine about it."

For good measure, Checketts protested Jackson's comments to the league, which fined Jackson $2,500.

Having been lectured in a champion's obligations, the Bulls bounced back in Game 5 in Chicago. Jordan, who had called Ewing "one of the best people I know, someone I'm really close to," squared off against Patrick in a chest-to-chest argument.

Another time, Jordan dunked over Ewing, then stood over him screaming in triumph and pumping his right fist. The Bulls shot 38 free throws, suggesting Jackson had gotten his $2,500's worth, and won, 96–88.

Back in New York for Game 6, the Knicks decapitated the Bulls, figuratively and nearly literally.

The Knicks won, 100–86. Starks hogtied Pippen around the neck on a breakaway and was assessed a flagrant foul. Ewing sprained his left ankle in the third quarter but limped back in to score 11 points in the fourth, reminding Knick fans of Willis Reed in the 1970 finals.

"That Game 6 against the Bulls was as much fun as New York had had for a basketball game since Red Holzman coached the '73 team," says Phil Mushnick, the *Post*'s TV critic.

"Everything was plugged in that night. It was an electric night and the only thing that could have messed it up was a loss to the Bulls.

"The celebrities at Elaine's that night—everybody had been at the game. It was like no one wanted to go home. Everyone's talking, like, beat the Bulls. The Madison Square Garden VIP suite had Paul Simon, Neil Simon, Ed Bradley, Robert Klein, Robert Wuhl, Holzman, Trump."

The series was going back to Chicago for Game 7 but the Bulls were teetering.

Jordan was on his own. McDaniel had taken possession of Pippen. In the last three games Scottie had missed 26 of 39 shots and X had outscored him, 74–41.

"You know how I knew I had him?" McDaniel says. " 'Cause when he had a good game, wasn't nothing wrong with his ankle. When he had a bad game, something was wrong with his ankle.

"He didn't want to drive because he felt myself or Oak or Pat or someone was gonna knock shit out of him. Just like the hit John Starks put on him. There's no fuckin' way that John Starks would have clotheslined me, almost knocked me out and just got a $5,000 fine for it. I would have told Michael or whoever was guarding him, 'Let him go to the hole, push up on him and force him to go to the hole and I'm going to rip his head off...'

"They were talking about our rough-housing play and that it wasn't good for basketball and the media really pumped on that. We were Darth Vader, they were Luke Skywalker.

"They [Bulls] were over there saying that. I said if I went over in their fucking locker room, they all would shut up.

"And Oak was like, 'Well, if you go, X, I'm going!' "

It was Riley's dream trying to come true and no one was more thrilled than he was.

"I can remember Game 6," he told Tom Brokaw later, "when there were 20,000 flag-waving New York Knick fans and we were beating the Bulls.... I mean, there's nothing like that. Nothing."

The buildup to Game 7 was appropriate to the fervor.

Gregory Hines, starring on Broadway in *Jelly's Last Jam*, promised when the Knicks won, he'd announce it from the stage.

Spike Lee, Knick diehard and Jordan intimate, announced: "I'm not flying to Chicago for the Knicks to lose."

■▌

They lost.

Bent on avoiding mayhem, the league assigned its top referee, Jake O'Donnell, who whistled two quick fouls on Wilkins to announce how tightly this game would be called. Jordan had 29 by halftime, 42 altogether, and the Knicks finally were blown out of a game, 110–81.

Riley didn't murmur a word of complaint about O'Donnell or anything else.

"Like I said, you play one game under any conditions," he said. "The conditions were Bulls' stadium, Michael Jordan, and Scottie Pippen. But we'll be back. There are no regrets, no tears."

Tears?

If pride were helium, he'd have floated home without a plane.

His players had walked a tightrope for weeks. If Joe Dumars had hit his free throws, they could have been gone in the first round. If Greg Anthony hadn't gone for Armstrong's fake, they might have slain the Bulls. They'd be back, badder than ever, and Riley had a whole, delicious summer to relish the thought.

He was back, too.

The magic still worked.

A Funny Thing Happened on the Way to the Parade

Maybe I haven't done anything yet. Maybe the stuff I did somewhere else was just a base. Maybe it was just a springboard to the opportunity of putting something together in New York.

—PAT RILEY TO MIKE LUPICA
NEW YORK DAILY NEWS, DEC. 24, 1992

A new era dawned in New York.

It was as if Riley had moussed Knick history. Now everything seemed gleaming and new, sleek and efficient.

If he'd had to make do with leftovers and grit in his first season, it looked like he was going to be blessed in his second.

From the Clippers came Charles Smith, a 27-year-old, 6–10 forward with an 18-point career average, plus veteran point guard Doc Rivers. From Dallas came sharpshooting Rolando Blackman. From Minnesota came Tony Campbell, from Indiana Herb Williams, from the draft Hubert Davis.

For all of them, Checketts gave up only Mark Jackson and draft picks.

Gerald Wilkins was allowed to leave. Xavier McDaniel left on his own. Checketts had wanted to sign X but for salary cap purposes had to make him wait until last. McDaniel's agent—Falk—took his client to Boston when the Celtics came up with a two-year deal.

The Bulls looked vulnerable. Michael Jordan had to give up half his summer, however reluctantly, to play on the Dream Team along with Scottie Pippen. The Bulls let Jordan report late so he could rest—actually he flew to Los Angeles and shot commercials—and held Pippen out of early drills. With John Paxson and Bill Cartwright injured, Horace Grant got huffy about being the only starter in two-a-days and Phil Jackson threw him out of a practice.

There were distress signals going up all over Chicago and the Knicks were poised to strike.

Celebrities began appearing at games in the Garden, not just long-time regulars like Woody Allen and Spike Lee but expatriate Bulls fans like Bill Murray and the down-on-their-luck Laker faithfuls like Jack Nicholson and Michael Douglas, as if to confirm this as the new capital of the basketball world.

All they needed for the coronation was someone to pass the scepter.

▌▌

The Bulls weren't quite done with it.

They were a strange crew, dominating—they were 30–9 in the two post-seasons—yet little feared. They weren't big, rough, or deep. Their center, Cartwright, didn't score. Their point guard, Paxson, was a creaky jump-shooter, who moved to open spots while Jordan drew the defense. Their second-best player, Pippen, was suspect.

Indiana's Reggie Miller, in a fit of pique but speaking for much of the league, sputtered, "Take Jordan away and what do they have?"

Of course, taking Jordan away was the problem.

At the top of a game the likes of which had never been seen before, Jordan had beaten all the raps—that he was too concerned with scoring titles, that he overwhelmed his teammates. But he was also a bare-knuckles competitor who wasn't loath to challenge his teammates, whom he sometimes called "my supporting cast."

Talking trash—or as the players called it— talking shit was a cherished NBA tradition. Johnson's Lakers and Bird's Celtics had raised it to an art form; now it was an accepted part of a star's game to psych out opponents. If a lower form of life, like Greg Anthony or John Starks, dared to talk some shit of his own to a star, the great man would burn with righteous indignation. Jordan couldn't get over the two Knicks' effrontery; he called them "two of the cockiest players in this league."

Aching to demonstrate their own greatness, the Bulls turned their guns on the Knicks.

In one spring, Chicago–New York had become the NBA's hottest rivalry, two major markets long positioned on an arrogance/jealousy axis, which now had marquee basketball teams to carry their colors. The Bulls had a case on the Knicks, whom they saw as over-hyped darlings of the Eastern establishment, and went out of their way to show their contempt.

"They've got Patrick who is, what, 30?" said Phil Jackson before the season. "And Rolando Blackman who's 33 or whatever? They're players with a lot of habits, an accumulation of personal failure."

"Same guys," said Pippen, "new address."

"Then there was Jackson's Knicks-as-Huns lament before a Christmas night meeting:

"Christmas is always a family day. It's a giving day, a holy day for Christians, and a meaningful day of peace and light. To mar it with a game in which you have to come out and fight with guys who are going to foul you on every play turns it into something else. We're not going to be able to enjoy the day."

When Riley was named Coach of the Year, Jackson ascribed it to thuggery, noting: "Not only is it accepted and condoned, it's *honored.* He's the Coach of the Year."

Before they'd meet again in the playoffs, Jackson would show his players scenes from the movie, *The Power of One,* a drama about South African racial conflict. Intercut with footage of the Knicks were images of a white South African jailer bashing a black prisoner's head against a wall.

They were an odd couple, Riley and Jackson. Jackson was a minister's son from North Dakota who'd become the house hippie on the great '70s Knick teams and he was still a committed political liberal.

However, the era of peace and music had never extended to Jackson's professional life. He was an awkward, physical player whose elbows were known around the league. He and Riley were friendly rivals as players, appropriately, since their games, if not personas, were similar.

Jackson's objection to the Knicks' style was, like Riley's objections to the Celtics in the '80s, grounded in self-interest. Like Riley, the former high priest of "Showtime" who now saw basketball as "a game of force," Jackson had once gone on record advocating the very tactic he now abhorred. Jackson had written a book, too, in which he detailed the proper use of the forearm in disrupting an offensive player's rhythm or vertebrae.

It was as if you took two completely different people, subjected them to similar pressures and circumstances and watched them move closer together. As coach of a successful, high-profile team, Jackson was battening down wherever he could, seeking to protect his control, like Riley. Bulls practices were routinely closed and the press wasn't allowed on charter flights or buses.

Like Riley, Jackson liked to say the things that set the agenda, that sent the press baying off to ask the other guy for a comment.

Like Riley, Jackson wanted to create an inviolate inner circle and wasn't above piping in a little paranoia. And, like Riley, Jackson could not take a rival lightly. Jackson regarded the Knicks as forces of darkness and Riley as the second coming of Richard Nixon.

"Pat's a tremendous opponent when it comes to a coach on the other side," said Jackson. "You feel his pressure when you coach and you know his teams are relentless....

"But you can see the differences in our styles. I believe that what we are trying to do with this ball club is genuine group dynmamics. He's turned a group around and he's got group dynamics going in a whole different value system—hard work ethic, maybe a little us against them.

" Like his players can't talk to my players. His coaches can't talk to my coaches. My style is open. I close my practices as he does but my style is open. Freedom with the basketball club, closed basketball team....

"I need the league's attention to what New York's doing defensively. I need people to say, 'Is this legal defense that's being played on Scottie Pippen and Michael Jordan?'

"That's all. I'm drawing attention to that. He knows it's a psychological warfare. He's big enough to know that."

It was hard to get to Riley but nobody had ever come after him personally before.

When they met again in the playoffs, Riley decided he'd had enough of being asked about what Jackson had said.

"Well, you know something?" Riley told writers, "that's for you to decide. That's for *you* to decide.

"That isn't for you to be, I think, a special delivery carrier of his messages to me and to have a comment from me. I think when somebody begins to make personal attacks on people, then that's up to you to decide whether or not...you know."

He gave a short, ironic laugh.

"I don't give a damn. I probably am all those things so...I don't know."

■

The season was anything but the warmup they'd hoped for.

It took Riley three months to get his new team to the level his old one had reached the preceding spring. Charles Smith, who'd spent years rolling up points for a losing team, had to move to small forward while learning what Riley meant by toughness and conditioning. The career 18-point scorer averaged 12 and Riley often used Anthony Mason in the clutch.

The schedule became a land mine as Riley's knife-between-the-teeth defense found itself an outlaw in a new, league-mandated era of nonviolence.

In February, Starks ended the season of the Nets' Kenny Anderson with a garden-variety hard foul. In March, Greg Anthony, in civilian clothes because of an injury, touched off a full-scale riot by sucker-punching the Suns' Kevin Johnson, resulting in an NBA record $294,173 in fines and lost wages.

In spite of Riley's attempt to portray them as honest workmen, the Knicks became gunfighters whose reputations preceded them everywhere.

In a late-season game at Miami, Heat Coach Kevin Loughery was overheard telling his players, "Knock 'em down! Knock 'em down!"

Referee Ronnie Nunn walked over and asked Loughery, "Did I hear correctly?"

"I didn't say anything," said Loughery, innocently.

Perhaps by coincidence, Heat forward Keith Askins then hit Ewing with a forearm, precipitating another melee. Four Miami policemen ran onto the floor but the Knicks, demonstrating their new-found discipline, kept their cool and got out of Dodge with the victory.

Models of focus, they finished 39–8, tying the franchise record of 60 wins set by the sainted '69–'70 champs.

The Bulls, meanwhile, lurched through their own trials, falling to 57 wins, 10 fewer than the season before.

"The confidence is still there," insisted Grant at one point, "but not the arrogance."

The year before, the Bulls had needed a seventh game on their floor to eliminate the Knicks but this spring it would be in New York.

In New York, the hype just kept happening.

The sprinkling of celebrities at Knick games swelled into a torrent of actors, comedians, singers, dancers, rappers, and news anchors: Danny Aiello, Tom Cruise and Nicole Kidman, Don Johnson and Melanie Griffith, Kim Basinger, Jerry Seinfeld, Tom Brokaw, Connie Chung and Maury Povich, Smokey Robinson, Bill Cosby, Kathleen Turner, Rick Moranis, Richard Lewis, Marky Mark.

John F. Kennedy, Jr. became an in-house legend in the Knick organization; he didn't ask for comps or choice locations but bought his tickets at the window like anyone else.

The Knicks kept a courtside section open for the stars, even if that meant telling the legions of the past-it and not-quite-there-yet they couldn't do anything for them tonight. The P.R. department listed that night's celebs—Rosie Perez!—on the post-game note sheet.

Player introductions were now made by spotlight before a darkened house with a laser beaming each Knick's signature onto the floor. On the scoreboard TV screens, the players performed a music video of the obligatory rap song: "Go New York, go New York, go New York, go!"

What was left? Oh yes, the actual championship.

■

They marched through the first two rounds.

The Knicks eliminated the Pacers and Hornets, although they had to go 10 tough games.

The Bulls, forgetting their squabbles and turning it back on, swept the Hawks and Cavaliers in seven.

The arrogance back, Bulls players again openly snubbed their noses at the Knicks.

Jordan said they were flawed. ("The Knicks have trouble scoring.")

Pippen dismissed them. ("They're not the team the Pistons were.")

Jackson exploded when told the Knicks were complaining the Bulls didn't respect them. ("Where's Aretha? Is Aretha Franklin here? 'Respect' again? They've been playing that tune for nine months. Give us a break! Get another song!")

The Knicks knew little of this since Riley told them not to read the newspapers, which was one even he hadn't thought of before.

The Knicks took Game 1, 98–90. Jordan missed 18 of his 28 shots and scored 27 points, two more than Starks who had the "impossible" task of guarding him.

They won Game 2 as Jordan missed 20 of 32.

It was a Knick tide now. They had their eyes on the prize and nothing was going to make them blink.

"Everybody just want to count us out and say how dirty we play, this and that, all that boolshit—boolshit, I gotta say it," said Oakley at the post-game press conference, launching into a stream-of-consciousness tour of the Knick psyche.

"And you know, everybody's down on us, the Bulls take us in five, you know, but we're just gonna keep playing.

"Awards for this and that come out, we never get nothing. [Ewing had finished fourth in the MVP balloting, announced that day.] We don't worry about it. Everybody says, well, shoulda this and that. I think Patrick Ewing is the MVP, he didn't get it so, you know, we didn't worry about it today. We had a game to play. Everybody's asking us about, you know, do you think Pat deserves it? Yes we do but, you know, he didn't get it so why keep talking about it?"

∎

Onto every grand design, no matter how meticulously planned, a little rain must fall.

What hit the Knicks was a monsoon.

While the series broke to change sites, the *New York Times* reported Jordan had gone gambling at Bally's Grand in Atlantic City the night before Game 2. Two anonymous sources claimed he was there at 2:30 A.M., which would have meant he wouldn't have been back in Manhattan before 4 A.M.

Jordan's gambling had come up before. In 1991, he skipped the team's trip to the White House to be honored for their championship to play golf in Hilton Head, S.C., with friends, some of whom turned out to be felons. Asked about a $57,000 check written on his account that was found in the possession of a convicted money launderer, Slim Bouler, Jordan said it was a loan.

When Bouler's case went to court, Jordan blithely admitted he had lied, that the check was to pay gambling debts.

The Atlantic City story was relatively harmless. The *Times*'s Harvey Araton, who wrote it, ran it several paragraphs down in a wrapup of the aftermath of the first two games. But the combination of circumstances—Jordan's fame, a marquee event—made it irresistible.

A feeding frenzy ensued. Writers streamed out to the Bulls' practice facility in suburban Chicago.

Jordan acknowledged he, his father, and two friends had taken a limo to Atlantic City but insisted they hadn't stayed late.

There were more questions. Did he go to Joliet, Illinois to gamble on the riverboats? Did he have a gambling problem?

When he heard the last one, Jordan stomped off, jumped into his Porsche, and burned rubber out of the parking lot. The next day, all the Bulls refused to talk to the press.

Back in New York where the Knicks were sitting out the three-day break, Riley waited uneasily. The Knicks had had everything their way. Now the apostle of constructive misery watched the Bulls corner the market. He didn't have to be told what to expect in Game 3.

Sure enough, the Bulls came out with a fearsome effort, took a 23-point lead before halftime and mopped up after that.

"All of them were strung up by their thumbs in the city square," Riley said later. "They were ready to play. They're the world champions.

"I'm not trying to be flip about it. We got our butts kicked. We've had eight, nine, ten days almost of relief. There hasn't been enough misery for us. Today maybe there's enough."

There was certainly enough attitude.

Charles Smith refused to touch fists with Jordan before the opening tip. Starks kicked the ball out-of-bounds in frustration and twice jumped into Pippen's chest, taunting him. Then Starks tried to fight Jordan, was led away, broke free, went after him again, and was, mercifully, ejected.

Riley stripped down his rotation to seven players for Game 4, trying to steal it but nothing the Knicks could think up mattered.

Jordan took over single-handedly, scoring 54 points, only eight of them on shots inside 17 feet. The Bulls won, 105–95 and it was 2–2.

Newsday ran a cartoon of Riley with horns, naming him its Game 4 goat for not double-teaming Jordan.

∎

Riley promised his players Game 5 would be the biggest in their lives.

For one of them, at least, it certainly would.

The game was played at a torpid pace as the pressure bore down on both teams. Jordan scored 17 straight points in the third and fourth quarters but the Knicks went up in the closing moments, 94–92.

Jordan passed to B. J. Armstrong in the corner for a three-pointer that put the Bulls up, 95–94.

But the Knicks would have the last possession. Riley put Ewing on the right wing and gave him the ball. Patrick started to drive on Stacey King, slipped and shoveled it to Charles Smith a few feet from the hoop.

Then came the four-second eternity.

Smith turned and put up a short shot. Horace Grant blocked it.

The ball came back to Smith. He head-faked Grant into the air and went back up but Jordan, zooming over to help, stripped the ball out of his hands.

It came back to Smith, now even more open on the other side of the hoop.

He went up a third time. Pippen blocked him from behind.

The ball came back to Smith, still open under the basket with Pippen still behind him.

Smith went up a fourth time. Pippen blocked it from behind again.

The ball squirted into the corner to Grant who threw it ahead to Armstrong whose layup at the buzzer made the final score Bulls 97, Knicks 94.

That's how precariously things are balanced.

The pivotal game had come down to four tries at a layup by a 6–10, player. The Knicks had lost. Their pain was undisguised.

"It hurts when you need something so much," said Riley.

Doc Rivers answered questions in the Knick room with tears in his eyes.

"You just keep thinking about all the work we put into it," he said, his voice trembling. "I never worked so hard in my life."

They couldn't even make their last stand in peace.

As the Knicks and Bulls flew back to Chicago, another story broke about Jordan's gambling. A San Diego man was publishing a book claiming Jordan had lost more than $1 million to him at golf. The media exploded anew. Somehow the Knicks' great crusade had become a subplot in a drama about the ubiquitous Michael.

Riley, once more summoning the ghost of Lee, said, "You get your back planted against the wall a number of times in your life and this is one of them and we'll just have to deal with that."

They tried, anyway.

They threw everything they had at the Bulls, out-rebounding them by a fearsome 25–7 in the first half, but it wasn't enough. Jordan staggered to a 25-point game. Pippen, the chump of the previous spring who'd shone throughout this series, hit three clutch jumpers in the last five minutes.

The Bulls won, 96–88.

"I'm glad the Knicks are going home," said a relieved Horace Grant. "The entire crew. Their GM, Pat Riley, everybody."

■

Summer came again but brought the Knicks no solace.

Doc Rivers told a friend that only winning could make Riley's regimen bearable. Having harvested heartache instead, the Knicks mourned, each in his own way.

"Emotionally we were drained," says Tony Campbell. "All that year, you feel like hey, we're going to be champions. We know we have to work hard, we know we're going to be the best-conditioned team, we know we're going to be the toughest team, you understand, we know that.

"We worked really hard, you know, the three-hour practices. Everybody knew about it, we didn't hide anything…. And then for it not to happen, wow, like you know, what went wrong?

"Then you start questioning: well, we believed this but maybe it wasn't really good for us to believe that. All the hard work, all the stress, the pressure mentally, was it really worth it?"

Within days, Charles Oakley, upset at diminished minutes and worried about trade rumors, shattered the Knick calm.

"I don't know if I'll be here next year," Oakley said. "I want to play more but I'm not going to kiss no one's butt.

"Ain't no problem me being in there, hurting my team by taking a crazy jump shot."

Hello, John Starks.

"The second half of the season," Oakley said, "I really fulfilled my role, making big plays down the stretch, keeping the ball alive. And a lot of times when I was in there, I was under the boards by myself. We've got three big men and I'm doing all the dirty work. That bullshit wears out sooner or later."

Hello, Patrick Ewing, Anthony Mason, and Charles Smith.

To Riley, this was not a faithful hand going on a drunk but more ballast than he could carry.

"If that was something he was carrying all year, that's not the spirit you go against the Chicago Bulls with," Riley said. "You've got to be totally pure and right. Oak, I think, simply had a great, great year for us but there has to be honor in your sacrifice."

This was only Oakley being Oakley and Riley being Riley. The real problem wore No. 23 and would never let them past while he had breath in its body.

And Riley knew it.

"When I was coaching the Lakers," he said after Game 6, jammed in a doorway in the tiny Chicago Stadium dressing room, smiling wanly, "there were some great players and great teams that had the misfortune of playing or living their careers in that decade. Because they knew they were never gonna beat us. That's very frustrating.

"We have to find a way to get better than the Bulls or we're going to be playing against a dynasty for four or five years because they're in their prime. They're gonna get more players.

"That's the frustrating part of it, knowing you can beat everybody else other than one team. That's why all those players used to come by the bench when I was coaching out there and say, 'Is there any way? Get me over here.' Because they knew they were never gonna beat 'em. We got to find a way to get above that."

It looked like it was going to be a neat trick.

CHAPTER FOURTEEN

The Animal That Has to Be Fed Every Day Just Dialed Room Service

"Those headlines are about unexpected losses and players who finally believe their coach makes mistakes...

"The emperor has no Armani tie. Riley can be wrong, finally, in his third season in New York. The arrow no longer points up all the time."

—FILIP BONDY
NEW YORK DAILY NEWS, JAN. 26, 1994

He just went away.

That was how the Knicks finally got past Michael Jordan. At 30, at the height of his power and fame, tired of all the hassle and grieving for his recently slain father, Jordan suddenly retired in the fall of 1993.

The news leaked out as he watched Game 1 of the Toronto–Chicago playoff series from White Sox-Bulls owner Jerry Reinsdorf's box in Comiskey Park, where he had thrown out the first ball.

Back in New York, Knick players watching the baseball game got a bonus. They spent the rest of the night calling each other, asking if they thought it was true, could they believe it, who was going to stop them now?

The next morning, Jordan made it official at a press conference televised around the world.

Riley, obliged to comment, gave a determinedly low-key response laying out the Knick party line: Their goal was already a title so nothing had changed, etc.

On WFAN, however, Deejay Don Imus imagined Riley's real reaction: *"Yessss!"*

It was ironic as ironic could be. As a player, Riley never got a break. In his coaching career, if he fell off a skyscraper someone would move a clover field beneath it.

Riley could barely contain himself. He opened training camp in Charleston at 12:01 A.M. while the rest of the NBA slept, the first pro coach to adopt college basketball's "midnight madness." The Knicks, he announced, intended to be the first team on the court and the last to leave.

No one disagreed. They appeared destined to play for a title, if for no other reason than default.

"The Knicks are going to win the East more than likely, unless they get upset," said the Suns' Charles Barkley, " 'cause they're playing against the Little Sisters of the Poor."

■

Riley had always had his own business—Riles & Co.—for his off-court enterprises. Now that was what the Knicks had become, too, Riles & Co.

He'd turned the program around, singlehandedly it seemed. In a league run by players, where coaches were transients and challenging players was a fast road to retirement, Riley was his franchise's star and ruled absolutely.

He was no longer subtle about jerking players back into place. The season before, he benched his wild bunch, John Starks, Anthony Mason, and Greg Anthony, en masse after they acted up in a loss to the Clippers and later mused: "If they feel ostracized by something I did, it's their problem."

The Knicks won their next game without them and Gotham swooned.

The sight of a coach so nakedly in charge in this era of the monster-athlete, willing to risk defeat for a principle, was refreshing, even thrilling. The *New York Post*'s Pete Hamill ranked Riley second in his annual Thanksgiving column of New York things to be grateful for.

"I'll give you a perfect example," said WFAN's Mike Francesa, host of a post-game show from the Garden's Play-by-Play nightclub.

"He [Riley] came to do my show. It's quite a large crowd, hundreds and hundreds of people. A lot of them have been to the game so they're kinda wild. I mean, you've got a lot of people in a bar-restaurant setting so not everybody's going to pay atttention to every guest.

"When Riley came in to do the show, you could have heard a pin drop when he spoke. And when he walked in, he got a standing ovation. This is the kind of weight he carries. The only time I heard the place that quiet was when Riley spoke and when Spike Lee spoke..."

Indeed, Riley, immersed as usual in his team, called himself a "high-profile recluse in New York City," but his fame multiplied, nonetheless.

General circulation magazines began sending media heavies to capture him: *Daily News* political writer Ken Auletta for *Vanity Fair*; Pulitzer prize winner and former Vietnam correspondent David Halberstam for *Esquire*, which ran the profile between one on architect I. M. Pei and actor Al Pacino. Tom Brokaw interviewed Riley for *Today*. PBS's Charlie Rose did an hour with him.

The underlying assumption seemed to be: Riley wasn't just a coach any more but something transcendent.

Riley embraced the notion. Putnam, the company that was publishing his second book, *The Winner Within*, had turned down some sports writers for interviews on his book promotional tour. This was a business book, a Putnam publicist said. Riley wanted to talk to business writers.

The Winner Within was dedicated to the concept that success doesn't have to carry the seeds of its own destruction. If Riley's experience in Los Angeles suggested otherwise, he was out to show it wasn't inevitable.

"Why can't a team go for twenty years?" he asked Charlie Rose. "Why does it always have to break down?"

At the book's conclusion, Riley laid down a "cycle of winning." Coincidentally or not, the cycle mirrored his Laker career.

In capital letters, courtesy of the author, the stages of the cycle were:

THE INNOCENT CLIMB (the Laker title under Westhead and Riley);

THE DISEASE OF ME (the collapse the next season);

THE CORE COVENANT (the rebound under Riley);

THUNDERBOLTS test our conviction (the reverses of his second season as coach);

THE CHOKE (the '84 loss to Boston);

BREAKTHROUGHS enable us to conquer our own self-devised handicaps (the '85 victory over Boston);

COMPLACENCY (losing to Houston in the '86 West finals);

MASTERY teaches us that we must always do more (the '87 title);

ANTEEING UP turns Mastery into unbeatable excellence [his guaranteed '88 title].

"Until the CORE CRACKS (the '90 Laker rebellion). And one must MOVE ON mentally—and perhaps physically, too—to a new rebirth (in New York)."

Reviews were generally polite although *Newsweek* dismissed it as a "271-page embarrassment."

"Its chief asset," wrote *Newsweek*'s David A. Kaplan, "is very wide margins." The review ran under a headline that said: "Riley suffers the 'disease of me.'"

❚

Some walkover.

The regular season was six months of hell. Even Riley, who often planned for contingencies no one else dreamed of, was caught off guard.

Charles Smith, a pariah after his four-blocked-layup farewell, went on the injured list twice and couldn't prove anything to anyone.

Aging but invaluable Doc Rivers blew out a knee and was lost for the season. The offense sagged to 98 points a game.

Dave Checketts and Ernie Grunfeld had been widely praised for acquiring Smith. Now hindsight, that great leveler, suggested they'd never been stronger than the spring of '91 with Mark Jackson and Xavier McDaniel.

"I think about that a lot," said Oakley. "I've made comments about that a couple of times. But they aren't here and we have to just live with what we have."

The tabloids took the gloves off.

A December slump led to a team crisis when two unnamed Knicks told the *Daily News's* Curtis Bunn that Riley's overreliance on Ewing was stifling the offense.

The *News* gave it the big treatment, a back-page headline, TEAM TURMOIL in letters 2¼ inches high.

This was garden variety turmoil at best. In another town, it might have been two paragraphs at the bottom of a story but the tabs were fighting for their lives. The *News* was rebuilding after a ruinous strike. The *Post* stumbled forward like a vampire, waiting for someone to pound a stake into its heart, with the staff even putting out a paper for a day when its publisher of the moment tried to close it.

Another coach might have ignored the *News* story but Riley had always hated leaks and was now going boldly where no coach had ever gone before.

The season before, he'd been incensed when Pete Vecsey, his old NBC teammate, reported that Knick veterans talked him out of sending Greg Anthony home from the trip on which he'd sucker-punched the Suns' Kevin Johnson.

Vecsey's report suggested only that Riley was furious with Anthony, a common sentiment in New York, but had taken his players' advice, a seemly act for a leader.

Nevertheless an angry Riley, knowing the story had to have sprung from his roster, snarled to Knick beat writers: "Anybody who talks to him [Vecsey] is a gutless fuck."

The day of the "Team Turmoil" headline, Riley called a team meeting and, according to Vecsey, still the thorn in his side, asked his players one by one if they'd been the source.

Not to miss out on the fun, the *Post* ran a headline that read: KNICKS: WE'LL FIND LOCKER ROOM RAT.

Speculation centered on noted grumbler Anthony Mason. The *Post* ran a head shot of Mason with his denial in the caption. It might have had an accompanying profile shot next to it, like a wanted poster, but didn't.

∎|

Checketts thought it was the rules changes put in to deal with the violence.

If the Knicks had made their bones, everyone else quickly tired of having theirs broken. After Oakley was fined $10,000 for leveling Indiana's Reggie Miller the season before, Pacer president Donnie Walsh complained Riley had "gone from an orchestra leader in L.A. to Hannibal Lecter with this team."

The Knicks gloried in their rough, tough image. Riley was approached by the marketing department, which had a "Tough Town, Tough Team" campaign for the 1992–93 season and wanted to illustrate it with a picture of a basket, looking down in the lane on a chalk line of a dead person.

"'Tough Town, Tough Team,' right?" said Riley, laughing. "Well, we didn't want to go that far, O.K.? I mean, driving the lane is one thing but we didn't want to draw chalk outlines in the lane."

Nor did NBA Commissioner David Stern but he wasn't chuckling about it.

Play as rough as the Knicks' was as old as the game. Until the late '80s, Stern seemed to accept a discreet level of violence as the league marketed the Bad Boy Pistons. But a confrontation was coming between the wrestlers and the artists, personified by the Pistons and Bulls. The artists—Jordan—were ratings heaven.

Stern began cracking down more each season.

It was one thing to be a Bad Boy in Detroit, another to do it in New York, which was already hated and feared on general principles.

By Riley's second season, the Knicks were going from hunters to hunted.

Starks was pilloried in his hometown press for breaking the Nets' Kenny Anderson's wrist. The Phoenix brawl in the spring of '93 made them all notorious.

"Our swagger has been missing since the start of this season," said Checketts in January, 1994, as the Knicks lurched from naught to juggernaut and back.

"I think some of the heart of this team was taken out by actions of the league, with everyone coming down on the Knicks as the bad boy."

■|

Actually, their defense had improved. They just couldn't score. They had little margin for error. They had to hold teams to 90 points or struggle to win.

Their faith in the system—and its author—was stretched to breaking point or, depending on one's place in the order, beyond.

"No question about it," said Tony Campbell at mid-season after getting exiled to Dallas in the Derek Harper deal, "guys are stepping back.

"The guys are practicing three hours a day like no other team in the league. Riley will tell guys how they're playing and make them feel real uncomfortable....

"Guys look at him and say, 'Hey, you're supposed to be this coach that's so great that it's supposed to happen.' And when you don't see it happen, you wonder, 'Do we really have what we say we have? Do we have what the media has portrayed us as having or what everybody sees we have?'

"I know guys are doubting it now. I mean, guys mumbled it all year long in the two years I was there. Guys were mumbling like, 'Who is this guy?' He dresses sharp, he has everybody fooled. A lot of people in New York think that he's a con artist....

"Everybody on the team questions him. Pat Ewing questions Riley sometimes. I mean, the whole team. Oakley questions him all the time. But that's just basketball. You're gonna have players do that....

"He's definitely a good coach, he's definitely a good motivator. I just don't think he has much sensitivity. I'm not saying he should be sensitive but to be a former player, you would think he'd have a better feeling for players. You can't treat everybody the same.

"The only problem that I can see that he has, he's just callous. It's like I'm it. I am. Me. Everything is just Riley. He's always right. But he's not always right."

■|

Riley tried everything and nothing worked.

He defended his players.

He told the fans to to go ahead and keep booing Smith and Anthony, and the newspaper guys to keep writing they were in a slump if they wanted to ruin them.

He challenged them.

He sneered at their title ambitions, noted they hadn't won a thing or proved a thing and if they didn't get it together, never would.

He coddled them.

After a depressing four-game losing streak on the West Coast, he whisked them off for an unscheduled night of fun. While the press guys searched for them, Riley directed the charter to fly, not to Sacramento, but to nearby Reno, where the players were surprised to see limos parked on the runway, waiting to take them to the casinos where they were given $250 and allowed to gamble into the wee hours of the morning. Two nights later they started a 15-game winning streak that stretched into April.

Even *that* didn't work.

Starks was lost during the streak with a knee injury, the margin for error was cut further, and reality dragged them down again.

Down the stretch they lost six of 10. After an embarrassment in Charlotte, Riley set upon his players anew, noting their failure to reach the next level—and his in reaching them.

"I have failed miserably," he said. "I've got to think about it, go home, go to a room, turn the lights off and think about it."

This was taken less as a heartfelt admission, more as a ploy to get the players up for their showdown two nights later with the Hawks. Back in New York, columnists whipped out *The Winner Within*—to look for straight lines.

The *New York Times*'s George Vecsey found one in the chapter called "The Temporary Insanity Textbook."

Wrote Riley, noting how he'd choreographed his 1988 blowup in Salt Lake City:

"A leader's aggrieved outburst is not an explosion, nor is it a regular or predictable event. It is the art of being angry at the right time, to the right degree, with the right people. T.I. requires plenty of advanced thought—a real and focussed mental plan, not emotion-driven monologue. A dose of T.I. demands a rapid follow-up of compassion."

Wrote Vecsey: "I liked the [post-Charlotte] anger part until I found it in the book. I'll check the book and see what we can expect next."

Next?

Riley suspended Mason.

Continuing their miserable failure, the Knicks blew a nine-point fourth-quarter lead to the Hawks, falling to No. 3 overall in the

East. Riley, desperate for offense, put the reviled Charles Smith back in and Mason complained to the press.

Daring to tweak the lion's nose twice, Mason kept it up the next day, saying of Riley:

"He always has his opinion and we have ours."

Mason was either using the royal "we" or suggesting mutiny. In either case, Riley shot him down.

If a protest about playing time was a thin pretext, Riley suspended Mason for the last three games, worth almost $50,000 in salary. The players pleaded for Mason's return for the post-season but Riley claimed he didn't decide until minutes before the deadline.

The team and Mason's agent agreed that Mason would forfeit not three but one game's pay—$13,414—and he didn't file a grievance. That was as close as he was coming to his "rapid follow-up of compassion."

Mason had long been the team hardhead. And the veterans didn't mind seeing Mase spanked. When it came right down to it, Mason wasn't crazy about Riley, although he wisely kept that out of the newspapers. If saying he wanted to play could get him suspended, the real story might get him locked away in a dungeon.

Reenergized or taking advantage of a lull in the schedule, the Knicks routed two nobodies and finished the regular season with a win in Chicago. The playoffs were coming. The celebs began calling. The seats on the bandwagon filled up.

He was Pat Riley, they were the New York Knicks, he'd think of something. Wouldn't he?

■|

Hadn't he seen this somewhere before?

If the Knicks were to win a championship, it would have to be like that bone-wearying spring of 1988 when Riley willed the Lakers through three seven-game series.

Starks returned five weeks after arthroscopic knee surgery. He had a big heart but when he first came back, he limped like Chester in Gunsmoke. Knick scoring dipped from the 90s into the 80s...and 70s...and 60s.

Nor did their draw offer any relief.

Surrendering best record in the East obliged them to open with the Nets, who were as big as they were, deeper and just as talented.

Chuck Daly had whipped his madcap youngsters into something resembling a basketball team but only a warden with cells and keys could have cleaned their act up altogether. In case anyone thought they'd grown up, Derrick Coleman and Jayson Williams were arrested in a late-night bar scuffle in Manhattan after Game 1.

Impetuous though they may have been, the Nets were hungry after years as poor cousins. They had won the season series, 4-1. Williams, a reserve forward, even guaranteed victory in the playoffs although his got less notice than Riley's or Joe Namath's.

The series was physical but brief. The Knicks won Game 2 after Ewing was ejected, while the Garden crowd went nuts, cheering them like the ghosts of the '70 champions finishing off the Lakers without Willis Reed.

The Nets won Game 3 but fell in four, like the warmup act they still were.

Bring on Da Bulls.

■|

These pains in Da Butts were on borrowed time.

Without Jordan, they'd posted a surprising 55–27 season. Only two home losses the last weekend, to the woeful Celtics and the Knicks, had cost them the East's best record.

But time was running out on them. Only six Bulls remained from the spring before. Bill Cartwright and John Paxson were retiring, Horace Grant and Scott Williams would be free agents. By next fall, they could be down to Scottie Pippen and B. J. Armstrong.

"Do I ever think about it?" said Pippen. "I think about it every day. Next year the whole championship squad could be done, the whole thing over....It's very depressing."

Not in New York, it wasn't.

The Knicks owed the Bulls something, for their insufferable arrogance as much as for ending their last three seasons. They had just held the Nets to 87 points a game and were feeling like titans once more.

Failing to swoon on cue, the Bulls led by 15 points in the third quarter of Game 1 and eight in the third quarter of Game 2. The Knicks won both with fourth-quarter rallies.

This wasn't a matter of bopping a bunch of Nets between the eyes. The Bulls' triangle offense spread out the Knick defenders.

Pippen, who could break any Knick down, did so repeatedly. The Knicks couldn't bump what they couldn't catch.

But the Knicks were 2–0 and this time, however, there'd be no Jordan, no gambling-story hysteria, no superstar to ride to the rescue.

Game 3 was one of those nights when the stars in the heavens and everything else seemed to collide. Derek Harper got into a fight with a scrub named Jo Jo English and body-slammed him into the courtside seats. Players piled on top of them, rolling over several customers, almost in the lap of a horrified David Stern, sitting four rows back.

The Bulls were up by 20 points in the fourth quarter. The Knicks caught them at 102–102 on Ewing's hook with :01.8 left.

There was a number destined to live on in memory, 1.8.

In a time-out huddle, Jackson designed a last shot—for rookie Toni Kukoc rather than Pippen. Pippen had gone cold and Kukoc had won three games at the buzzer that season.

Pippen had long resented management's coddling of the European star and may have been bummed out by the end of the dynasty that seemed to be arriving at warp speed. There was only a faint hope of winning the game in regulation, no matter who took the shot. Knick momentum would likely prevail in overtime and a 3–0 lead would be impregnable.

Pippen took himself out of the game.

He cursed at Jackson and sat himself down on the bench. Jackson, stunned, called another time-out. Pippen's buddy, Grant, and assistant coach John Bach tried to talk him into going in but Pippen refused. He was supposed to in-bound the ball to Kukoc but Jackson had to send in Pete Myers to do it.

Myers made a perfect pass to Kukoc, tightly guarded by Anthony Mason at the top of the circle.

The 6–10 Kukoc turned and launched a 21-footer that arched high into the smoky air of Chicago Stadium…and came down right through the net.

Bedlam.

Behind closed doors, Pippen apologized to his teammates but Jackson told the press what had happened. A day later, however, Jackson welcomed Pippen back to the bosom of the team and told his players not to say a word against Scottie.

"I think you saw how highly wrapped maybe New York is," Jackson said to the media, "and how highly wrapped the emotion is in this series and the pressures that are playing upon these players.

"We don't want to add to them. I know you don't either, as press people. And I know it's your job to expose and to make us all look human and naked. We're not going to do that, to our team or to any individual on our team."

Bill Wennington announced the Bulls wouldn't let the press pull "the family" apart.

What was this, a sequel? The Knicks up 2–0? Games 3 and 4 in Chicago? The besieged Bulls rallying around their disgraced superstar? The Knicks becoming a subplot in their opera?

Sure enough, the next day, Pippen was cheered wildly and played a great game—25 points, eight rebounds, six assists—as the Bulls routed the Knicks.

Back to New York for Game 5, last season's Little Bighorn.

Deja vu held for 47:58.

With :44 left, B. J. Armstrong, the big-eyed assassin who seemed to have been torturing the Knicks since he was an altar boy, hit an off-balance 17-footer and Chicago led, 86–85.

With :02 left, the Knicks took their last shot—Hubert Davis's three-pointer—and missed.

But fate is not always a predator. Now it turned into an angel in the form of referee Hue Hollins, who called a foul on Pippen for hitting Davis's wrist after the shot was gone.

There was no question there'd been some contact but NBA officials usually swallow their whistles in the final seconds rather than take the game from the players. But judgment is precarious. Hollins blew his, Davis sank two free throws and the Knicks escaped.

Jackson called the referees "harlots" as they left the floor. Bulls GM Jerry Krause yelled through their dressing room door: "You have to live with what you've done tonight for the rest of your life!"

In other words, it was just routine for the Knicks and the Bulls. Everyone was strung out and on the verge of losing it.

Back in Chicago, the Bulls put the Knicks to the torch yet again, winning, 93–79, to force Game 7.

All the Knicks seemed to have left was their home-court advantage. The Bulls had punctured their self-esteem once more. In Games 1–6, the Bulls had had leads of 15, 8, 22, 19, 9, and 19 points and the papers were all over the Knicks.

In the *Daily News*, the headline above Mark Kriegel's column read: "Win or lose, Knicks have lost."

"It is not just Chicago rooting against the Knicks now," wrote *Newsday*'s Mike Lupica. "It is the rest of the country looking at them as the guttersnipes of the NBA."

The alleged guttersnipes won, 87–77.

If this was end of the great Bulls–Knicks rivalry, it went graciously. Bulls players embraced the Knicks on the floor. Pippen stood in the hallway from the court, shaking hands with every Knick.

Even Riley and Jackson, passing each other in the interview room, stopped to shake hands.

Jackson mewed later, "The best team didn't win." But only one team advanced and it wasn't his.

"It has to be thought of as a beginning for us," said a relieved Riley, "because for some reason or other, it happened to us in Los Angeles with the Boston Celtics. We had to beat the world champions....

"Somewhere, some team had to put them [Bulls] away. It was fitting for us because we really aspire to what they worked so hard to achieve."

The last remark went all but unnoticed. His players were trying to win their first title. He wanted to replicate the Bulls' three-year run.

In case anyone had forgotten how narrow this victory had been, a Knick fan at Game 7 held up a sign:

"Hue Hollins Fan Club."

■|

Somewhere in this shining land there was a soft touch waiting for them, wasn't there?

But it wasn't Memorial Day weekend—Indy 500 weekend—in Indianapolis. It was the Hoosier version of hell: a parade downtown for 500,000 or so fans of racing and/or revelry; no hotel rooms within a 90-mile radius; press corps spread out over three states.

To top it off, there were the Pacers.

Once a happy meal for Eastern powers, the Pacers had one recognizable player, Reggie Miller, known as much for his provocateur antics as his jump shot. In the '93 playoffs, he'd gotten Starks ejected by suckering the Knick wild child into head-butting him, after which Ewing twirled Starks around and screamed at him and Riley had to grab Starks by the arm and walk him off before anything worse happened.

A lot had changed in a year.

The Pacer coach was now Larry Brown, a nomad but a card-carrying genius who had just taken his sixth pro team to its best

NBA finish. His Pacers, a humble No. 5 playoff seed, were the league's hottest team, having finished the season with a 31–12 run before ousting the Nos. 1 and 4 seeds, Atlanta and Orlando.

It was the basic Knick script: wins in Games 1 and 2 producing the usual euphoria; road losses in Games 3 and 4 bringing everyone back down. In Game 3, they set a playoff record for fewest points—68—of which Ewing had but one.

It was O.K., they'd been here before, they'd just whack the Pacers over the head in the Garden in Game 5. Sure enough, they opened with a 15–2 run and led by 12 starting the fourth quarter, their quarter all post-season.

Then Miller took them out, single-handedly.

He hit a three-pointer. He hit another. He hit a 26-footer with Starks between him and the three-point line. He gave Spike Lee, who was sitting courtside, the two-hands-around-the-neck choke sign. He scored 25 points in the fourth quarter, and the Pacers won. The Knicks' world collapsed around them.

"GAG CITY," read the back-page headline in the *Daily News*.

"CHOKERS," said the *Post*.

The day of Game 6 in Indianapolis, Phil Jackson interrupted his vacation to call the Knicks "ugly" and blast Riley in the *New York Times*. "I wasn't the guy who picked this fight," said Jackson. "…Hey, this is the guy who started whining in the first place. He tries to put a spin on everything. He's the media coach."

In the *Post*, Wallace Matthews called Knicks "bullies" who lacked "not only skill but character" and said of Riley: "Once you get past the cosmetics, there ain't much underneath."

The long knives were out but what's a funeral without a corpse? In a classic gut check, the Knicks won Game 6, 98–91.

An emotional Riley proclaimed his pride in his players.

"There was a massive, massive thud the other night with everyone jumping off the bandwagon," he said. "Now I'm sure there will be a massive thud with everyone jumping back on.

"We may not be the prettiest team and we may not be the most skilled team at times but I don't think see how anyone can question our heart. This team is all about heart."

They'd have to prove it again, too.

The Pacers didn't get it. They were supposed to trot onto the Garden floor for Game 7, hear the crowd howl and say good-by. Instead they were up by 12 and drawing away in the third quarter when Ewing picked up his fourth foul.

Riley rolled the dice and left Patrick in. The Pacers went after him but Ewing blocked Antonio Davis's jump hook cleanly, then stepped in front of Davis on a drive and got the charging call.

The Knicks closed the quarter with a 14-6 run. In the fourth, an inspired Ewing ran by the bench screaming at Riley, "Call 'em for me!" Riley did, the Knicks ran the Pacers down and won, 94–90.

They were finally in the finals, assuming there was anything left of them to go.

■

Fade in: A chunky middle-aged man stands on the ledge of a building, high above the street. Around one leg is a rope tied to an anvil. He's hunched over, listening to a portable radio.

Radio: Seconds left, Olajuwon shakes and bakes, he misses!

Man, straightening up in anguish: *That's…it…I…just… can't…take…it…any…more!*

He throws the anvil over the edge and the rope begins to play out.

Radio: But wait, he was fouled!

Man looks plaintively into camera.

Voiceover: Because everyone knows it's not easy being a sports fan in Houston.

■

It had been a difficult post-season in Houston, too.

The Rockets, champions of the West, had opened their second-round series against the Suns by blowing 18- and 20-point leads at home. The morning after they went down 0–2, they awoke to the same headline in both local papers: "CHOKE CITY."

When the first game hadn't sold out, Suns president Jerry Colangelo bought up the unsold tickets for Game 2 and flew in 300 fans from Phoenix. Rocket guard Vern Maxwell told Houston fans to go to hell.

The Rockets then surprised everyone and themselves by rallying to win the series from the Suns, 4–3. The organization rechristened itself Clutch City and began running TV commercials to let the fans know they understood.

The Rockets were a younger version of the Knicks, a good defensive team built around a great center, Hakeem Olajuwon. The Rockets had more firepower, though, and all the rest they needed. They had finished the Western Conference Finals eight days before and rested while the Knicks played games 5, 6, and 7 against the Pacers.

The Rockets would have the home-court advantage. They'd won 58 games to the Knicks' 57 and had beaten New York twice. In the two games, Olajuwon had outscored Ewing, 66–24.

The Knicks were running on fumes and Riley's will. They'd already played 18 playoff games of a possible 19. If the finals went seven, they'd break the record for the longest post-season, set by Riley's '88 Lakers.

After everything they'd been through, Knick players couldn't imagine their struggle had just begun. Relieved at shaking the Pacers, John Starks demonstrated his naivete, announcing: "The pressure was on us to get to the finals so the championship will be like a breeze compared to that."

How could they know?

No Knick player had ever been to the finals. None of them knew how it felt to come so far and lose. Half of them were in high school that endless night in Boston, June 12, 1984.

Riley knew how it felt. He had to reach them fast.

■

Game 1 went as expected. The Rockets were rusty, the Knicks tired. Starks went 3 for 18, the other New York guards 7 for 23 and the Rockets won, 85–78.

Riley began drawing lines and taking stands. He dismissed any notion they could be tired at a time like this. He told them they'd better not think of coming back next season with any of that getting-here-was-a-learning-experience stuff.

He *ordered* them to start making their shots.

"You're a professional player that gets paid a lot of money, you make those shots," Riley announced to the press. "You make 'em!

"I'm not using shooting as an excuse and let our team say, 'If only.' Last year against Chicago, I heard all summer long, if only we made 15 free throws. That's a losers' mentality. If you get the opportunity—the highest form of any player's sanity is the present moment, on the court, when the opportunity presents itself. Once you get the opportunity, you knock it down."

If only it were that easy. As a player, Riley shot 41 percent but maybe the problem was he never played for himself.

Embracing their highest form of sanity, the Knicks made shots in Game 2. Starks had 19 points, Derek Harper 18, including two threes in the stretch. They won, 91–83.

They went back to New York for the middle three games. A Rocket rookie named Sam Cassell promptly popped their balloon in Game 3, hitting a three-pointer with :32 left and the Rockets trailing by two. Houston won, 93–89.

The Knicks won Game 4. Ewing went 9 for 29 but Charles Oakley bailed them out with 16 points and 20 rebounds. Noted Oakley afterward: "I'm a true warrior."

Riley began reminding his players, "We're one win at home away from playing for the title." In Game 5, they got it, too.

While the press corps upstairs in the Garden watched the police chase O. J. Simpson on the TVs set up for replays, the Knicks went about their business, pulling another game out in the fourth quarter. As he had in Game 4, Starks hit a three-pointer to put them ahead to stay and they won, 91–84.

They were headed back to Houston for two games of which they needed but one.

"It seems like we've been out there forever," said Riley. "We started out at midnight October 6, 1993. We wanted to be the first team to hit the floor in '93 and hopefully, the last team to leave in '94....

"Right now we're on the brink of what they've been dreaming about."

■|

On the brink of a dream.

Like Columbus squinting anxiously at the New World...or Moses eyeing the land of milk and honey he wouldn't be allowed to enter?

Game 6 back in Houston was their chance, before the Rockets regrouped. It had been 12 years and 19 series since a home team had lost a Game 7. The Knicks weren't anxious to confront the Rockets and history, too.

The Rockets were there for the taking, too.

They had been feeling the heat late in games all series and the Knicks, 12 points down in the third quarter, were coming to get them again late in the fourth.

It was 86–84 with :05.5 left when the Knicks got the ball back the last time. They ran a high pick-and-roll, Starks off Ewing. Starks headed for the left wing, with Olajuwon, who'd been screened, trying to catch up.

Starks, 3 for 3 on threes in the period, went up for the NBA championship.

Olajuwon got a fingertip on it. It fell short like a bird with an arrow in its heart.

Afterward, Starks sat silent in the somber Knick dressing room, his feet on a chair, his eyes closed and a finger pointed at his right temple.

"Maybe this is the way it had to be for us to get to the Promised Land," said Riley. "If somebody told me on October 6 at midnight, 'We will guarantee you a seventh game at Houston, would you take it now?' I'd say yes."

Sure he would have.

The Most Unforgettable Man They Ever Met

Being the leader is a very difficult thing. It's a fine line.
While you have to keep on being one of the fellas—you have
to keep punching what I call that membership card—you have to
motivate players....

The only problem is, who gets him up?

Being a leader is a tough job 'cause you're out there alone.

—PAT RILEY

There was a parade that spring but the Knicks weren't in it.

It was the New York Rangers who were driven in the motorcade from Battery Park at the tip of Manhattan, up Broadway through the famed Canyon of Heroes like Lindbergh and MacArthur, picking bits of paper out of their wives' hair.

The Knicks flew home from Houston, met one last time in Purchase, packed their stuff in garbage bags, and drove themselves home.

Game 7 had gone much like the other Game 7s. Both teams were tight. The visitors were valiant, but the home team was triumphant.

John Starks went 2 for 18 but never backed away from a shot. Even Marv Albert, the Knick announcer doing the game for NBC, railed about his 10 misses in the fourth quarter. And later Riley second-guessed himself but his options were so limited as to have been nonexistent. Patrick Ewing had been badly out-played by Hakeem Olajuwon all series and in the final minutes of Game 7, when Riley was casting about for a shooter, he missed a wide-open 12-footer.

The remarkable thing was not that the Knicks had lost this title but that, after two exhausting seven-game series, they'd put themselves in a position to win it.

The truly amazing thing was that Riley had persuaded so many people—like Ewing who'd broken his Sphinx-like silence to an-nounce "This is our year"—that their quest was inevitable. If the emperor's clothes were splendid as ever, the troops were in rags.

After that game, Riley said he loved Starks "for his fighting nature."

It was a sad romance. He loved them all, in his way.

He said he'd never been prouder of a team in his life. In Indianapolis after Game 6, he'd been so moved at their heart, he recalled Lee Riley once more—"a hard-assed dad"—adding, "I'm the same way. And maybe I can't say those words to those guys but I have deep feelings for them…because I know what this team is about. I know how much they give. I know how where John Starks is from, where Anthony Mason came from.

"I know what these guys have gone through to get here. And regardless of what happens or how they're portrayed, I have that for them. You can't coach this game unless you feel for these guys."

So, the circle was unbroken, after all.

■|

Who knows why anyone does anything?

Once they said Ahab pursued Moby Dick because he wanted to look God in the eye. Now they'd say Ahab was trying to get his dead father off his back.

For whatever reason, Riley struggles heroically, pushing players farther than anyone has dared since they became adults with guaranteed contracts, trying to sooth the unruly mob, spinning the press on his nose like a seal. He dreams of doing things that have never been done, winning things that have never been won.

He turned 49 that spring.

Since returning to coaching, he'd begun referring to himself as a "lifer." But during the finals he started dropping hints that suggested he was asking himself if the price he was paying was worth it. He said he wanted this title for Patrick and Oak and the guys. But for him?

"It's not gonna change me," he said. "I'll be happy if we win it but another ring or whatever else comes from it is not going to change me.

"I mean, in the beginning it was wonderful. It was a different feeling the first time I won it. It was just like these guys feel right now and how desperate they all are to get that."

Desperate or not, his Knicks gave everything they had and it wasn't enough. They were old. Their window was either closing or closed. Or maybe this would be like 1987, after Houston's Twin Towers routed Riley's Lakers and everyone got off them and he turned them around and won back-to-back titles.

Were the Knicks ready for…Career Best Effort II?

■|

Riley was right, though. It wasn't going to change his life. If he still felt that itch to show 'em, the truth is, he had already shown 'em.

Magic Johnson, the man who meant the sun and the moon to him, called him the difference between the Lakers and Celtics in the '80s. No one else has ever compiled anything like Riley's run of 13 seasons without a second-place finish. He is the NBA's leader in winning percentage in the regular season and in playoff victories. He was already the game's best-paid coach, with salary and benefits adding up to some $2 million a year, but in the spring of 1994 Knick officials volunteered to give him a new, fatter, longer deal, to keep owners like the Clippers' Donald T. Sterling from luring him away with a part-ownership deal.

If Johnson and Larry Bird saved the NBA, if Michael Jordan took it to new heights, there was one other name from their era that could be mentioned with their's and it was Riley's, the NBA's first superstar coach.

He had gone from James Dean to the All-American boy to wandering minstrel-hoopster to beach dropout to announcer to coach's helper to coach to star, reinventing himself at every stage.

He won. Now he has to deal with that.

■|

No one who went through those last hard-burning Laker years will forget what a pain in the butt Riley could be, but time has healed those wounds. He was Riles. That was how it was. It was wonderful, wasn't it?

"Pat, let's face it, he wasn't just the coach," said his old trainer, Gary Vitti, watching the Lakers practice in the empty Forum three years after Riley's departure.

"He was as big as Magic. It wasn't just a bunch of superstars with a coach; it was the L.A. Lakers coached by *Pat Riley*. His name was on the marquee. And it should have been there. He had the whole image. He played it to the hilt. He didn't just play it; he lived it. I mean, it was true. It was real. He was exactly what the media portrayed him to be.

"The intensity was such—you were just trying to keep up with Pat. You were just trying to keep up with him. You never really stopped and smelled the roses or the flowers or whatever. And now I look back—it went by so fast for me. I never really enjoyed it. When people say, 'Hey those were the days,' and talk about the memories, I know what they're talking about because I have 'em now....

"I think when you run at that intensity level, you're going to wear the machine out. And that's basically what happened. I think it's surprising that it went that long. He should be commended. He went at top, top level for a decade. I mean, it's unbelievable. When Pat left, you could breathe a little easier. And I loved Mike Dunleavy, he was great to work with, but now, looking back on Pat—

I respected him then but now I have new-found respect for him. And in a way, I miss Pat.

"And there are things...the whole Magic [HIV] thing. I didn't talk about that much with anyone. Friends, family, my wife, teammates—I really didn't talk about it. And it really, really affected me.

"I think Pat, had he been here, would have been maybe the one guy I could have sat down with and maybe opened up a little bit about that situation because I would have known he would have understood, you know. He would have understood, suffice to say that.

"Even like my own wife, there isn't anything she could have said that would have made me feel better. But I know—I thought about calling Pat a bunch of times. But he had a whole new life back there and we were here. He had to deal with it, too, just like I did, you know what I mean, only he was removed from it. I don't know, I just didn't do it. But I've always thought about that."

Could he go through it all with Riley again?

"In a *second*," said Vitti. "Yes, I could."

∎

After Game 7 in Houston, Riley said good-by to the press corps—"We passed each other in the night in arenas"—and thanked them, "each and every one of you."

He said he appreciated everything they had done and apologized for any inconvenience he'd caused them. Sentimental as he got in the dying light of a season, he even loved the press guys for a moment.

He wished everybody a great summer and said he'd see them in the fall.

And so it continues.

Somewhere in America, Pat Riley is coaching his tail off tonight, putting it all back on the line. There's still a white whale waiting with his name on it.

INDEX